THE
ELIZABETHAN MALADY

*A Study of Melancholia
in English Literature
from 1580 to 1642*

THE
ELIZABETHAN
MALADY

A Study of Melancholia

in English Literature

from 1580 to 1642

BY LAWRENCE BABB

MICHIGAN-STATE UNIVERSITY PRESS

EAST LANSING

TO
TUCKER BROOKE
AND
JOSEPH QUINCY ADAMS

PREFACE

MY SUBJECT IS THE IMPRESSION left by a fashionable psychic malady upon the English literature of the late sixteenth and early seventeenth centuries. Melancholy was very much in vogue in the England of Elizabeth and the early Stuarts, especially among the intellectuals and would-be intellectuals. Elizabethan and early Stuart literature, consequently, abounds in references to melancholy and in melancholy characters. To understand these as the contemporaries of Shakespeare and Milton understood them requires study of the long-forgotten scientific theories which lie in their background. Modern scholars have for some time recognized this. Several of them have contributed to our knowledge of the old psychology in general and of melancholy in particular and have pointed out their literary influence. No one, however, has thus far published any comprehensive treatment of Elizabethan melancholy.

In this study, I have attempted to define what *melancholy* meant during the late Renaissance period in both scientific and popular usage, to describe the epidemic of melancholy in England, and to show in what manner it influenced thought and literary expression. I have chosen 1580 as my earlier limit because in the 1580's melancholy began to appear in English literature with some frequency. My terminal date is 1642. Melancholy did not cease to be a subject of interest in 1642—or in 1742—but one must stop somewhere. This is primarily a descriptive study, yet it will, I hope, contribute something toward the more complete understanding of Elizabethan thought and literature.

I should emphasize in the beginning that in Elizabethan usage the term *melancholy* did not commonly mean merely "sadness" or "despondency," as it does in modern speech. These are derived meanings—already in use in Shakespeare's day, to be sure, but not at that time very frequent. The word *melancholy* once had meanings and implications which, except perhaps in the technical language of psychology, it has long since lost. It is with these older meanings and connotations, most of them of a physiological or psychological character, that I am especially concerned. I have only a little to say, therefore, about the sobriety, depression, and disillusionment which developed among thoughtful Englishmen during the period under consideration. This development is a phenomenon related to my subject, but it is not the same thing.

In discussing the Renaissance theory of melancholy and its literary uses, I have not attempted to distinguish between fact and error. Even a psychologist, I am sure, would have difficulty in doing so. Many of the morbid psychic conditions which the elder physicians attribute to melancholy really do occur. There really are such things as morbid despondencies and bizarre hallucinations. Elizabethan writers who deal with these psychoses, however, write in the language of Renaissance science; they assume the truth of physiological and psychological principles which modern science has shown to be erroneous; they have derived from psychiatric works many symptomatic details which strain the credulity of the modern reader. Frequently it is plain that they owe more to the scientific lore of their period than to observation of realities. In interpreting their representions of melancholy, therefore, one must depend rather upon Renaissance psychology than upon modern psychology or upon firsthand knowledge of human behavior.

The scientific works which I have used for documentation are for the most part books which were available to Elizabethan or early Stuart Englishmen in their own language. In the bibliography I have included notes about the character of some of these works, about the dates of original publication, about their relative popularity (as indicated by the number of editions), and about their authors. I have made supplemental use of continental Latin treatises when these seemed more complete or more illuminating than anything that I found in English. Although I have not undertaken to write a history of melancholy in medical tradition, I have given some information in footnotes concerning classical and medieval sources. The works of Galen, Avicenna, and Bernard of Gordon were after all as much a part of Renaissance medical literature as those of Fracastoro and Fernel.

Acknowledgment of the work which other modern students have done on Elizabethan melancholy and related subjects has been a particularly awkward problem. There have been a great many studies in the field, and these have differed greatly in scope and in value. In preparing this study, I soon found that it would hardly be possible to refer to every existing discussion of every psychological theory or melancholy character. To do so would inflate the footnotes absurdly. I believe, however, that I have adequately acknowledged my debts. I should mention particularly my obligations to Miss Lily B. Campbell *(Shakespeare's Tragic Heroes: Slaves of Passion)* and to Miss Ruth Leila Anderson *(Elizabethan Psychology and Shakespeare's Plays)* for the instruction which they have given me in the general field of Elizabethan psychology. I have read two unpublished dissertations which to some extent were parallel to my own work: Harry K. Russell, *Certain Doctrines of Natural and Moral Philosophy as an Approach to the Study of Elizabethan Drama* (North Carolina, 1931), and Carmen L. Rogers, *Eliza-*

PREFACE

bethan Melancholy in the Writings of the University Wits (Cornell, 1933).

My conclusions have differed considerably at times from those of other investigators. If I had attempted to refute everyone with whom I disagreed, this book would have been far too long. It seemed best to omit controversy altogether.

The terminology which I have employed is of necessity often un-Elizabethan. I realize that *science* is used in a sense much narrower than the Elizabethan sense and that the Elizabethans seldom used *physiology* and never *psychology*.

I gathered a large part of the material included in this study during a year spent as a fellow at the Folger Shakespeare Library in Washington, D. C. I wish to thank the trustees of the library for the award of the fellowship and the Folger staff for their friendly assistance, which made the year both pleasant and rewarding. I am indebted to my colleague Professor Arnold Williams for his reading of the manuscript and for his valuable criticism and to Professor William M. Seaman for his assistance with translations from the Latin. In cases too numerous to mention, friends have directed me to passages in Elizabethan works which proved useful as documentation.

L. B.

East Lansing, Michigan
May, 1951

CONTENTS

Chapter I. THE PHYSIOLOGY AND PSYCHOLOGY OF THE RENAISSANCE

I

HAVING REDISCOVERED MAN as a physical and temporal creature, the Renaissance pursued the study of human nature with enthusiasm. The cunning complexity of man's physical and mental equipment and the excellence and efficacy of his faculties inspired scholars with wonder and pride. Man, they found, was a little world, a microcosm, the epitome of the great world, the macrocosm. He was "the head and chiefe of all that euer God wrought; the pourtraiture of the vniuersall world . . . [a] merueilous and cunning peece of worke";[1] "the last hand, the accomplishment, the perfection of the worke, the honor and miracle of Nature."[2]

The Renaissance derived its information concerning temporal man chiefly from writers of ancient times and from medieval writers indebted to classical thought. The principal authorities were Plato, Aristotle, Galen, Augustine, Avicenna, and Aquinas. Respect for authority was still profound. It occurred to only the very exceptional man to make scientific observation of human nature for himself. The rest studied philosophical and scientific works of elder times with fascinated interest. Many of them repeated the ideas which they found there in treatises of their own.

The concept of human nature which the Renaissance inherited from the past has at least one thing in common with that of modern science: the assumption that body and mind are closely related and mutually influential. Thus Renaissance psychology is a physiological psychology. It tends to explain mental conditions in terms of physical causes and vice versa. During the Renaissance, physiology and psychology were no more separable than they are today.

The principles of this physiological psychology were widely disseminated in sixteenth- and early seventeenth-century England. Many treatises on the subject, some of them translations, others original works by Englishmen, appeared in the native language. Poets did their share toward instructing their countrymen. Spenser's *Faerie Queene* contains an anatomy of human

---

[1] André du Laurens, *A Discourse of the Preservation of the Sight: of Melancholike Diseases; of Rheumes, and of Old Age*, tr. Richard Surphlet (London, 1599; Shakespeare Association Facsimiles, 1938), pp. 14–15.

[2] Pierre Charron, *Of Wisdome*, tr. Samson Lennard (London, c. 1607), p. 8.

nature (II, ix, 21–58). There are expository poems devoted entirely to the nature of man, including *Nosce Teipsum* by Sir John Davies, *Microcosmos* and *Mirum in Modum* by John Davies of Hereford, *The Purple Island* by Phineas Fletcher. Various plays, such as Tomkis' *Lingua* and Nabbes' *Microcosmus*, present the currently accepted psychology in allegorical form. Scientific theories of human nature, moreover, subtly and thoroughly permeate many literary works which have no expository purpose. One gets the impression that England of the time of Elizabeth and the early Stuarts thought a great deal about its physical and psychic states.

It will be necessary to review some of the principles of Renaissance physiology and psychology as an introduction to the discussion of Elizabethan melancholy.[3] First of all, I shall outline the conception of the human soul and its faculties which was generally current in late Renaissance England. In doing so, I shall simplify somewhat and ignore the authorities' multitudinous disagreements concerning details.

II

The soul[4] is the force which animates the inert matter of the body and directs its activities. It is one and indivisible. It is nevertheless, for purposes of analysis and description, divided into three sub-souls known as the vegetative (or vegetable) soul, the sensitive (or sensible) soul, and the rational (reasonable) soul.

The vegetative soul is seated in the liver. Its principal faculties[5] are those

---

[3] Many of the subjects included in this chapter have been treated before by modern literary scholars. See especially P. A. Robin, *The Old Physiology in English Literature* (London, 1911); Murray Wright Bundy, "Shakespeare and Elizabethan Psychology," *Journal of English and Germanic Philology*, XXIII (1924), 516–49; Ruth Leila Anderson, *Elizabethan Psychology and Shakespeare's Plays* (Iowa City, 1927); Lily B. Campbell, *Shakespeare's Tragic Heroes: Slaves of Passion* (Cambridge, 1930), pp. 51–78; John W. Draper, *The Humors & Shakespeare's Characters* (Durham, N. C., 1945).

[4] The following section is based mainly on: *Batman uppon Bartholome, His Booke De Proprietatibus Rerum* (London, 1582), fols. 12–17; Philippe de Mornay, *The True Knowledge of a Mans Owne Selfe*, tr. Anthony Munday (London, 1602); Thomas Wright, *The Passions of the Minde* (London, 1601), pp. 5–43; Charron, *Of Wisdome*, pp. 22–101; Pierre de la Primaudaye, *The French Academie*, tr. T. B. C. (London, 1618), pp. 401–43; F. N. Coeffeteau, *A Table of Humane Passions*, tr. Edward Grimeston (London, 1621), "Preface"; Robert Burton, *The Anatomy of Melancholy*, ed. A. R. Shilleto (London, 1926–27), I, 176–92.

[5] There are two popular classifications of the human faculties in Renaissance psychologies. The one which I am following groups them as powers of the three souls of the Aristotelian psychology; see *De Anima*, 413ª–414ª (II, ii–iii) and *Nicomachean Ethics*, 1102ª–1103ª (I, xiii). The other (see Anderson, *Elizabethan Psychology*, pp. 10–14) groups them according to their locations: natural faculties seated in the liver, vital faculties in the heart, animal faculties in the brain.

of nourishment, growth, and reproduction; in general, it directs the humbler physiological processes below the level of consciousness. Plants and animals as well as men have vegetative souls. The sensitive soul has the faculties of feeling and motion. It has the power of perceiving objects other than itself, it evaluates them as pleasing or repellent, and it directs motions of the body calculated either to obtain or to avoid them. It is seated in the brain and heart. Animals as well as men are endowed with sensitive souls. Man is distinguished from all other created beings by the possession of a rational soul, located in the brain, which is capable of distinguishing good from evil (not merely pleasure from pain), of contemplating itself, and of knowing God. The rational soul is the "self."

The faculties of sense and motion with which the sensitive soul is endowed are subdivided into various senses and motions. The senses are of two kinds, external and internal. There are five external senses—sight, hearing, smell, taste, and touch—and three internal senses—the common sense, the imagination (often called the *phantasy*, or *fancy*), and the memory. The internal senses are located in the brain.[6] The common sense receives impressions of the world outside from the external senses and assembles them into composite images. Its primary function, however, is apprehension. The eye does not know what it sees; the ear does not know what it hears. Sensory impressions are next conveyed to the imagination. This faculty can retain and consider them for some time. It evaluates them as pleasant or painful. It has the power of conceiving circumstances and situations other than those existing at the moment and of forming synthetic images from disparate elements as it pleases (hence, centaurs, griffons, and chimeras). This is the creative power of the imagination. It is a faculty which never rests; even when the other sensory and intellectual powers are in repose, a stream of images flows aimlessly through the imagination, and when one is asleep, this stream continues in his dreams. It is called the eye of the mind because the rational powers see the external world through it and through it alone; a new impression must pass successively through the external senses, the common sense, and the imagination before the reason may apprehend it.[7] The memory is a repository for sensory images delivered to it by the imagination and for ideas entrusted to it by the rational mind.

The motive powers of the sensitive soul are, like the senses, external and

---

[6] The brain is divided into cells, or ventricles. According to the most common opinion, there are three of these. Imagination and common sense occupy the foremost cell, reason the middle cell, and memory the hindmost. See Robin, *The Old Physiology*, pp. 53–54.

[7] This account of the imagination oversimplifies a complex and difficult subject. See M. W. Bundy, *The Theory of Imagination in Classical and Mediaeval Thought* (Urbana, 1927), Chap. IX.

internal. The internal powers, which operate in the heart,[8] are the precedent causes of the external. They are what in modern speech we call emotions. The sixteenth and seventeenth centuries called them *motions, affections, passions,* and *perturbations.* These terms are virtually synonymous, although *perturbations* sometimes seems to imply a greater degree of intensity than the others.

The internal motions fall into two categories: *concupiscible* and *irascible.* There are six of the former and five of the latter. Concupiscible passions arise when the imagination or the reasonable will perceives or conceives an object which appeals to it as pleasing or repellent. If the object is pleasing, the motion *love* is aroused; if painful, the motion *hatred.* From love arises *desire,* the inclination to possess whatever one loves; from hatred arises *aversion,* the inclination to shun whatever is abhorrent. *Joy* follows the fulfillment of desire; *sorrow* arises when inclination is thwarted. The irascible passions motivate effort toward the satisfaction of the concupiscible passions. *Boldness* inspires one to meet difficulties and dangers with confidence; *fear* prompts him to flee from dangers with which he apparently cannot cope; *hope* encourages him to persevere in his pursuits; *despair* persuades him to abandon fruitless endeavors; *anger* is the impulse to fight for the fulfillment of desire or aversion. These eleven principal passions are considerably subdivided. *Ambition, avarice,* and sexual *love,* for example, are subdivisions of desire; *pity, shame,* and *remorse* are subdivisions of sorrow. There are also compound passions; *envy,* for instance, is compounded of the desire for something and the hatred of its possessor.[9]

These, then, are the faculties of the sensitive soul, the faculties which rule the conduct of beasts. In man, the rational soul is the ruling power, and the sensitive faculties are its servants. It has two divisions—intellectual and volitional, that is, *reason*[10] and *will.* The former, which looks at the world through the medium of the imagination, is capable of perceiving the essence, not merely the appearance. It seeks truth through a logical train of thought. It draws conclusions regarding truth and falsehood, good and evil; in other words, it is capable of judgment. The reason determines what is

---

[8] Most authorities, following Aristotle (*De Anima,* 408[b]; *De Partibus Animalium,* 647[a], 665[a], 666[a]) place all the passions in the heart. According to Platonic tradition, the concupiscible passions are seated in the abdomen, the irascible in the breast (*Timaeus,* 69–71; *Phaedrus,* 253–54).

[9] The foregoing represents, in essence and in general outline, the classifications and definitions of the passions to be found in La Primaudaye, *Academie,* pp. 465 ff.; Charron, *Of Wisdome,* p. 74; Wright, *Passions,* pp. 41 ff.; Coeffeteau, *Passions,* pp. 32 ff.; Burton, *Anatomy,* I, 297 ff. These authors are following St. Thomas Aquinas (*Summa Theologica,* II [I], xxiii, 4). Not all of the authorities do so.

[10] *Reason* is very often used to designate the entire rational soul. I shall use the term in this broader sense hereafter.

good and what is evil and informs the will of its conclusions. The will, because of an instinct implanted in it by God, desires the good and abhors the evil which the reason represents to it. The will is sometimes called the rational appetite because it desires the good just as the sensitive affections desire the pleasing, and it abhors the evil just as they abhor the displeasing. When the will conceives a desire or an aversion, a corresponding passion normally arises in the sensitive soul. Thus the will causes physical action indirectly through the sensitive passions. Often the sensitive and rational desires conflict; the pleasant is not always the good. In such a case, the sensitive nature should yield, and passions corresponding to the promptings of the will should arise. For the reasonable will is the absolute mistress of the human soul.

III

The physical life of man "is stayed vpon two pillers, which are the radicall heate and moisture," that is, heat and moisture with which the body is endowed at birth. The radical heat, or natural heat,

is the principall instrument of the soule, for it is it that concocteth and distributeth our nourishment, which procureth generation, . . . which fashioneth all our parts, which maketh vs to liue. . . . This heate being a naturall bodie hath neede of nourishment, the humour which is called the radicall moisture, is the nourishment thereof, as the oyle which is put into the lampes, doth maintayne and feede the flame; this humour once failing, it must needes fall out, that the natural heate shuld perish, but this humor cannot last for euer, seeing the natural heate is daily threatning & consuming the same.[11]

As man grows older his body becomes gradually drier and colder. When the natural moisture is consumed and the natural heat fails, he dies. Natural heat is literally the flame of life. Heat and moisture, then, are the primary qualities of a living creature. Cold and dryness are hostile to life.

The Renaissance term for digestion is *concoction*. The liver, being a hot organ, "is to the stomake, as fyre vnder the pot."[12] The product of digestion

---

[11] Du Laurens, *Discourse*, p. 170. This theory regarding the nature of life and the reason for its decay has very ancient sources. A living creature, says Aristotle, is by nature warm and humid; old men and dead bodies are cold and dry (*Parva Naturalia*, 466ᵃ; *Problemata*, 955ᵃ). Dying is extinction of heat (*Parva Naturalia*, 469ᵇ). Man "is warmest on the first day of his existence and coldest on the last."—Hippocrates (?), *The Nature of Man*, Chap. xii (*Hippocrates*, tr. W. H. S. Jones [London, 1923–31], IV, 37).

[12] Sir Thomas Elyot, *The Castel of Helth* (London, 1541; Scholars' Facsimiles and Reprints, 1937), fol. 46ʳ.

in the stomach is a viscid, whitish fluid called *chyle*. This is conveyed to the liver, and there the nutrimental matter undergoes a second concoction,[13] the products of which are the four primary humors. *Blood* is the most plentiful of these. Mingled with the blood which the liver produces is a light and effervescent fluid, *choler*, which tends to rise. There is also a heavy and sluggish fluid, *melancholy*, which tends to sink. Melancholy consists of the less pure and less nutrimental parts of the chyle and is considered semiexcremental. One writer describes it as "dregges and durte remoued aparte from the principalles of lyfe, ennemy to ioye and liberalite, and of nere kinred to age and death."[14] The fourth humor, *phlegm*, is merely chyle only half digested. Phlegm further digested by the liver would be blood.

These four humors (with their abnormal varieties, of which more later) make up nearly all of the fluid content of the body. Each has two primary qualities: blood is hot and moist, choler is hot and dry, melancholy is cold and dry, and phlegm is cold and moist. The four humors of the microcosm, therefore, are analogous to the four elements of the macrocosm, for air is hot and moist, fire hot and dry, earth cold and dry, and water cold and moist. The humors also have their secondary qualities: blood is red and sweet; choler is yellow, bitter, thin, and volatile; melancholy is black, sour, thick, and heavy; phlegm is whitish or colorless, tasteless, and watery.

Each humor has its physiological functions. The blood is the carrier of the natural heat and moisture. It warms and moistens the whole body, and it nourishes most of the fleshy parts; that is, it is turned into flesh through the process known as the third digestion. Choler nourishes the parts of the body supposed to be hot and dry and has the function of provoking the expulsion of excrements. Melancholy nourishes "the parts which are melancholickely qualified, as the bones, gristles, sinewes, &c.,"[15] and it provokes appetite in the stomach. Phlegm nourishes the cold and moist members, notably the brain and the kidneys. Each humor has its particular seat. The seat of the blood is the liver; the seat of phlegm is sometimes said to be the lungs, sometimes the kidneys; the gall is provided for superfluous and excremental choler; the spleen is provided for superfluous and excremental melancholy.

---

[13] There are three digestions. The last is the process by which humors are utilized as nutriment, that is, the process by which humors become flesh. See Robin, *The Old Physiology*, pp. 76–77.

[14] *Regimen Sanitatis Salerni*, tr. Thomas Paynell (London, 1575), fol. cxxxii^v. The English matter in this volume consists of Paynell's translation of Arnoldus' commentary on the old Latin poem. Paynell prints the poem itself in Latin. All of my quotations from this volume are from the translated commentary.

[15] Thomas Walkington, *The Optick Glasse of Humors* (London, 1639; originally published 1607), p. 130.

Pathological conditions (barring wounds, fractures, dislocations, etc.) are due to humoral abnormalities: to superabundance or deficiency of a humor throughout the body, to improper concentration of a humor in one member, or to the presence, either through the body as a whole or in a single member, of noxious unnatural forms of choler, phlegm, or melancholy.[16] Renaissance medicine explains every disease by one of these conditions.[17] Each disease is classified as hot and dry, cold and dry, etc., according to the offending humor. A typical list of "diseases procedynge of melancolye," that is, cold and dry diseases, includes "madnesse, fallynge syckenesse [epilepsy], bleedynges [hemorrhoids?], quynces, poses, hoorsenes, coughes, lepries, scabbes, ache in the ioyntes."[18]

The fundamental principle of cure is, of course, the restoration of the normal. The most drastic method is bloodletting to evacuate the injurious humor from the veins. Purgation is supposed to serve the same purpose. Certain drugs are specific purgatives for certain humors. Black hellebore, for instance, is the favorite purgative for melancholy; rhubarb for choler. Various medicines ("alteratives") are used to change the character of a humor by moistening, drying, heating, cooling, thickening, thinning. Diet is important. A patient suffering from a hot and dry disease should eat cold and moist foods, such as lettuce and cress. In the Renaissance dietaries, the various foods are described in terms of heat, cold, moisture, and dryness[19] so that the reader may choose those foods which have a nature opposite to that of his complaint. The patient's daily manner of life also must be regulated. Idleness and sleep warm and moisten the body; labor and waking cool and dry it. The temperature and humidity of the atmosphere must be taken

---

[16] These arise through the burning of a natural humor by unnatural heat, through the putrifaction of a natural humor, or through improper mixture of natural humors. The medical writers distinguish many unnatural humors. Elyot's list is typical (*Castel of Helth*, fols. 8–9). See also *Claudii Galeni Opera Omnia*, ed. Kühn, (Leipzig, 1821–33), V, 108–9; XIX, 364–65, 490.

[17] "Videtur autem sanitatem eorum humorum aequalitate et symmetria consignare: his vero deficientibus vel exsuperantibus praeter modum vel quantitate vel qualitate vel locorum translatione vel complexu inordinato vel putredine vitiatis morbi oboriuntur; quemadmodum et dicitur, morbos humorum intemperie accidere: sicuti et sanitatem tum detractione et additione tum tenuitate et crassitie humorum atque omnino ipsorum temperie et commoderatione restitui. . . ."—Galen, *De Humoribus Liber*, in *Opera*, XIX, 491. Cf. *The Nature of Man*, in *Hippocrates*, IV, 11–13; Elyot, *Castel of Helth*, fol. 8ʳ.

[18] Elyot, *Castel of Helth*, fol. 83ʳ [85ʳ]. Quartan fever, cancer, and palsy are often listed as melancholy diseases. The authorities differ bewilderingly regarding the causes and classification of diseases.

[19] I have derived my information on this subject principally from Elyot, *Castel of Helth*, fols. 17ᵛ ff.; Thomas Cogan, *The Haven of Health* (London, 1589; originally published 1584); William Vaughan, *Approved Directions for Health* (London, 1612; originally published 1600); Tobias Venner, *Via Recta ad Vitam Longam* (London, 1628; originally published 1620).

into account. The patient should enjoy peace of mind, for mental perturbation breeds ill humors.

IV

The two digestions, or concoctions, by which food is refined into humors have already been mentioned. A third refinement (not strictly speaking a concoction) takes place in the heart. By this process the purest blood is made into a substance subtler and rarer than any humor ("subtilis vapor ... flammula ex purissimo sanguine in corde nata"[20]). This is called *vital spirit*, or *vital spirits*. The vital spirit is the vehicle of the natural heat and moisture which are essential to life.[21] The heart pours it into the arteries, and it is borne by the arterial blood to animate every part of the body. If for any length of time the supply of this spirit is meager, "the whole masse of bloud easily degenerateth" into melancholy.[22] If the flow of vital spirit is suddenly and completely interrupted, "then life ceaseth, as in a *syncope* or swooning."[23]

There is still a further step in the progressive rarification of matter, which takes place in the brain. Here the vital spirit is refined into an even subtler vapor, the *animal spirit*, or *animal spirits* (Latin *anima*). The animal spirit flows in the nerves ("in nervos infus[us] velut lumen"[24]). Its function is to act as messenger between the brain and the organs in other parts of the body. It is the link between mind and body.

For the proper functioning of mind and body, it is essential that the spirits be quick, lively, exquisitely subtle, and absolutely pure. The quality of the spirits depends naturally upon the quality of the blood. Unwise diet or ill digestion may produce blood of such a nature that good spirits may not be engendered from it. Superabundant or corrupted humors may vitiate the best spirits. By disturbing the operations of the heart, passions may prevent the production of good spirits: "manifestum est spiritum fieri meliorum in

---

[20] Philipp Melanchthon, *Liber de Anima*, in *Opera*, ed. Carolus Gottlieb Bretschneider (Halle, 1834–60), XIII, 88.

[21] The authorities commonly define the vital spirit as the vehicle of natural heat. It is of necessity the vehicle of natural moisture also, for the two are not independent entities. Natural heat is "a substance moist and very vaporous."—Juan Huarte, *Examen de Ingenios*, tr. R. Carew (London, 1594), p. 59. The "*Radicall humour* ... hath the celestiall and quickening heate brought immediatly and directly vnto it: so that when this moisture is extinguished, the heate also vanisheth."—La Primaudaye, *Academie*, p. 547.

[22] Timothy Bright, *A Treatise of Melancholie* (London, 1586; Facsimile Text Society Reprints, 1940), p. 249.

[23] Burton, *Anatomy*, I, 170.

[24] Melanchthon, *Opera*, XIII, 88.

cerebro, quando bonum est cordis temperamentum, et quando cor non tur-
batum est ira et moesticia."[25]

V

The ideal man would have the four humors mingled in his body in a very
exact proportion. Blood would be the most abundant humor, phlegm the
next in quantity, melancholy the next, and choler the least. Such a man would
enjoy perfect health of body and mind and would be richly endowed with
capabilities and virtues. But "This golden temperature must be onely understood and seen with the internal eies of reason, seeing it hath not a reall existence."[26] In actuality each man's constitution varies more or less from the
norm by a surplus of one humor or another; and his complexion, or temperament, is designated, according to the dominant humor, as sanguine, choleric,
phlegmatic, or melancholy. It should be noted that, according to Renaissance physiology, the temperatures and humidities of men's bodies differ
widely. The sanguine complexion is considered the most desirable, primarily
because heat and moisture are the qualities of life. The melancholy temperament is usually considered the least enviable, for cold and dryness are opposite to the vital qualities and cut "in twain the thred of . . . life long before
it be spun."[27] A man of hot and moist temperament is young at sixty; a man
of cold and dry temperament is old at forty.[28]

The dominant humor to a large extent determines the individual's appearance and behavior. The well-informed observer, consequently, can readily
classify men according to their complexions. The sanguine man is fleshy,
ruddy, fair-haired, amiable of countenance and manner, gladsome of spirit,
kindly, liberal, fond of good food and good wine, fond of music, amorous,
intelligent, courageous. The choleric person is lean, hairy, "saffron colored,"
rash, quick to anger, proud, revengeful, bold, ambitious, shrewd. The phlegmatic man is short and fat, pale, torpid, slothful, mentally dull.[29] Melancholy
men are "leane, dry, lank . . . crokenayled . . . the face becommeth pale,
yelowyshe & swarty . . . As touching the notes & markes of their minds, they
are churlish, whyning . . . obstinate, greedy . . . they vse a certaine slow pace
& soft nyce gate, holdinge down their heads, with countenaunce & loke . . .

---

[25] *Idem.*
[26] Walkington, *Optick Glasse*, p. 151. Cf. Du Laurens, *Discourse*, p. 169.
[27] Walkington, *Optick Glasse*, p. 126.
[28] Du Laurens, *Discourse*, p. 177; Edward Edwards, *The Analysis of Chyrurgery*
(London, 1636), p. 15.
[29] *Regimen Sanitatis Salerni*, fols. cxxxix–cxlii.

grim and frowninge."[30] They are taciturn, they love to be alone, and they are continually tormented by fears and sorrows.[31] Of all the four complexions, the sanguine is the happiest, and the most miserable is the melancholic. The sanguine man is the most attractive in appearance, whereas "The most deformed is the Malancholike," who is "swarte and ill fauored."[32]

If a man is dissatified with his complexion, there are means, especially dietary means, by which he may heat himself, cool himself, moisten himself, dry himself. If he follows the voluminous advice in the dietaries, he "may in time change and alter his bad complexion into a better."[33]

Renaissance scholars are notoriously fond of analogies. One finds a very complex system of analogies built about the four humors and the four complexions. The correspondency between the elements and the humors is only one of several. These may be conveniently presented by means of Diagram A.[34] This means, to take the melancholic segment (lower left hand) as an example, that the planet Saturn, the element earth, the north wind, the season winter, old age, and the melancholy temperament are all cold and dry. It means, moreover, that Saturn, the north wind, winter, and old age cause increase of the melancholy humor in all men.

Among these various associations, that which connects melancholy with Saturn probably appears more often than any other in Renaissance works, scientific and literary. One finds it, of course, in astrological treatises. According to one astrologer, Saturn is "Cold and drie, melancholick, earthie, masculine . . . maleuolent, destroyer of life." There follows a characterization of the saturnine man (the man born under Saturn's influence) which corresponds closely with the usual conception of the melancholy man.[35] *Saturnine* and *melancholic* are virtually synonymous.

---

[30] Levinus Lemnius, *The Touchstone of Complexions*, tr. Thomas Newton (London, 1576), fol. 146.

[31] *Regimen Sanitatis Salerni*, fol. cxliii.

[32] Thomas Rogers, *A Philosophicall Discourse, Entituled, the Anatomie of the Minde* (London, 1576), fol. 79r.

[33] Walkington, *Optick Glasse*, p. 61.

[34] This is copied, with minor omissions, from Walkington's *Optick Glasse* (opposite p. 76 in the 1639 edition). A similar diagram appears on the title page of Robert Anton's *Philosophers Satyrs* (London, 1616). The scheme shown here must be taken only as representative. One finds a great many disagreements among the various writers as to which is the melancholy season, which the melancholy age, etc.

[35] Claude Dariot, *A Briefe and Most Easie Introduction to the Astrologicall Judgement of the Starres*, tr. F. W. (London, 1598), sig. D2r. Cf. sig. C4r. Examination of other astrological works shows that Dariot's ideas are conventional. Similar material appears also in *The Kalendar & Compost of Shepherds*, a widely circulated book of science for the layman, first published in English in 1503. See the edition of G. C. Heseltine (London, 1930), pp. 141–42.

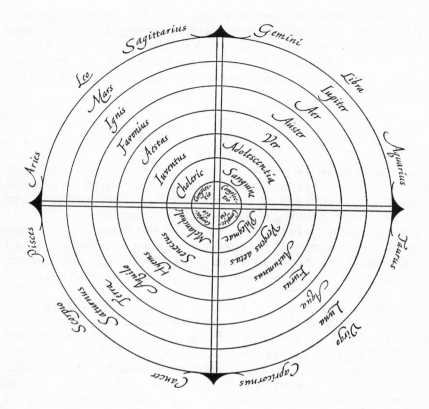

The melancholic character of old age[36] and the consequent decrepitude of the aged receive considerable attention in learned works. An affliction "natural to all, and which no man living can avoid," says Robert Burton, "is old age, which being cold and dry, and of the same quality as Melancholy is, must needs cause it, by diminution of spirits and substance."[37] Since mel-

---

[36] In Renaissance works one finds many descriptions of the various ages, or periods, of man's life. There is great disagreement concerning the number of these. Most frequently, however, the writers list four ages corresponding to the four humors (see the diagram from Walkington's *Optick Glasse*) or seven ages corresponding to the seven planets (see *As You Like It*, II, vii, 139–66), with Saturn ruling the seventh. There is fairly general agreement that youth is sanguine and old age melancholic. Franz Boll, in *Die Lebensalter (Neue Jahrbücher für das Klassische Altertum, Geschichte und Deutsche Literatur*, XXXI [1913], 89–145), investigates the classical and to some extent the medieval history of ideas regarding the successive periods of human life. The division into seven, he finds, was the most popular.

[37] *Anatomy*, I, 239–40. The physiology of the process of aging is discussed above.

ancholy is the humor most inimical to life, old men are subject to the most grievous infirmities of body and mind. Scholarly writers show deep concern for the hard lot of the aged, and in works like Du Laurens' essay "Of Old Age,"[38] Thomas Newton's *The Old Mans Dietarie* (1586), and Simon Goulart's *The Wise Vieillard*,[39] they offer advice on how to mitigate the evils of senility.

VI

I have characterized the passions as functions of the sensitive soul. They may be regarded also as physiological phenomena. A passion is a muscular expansion or contraction of the heart; the heart "doth alwaies either enlarge or shut vp it selfe according to those affections that are within it."[40]

This muscular action of the heart is most often a response to a mental state. When the mind is pleased or sees prospect of pleasure, it stimulates the heart to expand and open. A combative state of mind likewise stimulates dilation. When the mind is affected by something repellent or by the prospect of pain, it prompts the heart to contract and close.

Humors also cause motions of the heart. A hot humor provokes dilation. Tempered by moisture, heat excites passions associated with pleasure or the possibility of pleasure, such as joy, desire, and hope. These are "hot and moist," or "sanguine," passions. Accompanied by dryness, heat arouses combative passions—boldness and anger. These are "hot and dry," or "choleric," passions. Cold, in combination with dryness, provokes contraction of the heart and engenders passions associated with pain, such as sorrow, fear, and despair. These are "cold and dry," or "melancholy," passions. In combination with moisture, cold has little or no effect on the heart; phlegmatic men are unemotional.[41]

A passion is properly initiated by the reason. This function is sometimes usurped by the imagination, and it is possible for the humors to stimulate passion without authorization from any mental faculty. Normally, however, passion is a response to an injunction from the reason. When the reason sees occasion for emotion it communicates its will to the heart by the

---

[38] *Discourse*, pp. 168–94.

[39] Two issues of the English translation of this work appeared in 1621.

[40] La Primaudaye, *Academie*, p. 466. Melanchthon believes "ipsum cordis substantiam adfectuum fontem esse."—*Opera*, XIII, 129.

[41] The preceding paragraph is based especially on Melanchthon, *Opera*, XIII, 124–29; La Primaudaye, *Academie*, pp. 466–68, 471; Wright, *Passions*, pp. 60–68, 82–84, 101–6; Mornay, *True Knowledge*, pp. 158–60; Coeffeteau, *Passions*, pp. 15–17; Edwards, *Chyrurgery*, pp. 11, 20.

medium of the animal spirit. The heart responds as directed by expansion or contraction. Coincidentally there is a movement toward the heart of the humor whose qualities will stimulate the proper reaction in that organ (which is thus doubly stimulated). The heart does not "haue the temperature which all Passions require; for loue will haue heate, and sadnesse colde, feare constringeth, and pleasure dilateth." Thus "in pleasure concurre great store of pure [vital] spirites; in payne and sadnesse, much melancholy blood, in ire, bloud and choller; and not only . . . the heart draweth, but also the same soule that informeth the heart residing in other partes, sendeth the humours vnto the heart."[42] At the inception of a cold and dry passion, the spleen pours forth melancholy for the purpose of stimulating the heart; at the inception of a hot and dry passion, the gall pours forth choler.[43]

A passion is a definite sensation, felt first in the heart and subsequently throughout the body. Desire and joy are agreeable sensations. A joyful heart, says Melanchthon, dilates with pleasure as if to embrace the object, "ut amans laetatur amplectans puellam." In sorrow the heart suffers painful contraction: "constringitur, premitur, tremit et languefit cum acri sensu doloris."[44] When the heart is "stricken and beaten with some vnpleasant thing . . . then doth it retire, close vp it selfe & feele griefe, as if it had receiued a wound."[45] Sorrow is physical pain. In anger the heart swells belligerently and sends forth blood and spirit ("tanquam milites") to repel the offending object. In this operation it grows hot and inflames the blood and spirit, and the whole body trembles, even the bones.[46] The blood "boyleth round about" the heart, and "these burning flames and kindled spirits" rise to the brain[47] and vitiate the reason.

Each passion, we have noted, is associated with two of the primary qualities, namely the qualities which tend to incite it. Joy is stimulated by heat and moisture, sorrow by cold and dryness, etc. Each passion, moreover, alters the complexion of the entire body, which assumes, at least temporarily, the very qualities which excite the emotion. When the heart is opened by joy or a kindred passion, it "disperseth much naturall heate with the blood, besides great quantity of spirits."[48] The whole system is warmed and moistened. When grief or a kindred passion closes the heart, the blood and vital spirit are locked within it and thus are denied to the rest of the body. The whole system is cooled and dried both by lack of blood and vital spirit and

---

42 Wright, *Passions*, pp. 65, 83.
43 Melanchthon, *Opera*, XIII, 44, 129.
44 *Ibid.*, p. 126.
45 La Primaudaye, *Academie*, p. 466.
46 Melanchthon, *Opera*, XIII, 127.
47 La Primaudaye, *Academie*, p. 497.
48 *Ibid.*, p. 466.

by the melancholy humor issuing from the spleen.[49] During anger, choler issues from the gall: "ciet ardentissimum humorem scilicet rubram bilem, quae effusa, reliquum sanguinem inficit."[50] The body thus becomes hot and dry. Since any passion tends to establish the conditions which are favorable to its own continuation, it might conceivably prolong itself indefinitely.

Passions have a considerable influence upon physical health. Passions of "Content," says Edward Edwards, "dilate the heart & arteries," bring out vital spirit and natural heat, and if they are not immoderate, "comfort and strengthen all the parts of the body and minde, in all their actions."[51] Joy is "a medicine to the body: and foode to the naturall heate and moisture, in which two qualities life chiefly consisteth. . . . For this cause Phisicions alwayes exhort sicke persons to bee as merry as they may, and to auoide sorrow and sadnesse, which beeing colde and dry is contrary to life, and so consumeth men."[52]

Passions of "Discontent" divert "the vitall heat and spirits into the center of the heart." Because they deprive the system of "vitall heat and moysture," they are "destroyers" and "murtherers" "of body and minde," "hastners" of old age and death.[53] The constriction of the grief-stricken heart and the chill of the melancholy humor which surrounds the heart interfere with the production and distribution of vital spirit.[54] The blood, which should be heated and enlivened by the spirit, degenerates into melancholy; the body becomes cold and dry and withers away, "for colde extinguisheth heate, and drienesse moysture, which twoo qualities principally concerne life." Fear and sorrow "preuaile often so much with men, that they languish away and die."[55] Sorrow "is a maligne, colde and dry *Passion*" which wastes natural moisture, quenches natural heat, and withers the heart. When autopsy is performed upon "those that haue beene smothered with melancholy," it

---

[49] Fear and grief may have further physiological effects. Since the cold, dry melancholy humor has assembled about the heart, nature is "desirous to relieue and succour it [and] sendeth heat vnto it . . . she suddenly calleth backe the bloud and spirits vnto the heart, and then followeth a generall palenesse and colde in all the outward parts, and chiefly in the face, with a shiuering throughout the whole body."—*ibid.*, p. 471. This concentration of heat in the heart sometimes burns it. According to Melanchthon, "nisi desinat tristicia, tandem cor torrefactum extinguitur."—*Opera*, XIII, 126. Coeffeteau writes that the heat concentrated in the heart by fear may descend and burn the nether organs (*Passions*, p. 465). Elizabethan dramatists often associate sorrow and fear with burning.

[50] Melanchthon, *Opera*, XIII, 129.

[51] *Chyrurgery*, p. 20.

[52] La Primaudaye, *Academie*, p. 455. Cf. Elyot, *Castel of Helth*, fol. 68r; Burton, *Anatomy*, II, 137 ff.

[53] Edwards, *Chyrurgery*, p. 20. Cf. Elyot, *Castel of Helth*, fol. 64.

[54] La Primaudaye, *Academie*, p. 455; Wright, *Passions*, p. 105.

[55] Wright, *Passions*, p. 106.

reveals "insteed of a heart . . . nothing but a drie skinne like to the leaues in Autumne."[56]

Any immoderate passion may be harmful. Anger "stirreth vp the naturall heat, breedeth choler, and inflameth the blood and spirits . . . it vehemently heateth the bodie, drieth it, and resolueth the strengths." Even joy, the most salutary of the passions, is harmful if it is excessive, for it "relaxeth the heart, and causeth such effusion of the spirit, as that oftentimes ensue sicknesse, and great debility of the body, swoundings. . . ."[57] Any passion, if it is very sudden and violent, may kill outright. If joy "be sodayne and feruente, it oftentymes sleeth, for as moche as it draweth to sodeynly and excessiuely naturall heate outwarde"[58] and thus leaves the heart bloodless and cold. It happens "sometimes, that present death followeth a great and suddeine feare, because all the bloud retiring to the heart choaketh it, and vtterly extinguisheth naturall heat and the spirits, so that death must needes ensue thereof."[59] Sorrow may kill in the same fashion as fear.

> For both revoke the *sp'rites, bloud,* and *kind heate,*
> And to *harte's* Center doe the same direct,
> Which place bee'ng little, and their throng so greate,
> Expels the *Vitall spirits* from their *seate.*[60]

As a result of furious anger, "Some have broken their veines, supprest their urine, whereby present death hath ensued."[61] Sudden and violent passions, moreover, may break the heart. The heart "hath all manner of fibres right, oblique and transuerse, most strong and most compact and mingled one with another . . . as well for the better performance of his motion, as for a defence against iniuries."[62] In violently expanding or contracting the heart, a passion may break the heart strings.

The reader has doubtless noticed that the old physiology of the passions has contributed many common phrases to the language: "ardent love,"

---

[56] Coeffeteau, *Passions,* pp. 332–33.

[57] Venner, *Via Recta,* pp. 225–26. Hot passions, moreover, produce a noxious "unnatural" melancholy by burning the humors. This subject is treated in the next chapter.

[58] Elyot, *Castel of Helth,* fol. 68.

[59] La Primaudaye, *Academie,* p. 471.

[60] John Davies of Hereford, *Microcosmos* (in *Works,* ed. A. B. Grosart [Edinburgh, 1878], vol. I), p. 35. Fortunately the sighs and lamentations which usually accompany grief lessen the danger of its proving fatal: "For howsoeuer griefe shutteth vp the heart . . . yet by groning, sighing, and weeping, the heart doth in some sort open it selfe, as if it would come foorth to breathe, least being wholly shut vp with sorrow it should be stifled."—La Primaudaye, *Academie,* p. 468. It is dangerous to repress grief.

[61] Charron, *Of Wisdome,* p. 88.

[62] Helkiah Crooke, *Microcosmographia* (London, 1616), p. 370. See Miss Anderson's discussion of heartbreak, *Elizabethan Psychology,* pp. 13, 86–87.

"blazing anger," "boiling blood," "chilling fear," "cold-blooded murder," "broken heart," and the like. These expressions were not figures of speech in Queen Elizabeth's day.

VII

The reasons for the sanguine man's characteristic gaiety, the choleric man's anger, and the melancholy man's sadness should now be clear: "euery one is most subiect to those affections that come neerest to the nature, temperature, and complexion of his body." The sanguine constitution is predisposed to certain passions and is resistant to others.

As for example, the affection of ioy is hote and moist, and therefore they that are hot and moist, as children, young men, sound and healthy folkes, and idle persons, are most easily inclined to that affection. Contrariwise, sorrow is a cold and dry affection, and therefore they that are colde and drie are most giuen to that affection; and such are old folkes and they that are of a melancholy humour.[63]

Choleric men are by physical necessity inclined to be angry. Phlegmatic men necessarily are dull and passionless.

It is possible for the dominant humor to cause a passion without external stimulus. Some men "are alwayes, almost, merry, others, for the most part, melancholy, others euer angry: this diuersity must come from the naturall constitution of the body, wherein one or other humor dooth predominate."[64] Also

wee prooue in dreames, and physitians prognosticate by them what humour aboundeth, for choller causeth fighting, blood, and wounds; melancholy disgrace, feares, afrightments, ill successe, and such like: these dreams are caused by the spirits which ascend into the imagination, the which being purer or groser, hotter or colder, more or lesse, (which diuersitie dependeth vpon the humors of the bodie) mooue diuerse passions according to their nature.[65]

Just as the temperament influences the passions, so the passions may affect the temperament. If a passion is very strong or if it continues long, it tends to establish the humor of corresponding qualities as the dominant humor, and the humor in turn may make the passion which produced it habitual.

---

[63] La Primaudaye, *Academie*, p. 455.
[64] Wright, *Passions*, pp. 111–12.
[65] *Ibid.*, p. 111. Cf. Chaucer's "Nun's Priest's Tale," ll. 103–16. The humors or fumes rising from them are sometimes said to discolor the animal spirits or even the substance of the brain. Melancholy, for example, would blacken the images in the brain.

Passions may thus modify personality profoundly, even effect a permanent change in complexion. "When the *Affections' Acts* are *habits* growne," they become "*Vertues* or els *Vices*."[66]

Once more, the linguistic contribution of the old physiology should be noted. When we describe a personality as "sanguine," "choleric," or "phlegmatic," we mean something very close to what the Elizabethans meant by the same adjectives, although they have now lost their scientific connotations.

VIII

The physical dangers which lie in the passions are grave, but the moral dangers are graver. Moralists of the Renaissance subscribe to a fundamental principle of classical ethics: conduct motivated by reason is virtuous conduct; conduct motivated by unregulated passion is vicious conduct. Reason is the faculty which distinguishes man from beast. In man it is, or should be, the ruling power. If one follows its dictates, he will achieve virtue and happiness. The passions, however, are turbulently rebellious servants. Often they overrule reason and impel one into evil and misery.

As it is ... a poynt of treason, that suche lewed perturbations ... shoulde rage rebell & take vpon them the rule of the hole man, contemptuously despysynge the auctorytie of the mynde, so it is extreme foly for the mynde, to be slaue vnto fonde affections, and to serue at a becke, the vyle carkeys, neyther the dignitie of nature, neyther the expresse lawe of god, any thyng regarded.[67]

This doctrine had wide currency and influence in Elizabethan and early Stuart England.[68]

The passions are strong and violent. Sometimes they compel one to act against his better judgment; "haling to ilnesse, they tosse and turmoyle our miserable soules, as tempests & waues the Ocean sea."[69] At other times they confuse or blind the reason and win its assent. They are like "greene spectacles, which make all things resemble the colour of greene; euen so, hee

---

[66] John Davies of Hereford, *Microcosmos* (in *Works*, vol. I), p. 37.

[67] Juan Luis Vives, *An Introduction to Wisedome*, tr. Rycharde Morysine (London, 1540), sigs. Dii–Diii.

[68] See Bundy, "Shakespeare and Elizabethan Psychology"; Anderson, *Elizabethan Psychology*, especially pp. 132–53; Campbell, *Shakespeare's Tragic Heroes*, pp. 63–72, 93–102; Theodore Spencer, *Shakespeare and the Nature of Man* (New York, 1942), pp. 21–28. The chief authorities from whom this ethical system was derived were Plato, Aristotle, Plutarch, Cicero, Seneca, Augustine, and Aquinas.

[69] Wright, *Passions*, pp. 301–2.

that loueth, hateth, or by anie other passion is vehemently possessed, iudgeth all things that occurre in fauour of that passion, to bee good and agreeable with reason."[70] In their insurrections against reason the passions have the imagination for an ally. The imagination, like the passions, is a sensitive faculty and is capable only of distinguishing pleasure and pain, not right and wrong. Whatever the reason can see of the world without "passeth by the gates of our imagination, the cosin germane to our sensitiue appetite." As the rising or setting moon is magnified by vapors, "euen so, the beauty and goodnesse of the obiect represented to our vnderstanding, appeareth fairer and goodlier than it is, because a clowdie imagination interposeth a mist."[71]

The sensitive powers not only may win temporary mastery over the intellect but may permanently vitiate and dominate it. They "trouble woonderfully the soule, corrupting the iudgement, & seducing the will."[72] When reason has once yielded to passion, it seeks justification for passion: "the *Wit* on the one side labours to find out reasons presently, that may countenance & grace it: and the *Imagination* on the other side, like a deceitfull Counsellor, [seeks] to blinde the eyes of the Iudge."[73] Thus the master becomes the servant. And by degrees it happens that "what was done in the beginning with some scruple and doubt, hath beene afterwards held and maintained for a veritie and revelation from heaven: that which was onely in the sensualitie, hath taken place in the highest part of the understanding."[74]

It may seem strange that, in a creature as ideally endowed as man, the lower nature should thus subvert the God-ordained order of things and win the mastery over the higher. The explanation is the corruption of man and the enfeeblement of his intellectual powers which resulted from the Fall. "The things that were made to obey vs seeme now, through the curse that followed our fall, to rebell against vs. Reason should rule our affections, but now contrariwise our affections beare rule ouer reason."[75] The light of our reason is "by Mans Fall much dimmed and decayed," and "our unruly *Appetite* . . . laboureth against us . . . to deprive us of those Reliques of Sight which we yet retaine."[76]

In human nature, then, there is continual warfare between the rational and the sensitive, the human and the bestial, the intellectual and the physical.

---

[70] *Ibid.*, p. 88.
[71] *Ibid.*, pp. 91–93.
[72] *Ibid.*, p. 14.
[73] Daniel Tuvil, *Essaies Politicke, and Morall* (London, 1608), fol. 19ᵛ.
[74] Charron, *Of Wisdome*, pp. 64–65.
[75] Sir Richard Barckley, *The Felicitie of Man* (London, 1631; originally published in 1598), p. 3.
[76] Edward Reynolds, *A Treatise of the Passions and Faculties of the Soule of Man* (London, 1640), p. 63. Cf. La Primaudaye, *Academie*, p. 12; Wright, *Passions*, pp. 2–3, 322–23.

The passions are very likely to be not good servants, but intestine enemies always ready to rise and reverse the normal order of the soul. When they do so, they are diseases of the soul. Writers of the Renaissance attribute to them most of man's vices and sins. The passions, moreover, are the principal cause of human misery. Men are "slaves to their several lusts and appetite, they precipitate and plunge themselves into a labyrinth of cares, blinded with lust, blinded with ambition. . . . By giving way to these violent passions . . . they are torn in pieces, as *Actaeon* was with his dogs, and crucify their own souls."[77] Virtue and happiness are coexistent spiritual states: "happiness consisteth in a minde endued with vertue, voide of all perturbations and vnquietnesse."[78] The *summum bonum*, the greatest good possible to man in his earthly life, is "tranquillitie of the spirit. . . . This is that great and rich treasure, which . . . is the fruit of all our labors and studies, the crowne of wisdome."[79] To achieve this enviable condition, the reasonable soul must keep continual watch over the sensitive powers and must continually exert itself in curbing them.

Since man's greatest enemies lie within himself, his greatest moral problem is self-mastery. Before self-mastery must come self-knowledge, for no man can govern his lower nature without an understanding of it. For this reason the moralists write treatises on psychology, and through these there echoes the ancient exhortation *nosce teipsum.*[80] Melanchthon's *Liber de Anima*, Roger's *Anatomie of the Minde*, Wright's *Passions of the Minde*, Charron's *Of Wisdome*, Sir John Davies' *Nosce Teipsum*, Mornay's *True Knowledge of a Mans Owne Selfe*, Walkington's *Optick Glasse of Humors*, Reynold's *Treatise of the Passions*, and many other works have the avowed purpose of instructing the reader on the subject of his own nature so that he may be armed with the knowledge which is necessary to virtue and happiness. Ethical treatises are, in fact, our chief source of information on Renaissance psychology. Psychology and ethics were not distinguishable subjects in that period.

He who "throughly would know him selfe, must as well knowe his boddie, as his minde."[81] Instruction in psychology necessarily includes instruction in physiology and in the means of maintaining physical health. Treatment of diseases of the soul may involve, first of all, cure of diseases of the

---

[77] Burton, *Anatomy*, I, 298.

[78] Barckley, *Felicitie*, p. 506. Cf. pp. 491, 513–14.

[79] Charron, *Of Wisdome*, p. 346. Cf. La Primaudaye, *Academie*, pp. 14–15; Burton, *Anatomy*, II, 117–18.

[80] "Know thyself," it is said, was inscribed above the portals of the temple of Apollo at Delphi. See Plato, *Charmides*, 164–65, *Phaedrus*, 229, *Alcibiades*, 129 ff.; Cicero, *Disputationes Tusculanae*, I, xxii; V, xxv.

[81] Rogers, *Anatomie*, "To the Reader," p. 5.

body. A virtuous mind is not likely to be found in a distempered body: "the temperance or intemperance that may be in our bodies, extendeth it selfe vnto the estate of our soule."[82]

Thus the physician shares the responsibility of the moral teacher, and many physicians are conscious of this responsibility. Timothy Bright believes that "Of all other practise of phisick, that parte most commendeth the excellency of the noble facultie, which not only releeueth the bodily infirmity, but after a sort euen also correcteth the infirmities of the mind."[83] The elaborate dietaries and regimens which medical writers offer have the twofold purpose of preventing bodily infirmity and regulating the passions of the mind. Physicians, moreover, earnestly recommend intellectual control of the emotions, for in "mediocritie" of passion "consisteth the tranquillity both of mind and body, which of this life is the chiefest happinesse ... beware chiefly of sadnesse, for it drieth the bones; and embrace moderate ioy, for both body and minde are bettered thereby."[84]

---

82 La Primaudaye, *Academie*, p. 456.
83 *Treatise*, dedicatory epistle.
84 Venner, *Via Recta*, p. 226.

Chapter II. THE SCIENTIFIC THEORY OF MELAN-CHOLY

I

MELANCHOLY, AS I HAVE EXPLAINED, is the name of one of the four primary humors. It is cold and dry, black, thick, sluggish, semiexcremental (for it is the dregs of the blood). It "is not vnlike vnto Beasts feete when they be sodden and brought into a Jellie, which in eatinge, cleaue to the fyngers and lyppes, as tough as Byrdlyme: whereby it causeth Bloud to haue a good power retentyue, and to be thicker."[1] It has the physiological functions of nourishing the cold and dry parts of the body, especially the spleen and bones, and of provoking appetite. The spleen is supposed to absorb any surplus of it which may develop. If there is a comparatively high proportion of it in the body, the complexion of the body is said to be melancholy.

This humor is physiologically normal. There are also melancholic humors which are abnormal and morbid.[2] Since *melancholy* means "black bile," it may accurately be applied to any bilious humor which is black.[3] Certain black bilious humors arise from the scorching or burning of normal humors by unnatural heat, which is due to such causes as improper diet, physiological disorder, or immoderate passions.[4] The "straunge and forreyne heat" burns the natural humors (or their abnormal varieties) "into Ashes, like Wood, or other combustible substaunce burnt, & wyth the force of fier brought into Cinders." The product of this combustion "is farre worse and more pernicious" than natural melancholy.[5] It is "of such an exulcerating, and fretting qualitie, that it wasteth those partes, where it lighteth."[6] Its effects upon body and mind are diverse and prodigious. The terms which

---

[1] Lemnius, *Touchstone*, fol. 136ᵛ.

[2] Miss Campbell has pointed out the importance of unnatural melancholy in Renaissance medical theory (*Shakespeare's Tragic Heroes*, pp. 75–78).

[3] Bile is distinguished from blood by the fact that it does not coagulate (Galen, *Opera*, V, 110; Luis Mercado, *Opera* [Frankfurt, 1619–20], I, 220). There are two natural forms of bile—yellow bile (choler) and black bile (melancholy).

[4] "Ac . . . caloris exsuperantia resiccans ac consumens humiditates, a quibus calor nutritur, humores nigrefacit, quemadmodum etiam sol fructus et hominum corpora."— Aëtius, *De Melancholia . . . Libellus*, in *Galeni Opera*, XIX, 706. Aëtius is quoting Rufus. A natural humor undergoes various changes before it becomes black bile. According to François Valleriole, there are three intermediate stages between choler and unnatural melancholy (*Enarrationum Medicinalium Libri Sex* [Lyons, 1604], p. 424).

[5] Lemnius, *Touchstone*, fol. 146ᵛ.

[6] Bright, *Treatise*, p. 32.

English writers apply to it are *unnatural melancholy, melancholy adust* (Latin, *aduro*), *burnt choler, black choler, atra bilis,*[7] and of course simply *melancholy.*

The genus of humors called *unnatural melancholy* has logically four species to correspond with the four natural humors, and in many treatises[8] these four are listed. Occasionally one finds descriptions of their respective physical qualities. Natural melancholy adust, for instance, "is sower as vineger. And if it fall vpon the earth, it boyleth, and the smel thereof is heauie and sower as vineger, the which flyes shun and voyde for horrible sauor thereof."[9] Since phlegm is cold and moist, it resists adustion. There are, in fact, authors who doubt the existence of the phlegmatic species of melancholy.[10] Others mention a salt phlegm, a degenerate form of the humor, which may undergo adustion.[11]

In its physical character, unnatural melancholy (any variety) "may after a sort be resembled vnto Iron, Seacoales or Charcoales, which beinge fiered, appeare glowing hoate, shyning lyke burnished Golde, and burninge the members of the touchers: but being quenched, they looke blacke, cankered & rustie."[12] When it has cooled, unnatural melancholy on the whole resembles natural melancholy: "if it happens that yellow bile becomes overheated, there remains, when the heat has at length passed from it, a substance like ashes which is called *atra bilis.* This is much drier than the fluid which is properly called melancholy, and not so thick. Superabundance of it does not render the complexion warm, for it is cold and dry."[13] The physical

---

7 Some writers, English and continental, confine the term *atra bilis* to unnatural melancholy, for instance Bright and Lemnius (in the Latin original). Others, for instance Ficino and Melanchthon, make no such distinction.

8 Among them: Avicenna, *Liber Canonis,* tr. Gerard of Cremona (Basel, 1556), p. 14; Bernard of Gordon, *Lilium Medicinae* (Paris, 1542), fol. 107r; *Batman uppon Bartholome,* fol. 33r; *Regimen Sanitatis Salerni,* fols. cxxxviii–cxxxix; Marsilio Ficino, *De Vita Libri Tres* (Basel, 1549), p. 15; Elyot, *Castel of Helth,* fol. 72v; Lemnius, *Touchstone,* fols. 146–47; Bright, *Treatise,* pp. 2, 32–33, 101, 110–11; Burton, *Anatomy,* I, 197–99, 459–63.

9 *Batman uppon Bartholome,* fol. 33r. Cf. Galen, *De Atra Bile,* in *Opera,* V, 110; Avicenna, *Canon,* p. 14.

10 See Burton, *Anatomy,* I, 198.

11 See, for instance, Elyot, *Castel of Helth,* fol. 72v; Bright, *Treatise,* pp. 32–33.

12 Lemnius, *Touchstone,* fols. 147–48. "Nam quale quiddam patiuntur carbones, qui dum uruntur lucidissimi ob flammam existunt, extincta vero flamma atri redduntur; tale quiddam etiam circa clarum sanguinis colorem frigus molitur."—Aëtius, *De Melancholia,* pp. 705–6 (from Rufus).

13 Si "flauam bilem superassari contingat, calore tandem euanescente, quidpiam cineri simile effectum relinquitur, quam atram bilim vocant, succo melancholico proprie dicto multo siccior & minus crassa, qua in corpore superabundante, calidum propterea eius non euadit temperamentum, cum frigida . . . sit & sicca."—Joannes Baptista Silvaticus, *Controversiae Medicae Numero Centum* (Frankfurt, 1601), p. 2.

and psychic effects of cold adust melancholy are not readily distinguishable from those of natural melancholy in excess.[14]

II

The term *melancholy* is used also to designate a disease (or genus of diseases[15]) due to the presence of a melancholy humor abnormal in quantity or quality. The melancholic malady is fundamentally a physical condition. Yet its symptoms are so largely psychological that it is ordinarily regarded as a mental disease.

The causes of this malady include everything which may engender a melancholy humor. Diet is a frequent cause: "chieflie meates and drinkes do yeeld matter to this humour."[16] The foods which engender melancholy, as we have seen in the preceding chapter, are primarily those which the authorities classify as cold and dry. Yet hot aliments may produce unnatural melancholy; "strong wine," for instance, "burneth the humours, & turneth them into ashes."[17] Other causes are the climate, the weather, the situation of one's dwelling, too much or too little sleep.[18] Either idleness or overexertion may engender natural melancholy, "the one causing the blood to be thicke through setling: and the other, by spending the bodie ouermuch, & drying it excessiuely."[19]

There are psychological as well as physical causes. Passions are very likely to produce black bile: "Nothing certainly engenders melancholy

---

[14] In the foregoing discussion of the melancholic humors, I have tried to present what seems to be the orthodox pattern of Renaissance medical thought. I have, however, come upon various opinions which do not altogether conform to this pattern. Galen distinguishes four kinds of black bile (including the natural): see *De Atra Bile*, in *Opera*, V, 108–9; *Definitiones Medicae*, in *Opera*, XIX, 464–65; *De Humoribus Liber*, in *Opera*, XIX, 490. These three passages, incidentally, are not altogether in agreement with one another. Mercado says that there are three black humors: natural melancholy, which he subdivides into three species; melancholic blood; and *atra bilis*, that is, melancholy adust (*Opera*, I, 218–20; III, 88–89). Jason Van der Velde distinguishes two sorts of unnatural melancholy, one produced from blood by overcooling, the other produced from blood by overheating (*De Cerebri Morbis . . . Liber* [Basel, 1549], p. 259). And so forth.

[15] The species most frequently listed are *head melancholy, body melancholy,* and *hypochondriacal melancholy*. The distinction between the first two does not seem very useful, for the causes, symptoms, and cure of the one are never clearly differentiated from those of the other. The psychological symptoms of all three are very similar. For reasons which will be obvious, I shall discuss hypochondriacal melancholy separately.

[16] Bright, *Treatise,* p. 25. Bright proceeds to specify the foods which produce melancholy (pp. 26–30). Cf. Burton, *Anatomy,* I, 247 ff.

[17] *Batman uppon Bartholome,* fol. 89ʳ.

[18] Bright, *Treatise,* pp. 25, 30–31; Burton, *Anatomy,* I, 272–77, 286–87.

[19] Bright, *Treatise,* p. 31.

more quickly or more readily causes existing melancholy to linger than passions of the mind, for they both dry the body and disturb the spirits and humors beyond nature."[20] For just as physical disease affects the mind, "so . . . the mind most effectually works upon the body, producing by his passions and perturbations miraculous alterations, as melancholy, despair, cruel diseases, and sometimes death itself."[21]

All immoderate passions "consume the spirits"[22] and thus cool and dry the body and engender the natural melancholy humor. Cold and dry passions engender natural melancholy also, as explained in the first chapter, by preventing the production and distribution of vital spirit. Grief especially has pernicious effects: "There is nothynge more ennemye to lyfe, than sorowe . . . for it exhausteth bothe naturall heate and moysture of the bodye, and dothe extenuate or make the body leane, dulleth the wytte, and darkeneth the spirites. . . . And Salomon sayth [Proverbs 17:22], that sorowe drieth vp the bones."[23] Sorrow is *the mother and daughter of melancholy, her epitome, symptom, and chief cause. As Hippocrates hath it, they beget one another, and tread in a ring."* "Cousin-german to *sorrow* is *fear* . . . an assistant and a principal agent in procuring of this mischief, a cause and symptom as the other."[24]

Hot passions, if they are excessive, engender adust melancholy by burning the humors. Anger is very likely to do so. If anger continues long, the choler in the system "becommeth blacke, and seething strongly, dries vp and burnes, whereby oftentimes it happens that some becom frantique, mad and desperate."[25] Even joy, the most healthful of the passions, results in adustion if it is immoderate: "the heart beeing continually enuironed with great aboundaunce of spirites, becommeth too hote and inflamed, and consequently engendereth much cholericke and burned blood." As a consequence, "after much pleasure and laughter men feele themselues both to languish, and to be melancholy."[26]

Intent thinking is another psychological cause of melancholy. "The first doctrine" of the *Regimen Sanitatis Salerni* "is that he that desireth health of body, must eschew and auoide great charges [of] thought and care. For

---

[20] "Nihil profecto citius melancholiam accersere solet, & iam praeexsistentem remorari, quam animi passiones, quae . . . vel corpus exsiccant, vel spiritus & humores praeter naturam exagitant."—Mercado, *Opera*, III, 102.

[21] Burton, *Anatomy*, I, 288.

[22] *Ibid.*, 297. For reasons given below, any mental activity expends spirit. Passion is a particularly agitating kind of mental activity.

[23] Elyot, *Castel of Helth*, fol. 64. Many similar passages on sorrow appear in Renaissance scientific and moralistic works.

[24] Burton, *Anatomy*, I, 298, 301.

[25] Mornay, *Knowledge*, p. 160.

[26] Wright, *Passions*, pp. 103, 105.

thought dryeth vp mans body [and through impairing the spirits] drieth vp
the bones."[27] Marsilio Ficino explains in some detail how this happens: Mental labor consumes animal spirit;[28] and since animal spirit must be renewed
at the expense of vital spirit, thinking indirectly draws the heat and moisture
from the blood: "ob frequentissimum inquisitionis motum, spiritus quoque
moti continue resoluuntur: Resolutos autem spiritus, ex subtiliore sanguine
instaurari necessarium est. Quapropter subtilibus clarioribusque sanguinis
partibus saepe consumptis, reliquus sanguis necessario densus redditur &
siccus & ater." Thus brain and body become melancholic. While the mind
is active, moreover, nature neglects the stomach and liver, with the result
that digestion is poor and its product melancholic. Finally, the physical in-
activity which meditation involves hinders proper evacuation. For these
various reasons the animal spirit becomes tainted with melancholy and the
mind grows sorrowful and fearful ("Haec omnia melancholicum spiritum,
moestumque & pauidum animum efficere solent").[29] It is small wonder that
melancholy often afflicts

Magistrates and Officers in the Commonwealth, or Studentes which at vnseason-
able times sit at their Bookes & Studies. For through ouermuch agitation of the
mynd, natural heat is extinguished, & the Spyrits aswell Animall as Vitall, attenuated and vanish away: whereby it commeth to passe, that after their vitall iuyce
is exhausted, they fall into a Colde & Drye constitution.[30]

Studies "haue great force to procure melancholie: if they be vehement, and
of difficult matters, and high misteries."[31]
    Scholars necessarily are inclined to melancholy because of their arduous
mental activity and their sedentary life. Melancholy is the scholar's occu-
pational disease. Men of letters, says Ficino, either are melancholy by innate
temperament or become so through study.[32] One may add that poverty,

---

[27] Fol. i[v].
[28] Labor of any kind consumes heat (and therefore moisture) as fuel. Physical labor
cools and dries the body (Bright, *Treatise*, p. 248).
[29] *De Vita*, pp. 12–13. This celebrated work of Ficino's seems to have been at least
partially responsible for the general interest in the scholar's melancholy. The association
between pathological melancholy and intellectual activity, however, antedates Ficino by
many centuries. Constantinus Africanus (eleventh century) writes that mental labors
breed melancholy (*De Melancholia*, in *Opera* [Basel, 1536], pp. 283, 284). Rhazes (Arabian, ninth century) quotes a similar opinion from Rufus (Greek, first century): "*Dixit
quod multa cogitatio et tristitia faciunt accidere melancoliam.*"—*Oeuvres de Rufus
D'Éphèse*, ed. Charles Daremberg and Charles Emile Ruelle (Paris, 1879), p. 455.
[30] Lemnius, *Touchstone*, fol. 136[v]. Cf. fol. 143[v].
[31] Bright, *Treatise*, p. 243. Bright, like Ficino, goes into considerable detail (pp.
243–45).
[32] *De Vita*, pp. 11–13.

hard fare, disillusionment, and discouragement contribute to the scholar's melancholy. The days are long past when intellectual achievement was encouraged and rewarded by such great patrons as Augustus Caesar and Maecenas. In this later, degenerate age, men of letters are slightly regarded and slenderly rewarded. The scholarly life is one of sorrow and hardship, and both of these breed melancholy.

The scientific writers of the Renaissance (scholars themselves) show great concern for the scholar's hard lot. Ficino's *De Studiosorum Sanitate Tuenda*, the first book of *De Vita Libri Tres*, expounds a regimen of life calculated to mitigate the melancholic infirmities of the studious life. The Dutch physician Jason Van der Velde recommends his *De Cerebri Morbis . . . Liber* as useful "non tam Medicis quam Studiosis."[33] A work by Thomas Lorkyn, an English physician, is entitled *Recta Regula & Victus Ratio pro Studiosis & Literatis* (1562). Thomas Cogan's *The Haven of Health* is "Chiefly made for the comfort of Students."[34] Burton includes in the *Anatomy* a long discourse on "*Love of Learning, or overmuch Study*" as a cause of melancholy, "*With a Digression of the Misery of Scholars, and why the Muses are Melancholy*."[35] In dealing with these subjects, he displays considerable personal feeling: "How many poor scholars have lost their wits, or become dizzards, neglecting all worldly affairs and their own health, *esse & bene esse*, to gain knowledge!"[36]

The melancholic malady may be due to any of the foregoing circumstances which engender black bile. It may be due also to functional failure in any one of a group of abdominal organs known collectively as the *hypochondria*, or *hypochondries*. These include notably the liver, gall, bladder, spleen, and uterus. When melancholia is a consequence of disorder in any hypochondriacal organ, it is called *hypochondriacal melancholy*.[37]

The spleen is the most frequent seat of hypochondriacal melancholy.[38]

---

[33] From the title page of the first edition, Basel, 1549.

[34] From the 1589 title page.

[35] I, 348.

[36] I, 351.

[37] Some authorities use *hypochondriacal melancholy* as a more inclusive term than others. They disagree greatly in their opinions concerning the physiology of the disease (see Burton, *Anatomy*, I, 436–37).

The offending humor in hypochondriacal melancholy may be either natural melancholy, adust melancholy, or a "crudity" (underdigested chyle). According to Du Laurens (*Discourse*, p. 126), the humors involved always become heated, apparently, however, not always to the point of adustion. In hypochondriacal melancholy there is not necessarily any increase in the quantity of black bile.

[38] Renaissance physicians have ample classical authority for their opinions concerning splenetic melancholy. See, for instance, Galen, *Opera*, VIII, 185–93; Aëtius, *De Melancholia*, pp. 699–702; *The Seven Books of Paulus Aegineta*, tr. Francis Adams (London, 1844–47), I, 383, 577.

The spleen is a spungy structure in the lower left side. It is supposed to absorb all superfluous black bile from the liver and blood. It uses the more nutritive part of this to nourish itself, discharges a part into the stomach to provoke appetite, and excretes the rest. Sometimes, however, "either for feeblenes, or obstruction," the spleen fails "to suck the melancholie from the blood."[39]

It chanceth sometime not onely through weakenes of attractiue vertue, which is in the spleene, but also through stopping of the passage, by which the dreggie humour of melancholy is deriued from the liuer vnto the spleene there followeth obstruction. Afterward that vnpure and naughtie blood is distributed all ouer the whole bodie, which if it chance, then the colour of the bodie is corrupt, and enclineth to blacknesse. . . . This euill is knowne by heauines . . . about the left side.[40]

Sometimes, moreover, through loss of its expulsive faculty, the spleen fails to "discharge itself into those passages, which nature hath therto ordained."[41] In this case it swells and exudes melancholy into the veins. The swollen spleen has become a cesspool of feculent humor, from which black, "fulsome vapours" ascend "as it were out of a dampishe Marshe or stinkinge Camerine."[42] Medical writers manifest no small disgust with the spleen: "This member, of the whole bodie is the grossest, and euill fauouredst to be held, blacke of colour, and euill sauorie of taste."[43]

Humors which are confined and compressed within a narrow space are believed to putrify and generate heat.[44] When melancholy is imprisoned within the spleen, it is likely to become hot. If so, "on the side of the spleene, there is something which biteth and beateth continually"; patients feel a "heate and burning . . . on the spleene side."[45] This heated melancholy is pervaded by gas. The idea that hot melancholic humors are "windy" seems to be based on an analogy with boiling water. The heated humor, "comming as it were to boyle, is puffed vp and sendeth his vapours into all the parts neere thereabout."[46] If the spleen fails to discharge itself, therefore, there is "an vnnaturall boyling of heate, with wyndines vnder the left side."[47] In Bur-

---

[39] Bright, *Treatise*, p. 31.
[40] Philip Barrough, *The Method of Phisick* (London, 1590), p. 151. Cf. Lemnius, *Touchstone*, fols. 138ᵛ, 141ᵛ–42ʳ; Christopher Wirtzung, *Praxis Medicinae Universalis*, tr. Jacob Mosan (London, 1598), p. 409.
[41] Bright, *Treatise*, p. 32. Cf. Wirtzung, *Praxis*, p. 409.
[42] Lemnius, *Touchstone*, fol. 142ᵛ.
[43] Bright, *Treatise*, p. 32.
[44] See Du Laurens, *Discourse*, pp. 127, 128.
[45] *Ibid.*, p. 129.
[46] *Idem.*
[47] Bright, *Treatise*, p. 125.

ton's frontispiece, which represents various types of melancholy men, there appears a picture of "Hypocondriacus," who is bent toward the left. "Wind in his side doth him much harm."[48] Because the hot melancholic humors involved are gaseous, hypochondriacal melancholy is often called *windy melancholy*, or *flatulent melancholy*.

Hypochondriacal organs other than the spleen may be the seat of hypochondriacal melancholy. Du Laurens informs one that, next to the spleen, the liver and the mesenterium (mesentery) are most frequently at fault. The veins of these organs, through some obstruction, "are stuffed and filled" with noxious humors, and there follows "a drie inflammation of the veines."[49] Inflammation makes the compressed humors flatulent, and from them "windy vapours ascend up to the brain, which trouble the imagination."[50] Some authors mention a uterine melancholy, and there are other varieties. In any case, most hypochondriacs "feele a burning in the places called *Hypochondria*, they heare continually a noyse and rumbling sound throughout all their bellie, they are beaten with winde on both sides."[51]

Hypochondriacal melancholy is notable among melancholies for the fact that it furnished the late seventeenth century and the eighteenth century with a set of terms. Before the time of Queen Anne, *melancholy*, as the name for morbid depression, had been largely replaced by *hypochondria*, *spleen*, *hysteria*, and *vapors*, all four terms denoting the same disorder.[52] The terms *hypochondria*, *spleen*, and *vapors* originated in the medical theories which I have just reviewed, although these theories had been abandoned by advanced physicians before 1700. *Hysteria* had a different origin.[53]

III

The psychological effects of black bile in the system are due chiefly to two physiological facts. One is that the humor (unless it happens to be hot) in-

---

[48] From "The Argument of the Frontispiece."

[49] *Discourse*, pp. 126–27.

[50] Burton, *Anatomy*, I, 474.

[51] Du Laurens, *Discourse*, p. 129. Cf. Barrough, *Phisick*, p. 46.

[52] See Thomas Sydenham, *Works*, tr. R. G. Latham (London, 1848–50), II, 85. Sydenham's treatise on hypochondria was written in 1682. The first two of these terms were used only when the patient was a man; the last two when the patient was a woman. *Hypochondria* and *hysteria*, of course, survive in modern psychiatric terminology.

[53] Hysteria was originally supposed to be a nervous disorder arising from disaffection of the uterus. See Galen, *Opera*, VIII, 413–37; *The Extant Works of Aretaeus, the Cappadocian*, tr. Francis Adams (London, 1856), pp. 285–87; Paulus Aegineta, *Seven Books*, I, 633–34. By the end of the seventeenth century it had merged, in medical theory, with melancholy.

clines both heart and brain to cold and dry passions and thus produces such passions without objective cause. The reasons for this have been previously set forth. The other is that black bile or its vapors disorder the physical instruments of perception and thought. The melancholy humor "tainteth and brandeth with blackenes [the animal spirit], which passing from the braine to the eye, and from the eye to the braine backe againe, is able to moue these blacke sights, and to set them vncessantly before the minde." Indeed, if the spirit "be blacke and ouercooled also," it troubles the mind's "most noble powers, and principally the imagination, presenting vnto it continually blacke formes and strange visions."[54] Ocular impressions are not the only ones affected. "All [the] senses are troubled"; melancholy men "think they see, hear, smell, and touch, that which they do not."[55] There are many cases, one authority writes, "in which one sees all the senses diversely corrupted either by this humor alone or by a sooty atrabilious vapor. This imbues the seat of the mind, and by it those imaginary monsters evidently are begotten."[56]

The melancholic vapors commonly mentioned in connection with these sensory disturbances very often rise from a disordered spleen. These "greeuous and odious fumes" annoy the brain "and distemper the Spirits Animall wyth a straunge and forreine quality. Hereof commeth disquietnes of mynde and alienation of right witts, absurde cogitations, troublesom Dreames ... a mynde sorowfull, comfortlesse, perplexed, pensiue and fearefull."[57] Atrabilious vapors pollute "both the substance, and spirits of the brayne." If the brain is exposed to them over a considerable period, it becomes saturated with "that spleneticke fogge, whereby his nature is become of the same quality, and the pure and bright spirites ... defiled, and eclipsed." Thus there develops "an habite of depraued conceite."[58]

---

[54] Du Laurens, *Discourse*, pp. 91–92.

[55] Burton, *Anatomy*, I, 442.

[56] "Infinita alia huc coaceruari possent exempla, ubi sensus omnes multifariam uitiatos cernas, ex unico illo humore, uel fuliginoso atrae bilis uapore, mentis sedem inficiente, unde phantastica illa procreari monstra constat."—Johann Weyer, *De Praestigiis Daemonum ... Libri Sex* (Basel, 1568), p. 228. Weyer gives examples of melancholy men whose senses of hearing and smell have been vitiated. While the authorities give a definite reason for the blackening of ocular images, they give no such specific explanation for other sensory falsifications. One learns from them simply that the animal spirit and sometimes the substance of the brain have been corrupted.

[57] Lemnius, *Touchstone*, fols. 142–43.

[58] Bright, *Treatise*, pp. 102–3.

IV

Pathological melancholy is hard to distinguish from the relatively normal condition of the man of melancholy complexion. The symptoms of the disease are very similar to the traits which characterize the temperament. The disease, however, is adventitious, whereas the melancholy temperament is innate; and though there is a resemblance in kind, there is usually a considerable difference in degree.

Although there is great diversity among melancholic disorders, fear and sorrow are the primary mental symptoms in most of them. Melancholy is often defined as a kind of dotage accompanied by fear and sorrow without apparent cause.[59] One "may as well bid him that is diseased not to feel pain, as a melancholy man not to fear, not to be sad: 'tis within his blood, his brains, his whole temperature."[60] Like "tirannous executioners," fear and sorrow set the mind "on the racke."[61] The melancholy man is "alwaies fearefull and trembling . . . afraid of euery thing, yea and maketh himselfe a terrour vnto himselfe . . . with an vnseparable sadnes, which oftentimes turneth into dispayre."[62]

There are many secondary symptoms. The melancholy person is bashful: "He dare not come in company for fear he should be misused, disgraced, overshoot himself in gesture or speeches, or be sick; he thinks every man observes him, aims at him, derides him, owes him malice."[63] He is extremely cautious: "doubtfull before, and long in deliberation: suspicious, painefull in studie, and circumspect."[64] Suspicion colors all his observations and thoughts: "if he see three or foure talking together, he thinketh that it is of him . . . being alwaies in feare, he thinketh verely that one or other doth lie in wait for him, and that some doe purpose to slay him."[65] Melancholics are "enuious, and ielous, apt to take occasions in the worse part";[66] "testy, pettish, peevish, and ready to snarl upon every small occasion . . . waspish and suspicious."[67] They are wayward, whimsical, and intractable: "*Inconstant* they are in all their actions, vertiginous, restless, unapt to resolve of

---

[59] See Du Laurens, *Discourse*, pp. 86-87; Bright, *Treatise*, pp. 1, 3; Wirtzung, *Praxis*, p. 130; Burton, *Anatomy*, I, 443.
[60] Burton, *Anatomy*, II, 121.
[61] Du Laurens, *Discourse*, p. 89.
[62] *Ibid.*, p. 82.
[63] Burton, *Anatomy*, I, 445.
[64] Bright, *Treatise*, p. 124.
[65] Du Laurens, *Discourse*, pp. 93–94.
[66] Bright, *Treatise*, p. 124.
[67] Burton, *Anatomy*, I, 450.

any business, they will and will not."[68] They can be very stubborn: "firme in opinion, and hardly remoued wher it is resolued."[69]

The melancholy person is subject to hallucinations, usually of a fearsome character. He "imagineth a thousand chimaeras and visions, which to his thinking he certainly sees, bugbears, talks with black men, ghosts, goblins, &c."[70] He clings to his delusions with great tenacity.

Melancholy men suffer grievously from insomnia because of the dryness of their brains.[71] Du Laurens has "seene some that haue abode three whole moneths without sleepe."[72] When they chance to sleep a little, they are "assayled with a thousand vaine visions, and hideous buggards."[73] For the melancholic humor blackens the spirits and the brain.

When black bile is superabundant it cools and deadens both the vital spirit, which gives the body life, and the animal spirit, which serves the mind and the perceptive faculties. Black bile, moreover, prevents the generation of spirits with such warmth, subtlety, and celerity as are requisite to their functions. Melancholics consequently tend to be physically and psychologically sluggish, "slow, silent, negligent," "dull, both in outward senses, and conceite."[74] "They haue their eyes fixed . . . and oftentimes cannot speake."[75] A characteristic condition is a lethargic despondency: When the blood is "melancholie of qualitie," it is

grosse, dull, and of fewe comfortable spirits; and plentifully replenished with such as darken all the clernesse of those sanguineous [spirits], and ingrosse their subtilnesse, defile their purenesse with the fogge of that slime, and fennie substance, and shut vp the hart as it were in a dungeon of obscurity, causeth manie fearefull fancies, by abusing the braine with vglie illusions, & locketh vp the gates of the hart, whereout the spirits should breake forth vpon iust occasion, to the comfort of all the family of their fellowe members: whereby we are in heauinesse, sit comfortlesse, feare, distrust, doubt, dispaire, and lament, when no cause requireth it.[76]

The melancholy humor "taketh away from a man his sharpenes of witte and vnderstandinge, his assured hope and confidence, and all his manlye strength

[68] *Idem.*

[69] Bright, *Treatise*, p. 124.

[70] Burton, *Anatomy*, I, 445.

[71] The material cause of sleep is a moist vapor (Du Laurens, *Discourse*, p. 95).

[72] *Ibid.*, p. 94. According to Burton, they sometimes wake "for a month, a year, together" (*Anatomy*, I, 441).

[73] Du Laurens, *Discourse*, p. 82. Cf. Burton, *Anatomy*, I, 440, 446. Bernard of Gordon says that in their dreams melancholy persons see "daemones, aut monachos nigros, aut suspensos, aut mortuos, & omnia talia consimilia."—*Lilium Medicinae*, fol. 107v.

[74] Bright, *Treatise*, p. 124.

[75] Du Laurens, *Discourse*, p. 96.

[76] Bright, *Treatise*, p. 100.

and courage, so that he hardly eyther attempteth or atchieueth any matter of excellency & worthynes: for such be doltish, dull, slow, and lumpishe."[77]

Persons affected by black bile are continually wrapped in their thoughts and fancies, "surly, dull, sad, austere, *cogitabundi* still, very intent." A melancholy man "doth not attend what is said, if you tell him a tale, he cries at last, what said you?"[78] Melancholics are extremely taciturn. They have "a drop of words, and a flood of cogitations."[79] Yet they are subject to "sodayn incontinencie of the tongue";[80] they "holde their peace when they should speake, and speake too much when they should be still."[81] In speaking, they are inclined to trip and stammer.[82]

Melancholy men love solitude and darkness. They seek out "desert places ... orchards, gardens, private walks, back-lanes, averse from company ... they abhor all companions at last, even their nearest acquaintance, & most familiar friends."[83] They "shunne the light, because that their spirits and humours are altogether contrary to the light."[84] A melancholy man *"loves darkness as life, & cannot endure the light,* or to sit in lightsome places; his hat still in his eyes."[85] In more extreme cases melancholy "maketh men sullen, morose, solitary, averse from all society, and Haters of the light, delighting onely like the Shrieke Owle or the Bitterne in desolate places, and monuments of the dead."[86] The melancholic's unsociability sometimes develops into a venomous hatred of humankind. Those that harbor this melancholic misanthropy "abhorre all the honest pleasures of life, fly the light of men, and wish euill vnto themselues, so as they cannot indure to bee seene, neither will they speake to any man, but seeke desarts & solitary places, where they confine themselues, and consume themselues with the discontent and *Hatred* they beare to mankind."[87] Thus melancholy "causeth men to be aliened from the nature of man, and wholly to discard themselves from all society,

---

[77] Lemnius, *Touchstone*, fol. 148ᵛ. Lemnius is writing of adust melancholy which has cooled.

[78] Burton, *Anatomy*, I, 451, 468.

[79] Walkington, *Optick Glasse*, p. 131.

[80] Elyot, *Castel of Helth*, fol. 73ʳ.

[81] *Batman uppon Bartholome*, fol. 33ʳ. Cf.: "cum loqui incipiunt, & si diu locuti fuerint, silere tamen nequeunt."—Peter van Foreest, *Observationum et Curationum Medicinalium ... Libri XXVIII* (Frankfurt, 1602), p. 343.

[82] "Veloci plerumque lingua sunt et balbi et gracili voce praediti ob linguae incontinentiam."—Aëtius, *De Melancholia*, p. 705 (from Rufus).

[83] Burton, *Anatomy*, I, 455.

[84] Du Laurens, *Discourse*, p. 96.

[85] Burton, *Anatomy*, I, 455.

[86] Reynolds, *Treatise*, p. 130. "Plerique ... in tenebrosis locis degere cupiunt ac in monumentis et solitudinibus."—Aëtius, *De Melancholia*, p. 702.

[87] Coeffeteau, *Passions*, pp. 192–93. Cf. Felix Plater, *Praxeos* (Basel, 1602), p. 100; Lemnius, *Touchstone*, fol. 143ʳ. Melancholy men, says Areteaus, "flee to the desert from misanthropy."—*Works*, p. 299.

but rather like hermits and old Anchorits, to live in grots, caves, and other hidden cels of the earth."[88]

The victims of melancholy suffer such torments of mind that they long for death: they become "weary of their lives, and feral thoughts to offer violence to their own persons come into their minds; *taedium vitae* is a common symptom."[89] Some "grow so far as to hate themselues, & so fall to despaire, yea many kil & destroy themselues."[90]

Melancholy degrades its victims as much as it tortures them. The melancholy man is "the most caitife and miserable creature that is in the world, spoyled of all his graces, depriued of iudgement, reason and counsaile, enemie of men and of the Sun, straying and wandring in solitarie places." The reader may "iudge and weigh if the titles . . . giuen to man . . . a diuine and politique creature, can any way agree with the melancholike person."[91]

In appearance, the melancholy patient is "of colour blacke and swart, of substance inclyning to hardnes, leane, and spare of flesh: which causeth hollownes of eye, and vnchearefulnes of countenance . . . countenance demisse, and hanging downe, blushing and bashfull, of pace slow, silent, negligent."[92] He is likely to be very hairy.[93]

V

"Melancholike men by adustion are variable and vnequall in their complexion: for that choler adust is verie vnequall, inasmuch as somtimes it is ex-

---

[88] Walkington, *Optick Glasse*, p. 132.

[89] Burton, *Anatomy*, I, 448–49.

[90] La Primaudaye, *Academie*, p. 467.

[91] Du Laurens, *Discourse*, pp. 80, 82. The conception of melancholic distraction outlined in the two foregoing sections enjoyed a very long life in medical tradition. Most of the symptoms which become so familiar to the reader of Renaissance medical works appear in Galen's *De Locis Affectis*. I quote a sample: All persons disordered by melancholy ". . . timent, moerent, vitam damnant, odio habent homines . . . quosdam etiam alieno admodum videbis animo, utpote qui simul et mortem metuant et mori cupiant. Proinde recte videtur Hippocrates omnia ipsorum symptomata in duo haec coëgisse, metum et moestitiam [*Aphorisms*, VI, xxiii]. Moestitia nimirum eos inducit, ut odio prosequantur omnes, quos viderint, perpetuo moestitiam prae se ferant, ac terreantur, ut in tenebris profundis pueri, atque ex adultis indocti. Quemadmodum sane externae tenebrae omnibus fere hominibus pavorem inducunt, nisi vel audaces admodum, vel docti fuerint, sic atrae bilis color, mentis sedem peraeque ac tenebrae obscurans, timorem efficit."—*Opera*, VIII, 190–91. Cf. Rufus, *Oeuvres*, p. 455; Alexander of Tralles, *Libri Duodecim* (Venice, 1555), fols. 33–34; Aëtius, *De Melancholia*, pp. 702–3; Avicenna, *Canon*, pp. 375–77.

[92] Bright, *Treatise*, p. 124.

[93] See Burton, *Anatomy*, I, 441, 475. "Hirsuti vero ipsorum plures sunt propter crassorum excrementorum multitudinem."—Aëtius, *De Melancholia*, p. 705 (from Rufus). Cf. Galen, *Opera*, VIII, 182. The old physiology regards hair as an excrement.

ceeding hot, and somtimes cold beyond measure."[94] When it "is hotte, it maketh menne madde, and whan it is extincte, it maketh menne fooles, forgetfull, and dulle."[95] A case of melancholy due to an adust humor, therefore, has two phases: a hot phase characterized by energetic extravagances and a cold phase with such dull and passive melancholic symptoms as those already described.

In its hot stage adust melancholy produces a diversity of symptoms. It may incite extravagant fury ("concitatos furentesque facere solet"). Upon cooling, however, the humor, since its subtler and purer elements have been burned away and there remains only a foul, sooty substance, renders men heavy and stupid ("At quando iam extinguitur, subtilioribus clarioribusque partibus resolutis, solaque restante fuligine tetra, stolidos reddit et stupidos").[96] It may engender an exaggerated gaiety, causing patients to be "exceedingly set vpon their mery pin, & (past al godsforbod) iocund, & pleasurably geeuen to singing, dauncing skipping & sporting." They are amorous, and their minds run upon marriage and children. "But when this great heat is cold ... & their spyrites at reste, they ... condemne and deteste yesterdayes deedes, and are much ashamed."[97] Other possible symptoms are insane fear and grief and torpid stupidity.

The nature of the symptoms, one learns from Bright, depends upon the variety of the humor. If unnatural melancholy "rise of the naturall melancholy," it causes

monstrous terrors of feare and heauinesse without cause. If it rise of choler, then rage playeth her part, and furie ioyned with madnesse, putteth all out of frame. If bloud minister matter to this fire, euery serious thing for a time, is turned into a iest, & tragedies into comedies, and lamentation into gigges and daunces.[98]

Thus the passions which a humor fosters in its natural state are extravagantly exaggerated when it becomes adust. Burton describes the same three species of melancholy and adds a fourth, the melancholy arising from phlegm adust. The phlegmatic melancholy, not so frequent as the others, "stirs up dull symptoms, and a kind of stupidity, or impassionate hurt."[99] If a melancholy disease "proceed from the severall combinations of these four humours, or

---

[94] Huarte, *Examen*, p. 147.

[95] Elyot, *Castel of Helth*, fol. 73r.

[96] Ficino, *De Vita*, p. 15. Valleriole repeats Ficino almost verbatim (*Enarrationum Medicinalium Libri Sex*, p. 425). Cf. Aëtius, *De Melancholia*, pp. 706–7 (from Rufus).

[97] Lemnius, *Touchstone*, fol. 148.

[98] *Treatise*, p. 111. Bright does not mention the cold phase. Similar melancholic disorders are described in Alexander, *Libri Duodecim*, fols. 31–34; Bernard, *Lilium Medicinae*, fol. 108r; Foreest, *Observationum*, p. 343b.

[99] *Anatomy*, I, 459.

spirits . . . the symptoms are likewise mixt." One can see that "The Tower of *Babel* never yielded such confusion of tongues, as this Chaos of Melancholy doth variety of symptoms."[100]

Some authorities seem to think of the hot-and-cold sequence as occurring only once. When the humor has cooled, according to this view, it remains cold ever thereafter. Others[101] evidently think of the sequence as a cycle, heat alternating with cold indefinitely. The patient's moods, therefore, are diverse, inconstant, and unpredictable. Clearly the idea of the hot-and-cold cycle is at the basis of the notion that melancholics are "*Humorous* . . . beyond all measure, sometimes profusely laughing, extraordinary merry, and then again weeping without a cause."[102] Burton has a good deal to say about the ups and downs of melancholy, both in "The Author's Abstract of Melancholy," a poem which serves as preface to the *Anatomy*, and in the book itself. It is most pleasant at first, he writes,

to walk alone in some solitary Grove, betwixt Wood and Water, by a Brook side, to meditate upon some delightsome and pleasant subject. . . . A most incomparable delight it is so to melancholize, & build castles in the air, to go smiling to themselves, acting an infinite variety of parts . . . they could spend whole days and nights without sleep, even whole years alone in such contemplations, and phantastical meditations.

But there comes a time when suddenly "this infernal plague of Melancholy seizeth on them, and terrifies their souls."[103] Although Burton fails to explain, this alternation of pleasant exhilaration and excruciating despondency could be due only to the hot-and-cold cycle of a sanguine melancholy humor.

There are, then, diverse kinds of melancholy men. "Of all the other humours melancholie is fullest of varietie of passion, both according to the diuersitie of place where it setleth . . . as also through the diuerse kindes, as naturall, vnnaturall . . . [the unnatural arising] either of bloud adust, choler, or melancholie naturall."[104] Most melancholy men, perhaps, are moderately

---

[100] *Ibid.*, pp. 463, 456.

[101] See especially Huarte, *Examen*, p. 147. According to Alexander, "Interim . . . rident aegri, interim audacius loquuntur, & alias alios motus, interuallaque &'accessiones habent, quemadmodum in febribus accidit quae circuitu mouentur. Atque in his nonnunquam isto humore cerebrum repleri, nonnunquam illo, pro diuersis ipsorum mutationibus, motibusque."—*Libri Duodecim*, fol. 32ᵛ. Bernard says of the melancholy patient, "modo ridet modo flet, & timet de non timendis, & ridet de non ridendis."—*Lilium Medicinae*, fol. 107ᵛ.

[102] Burton, *Anatomy*, I, 452.

[103] *Ibid.*, pp. 283–84. See also p. 467.

[104] Bright, *Treatise*, p. 101.

sorrowful and timorous, passively unsociable and taciturn. Yet medical writers refer to some who are tortured by the wildest pathological griefs and terrors, who seek darkness and the seclusion of desert places, like Bellerophon, and who hate humankind with a venomous hatred, like Timon Misanthropos. There are others, moreover, who are subject to insane anger, who rage, clamor, and do violence to others and to themselves, like Heracles and like Ajax after his disgrace. There are melancholy men who continually laugh, even at tragic spectacles, like Democritus, the laughing philosopher.[105]

Clearly the melancholic category is very indefinitely bounded. When one attempts to lay down its limits, he becomes involved in terminological difficulties. Some authorities use the term *melancholy* in referring to the mental diseases due to adust humors; others, however, call the same diseases *mania*, or *madness*.[106] There is, indeed, no discoverable line of distinction in the old psychiatry between melancholy and madness.[107] The difference, if any, is one of degree. Next to melancholy and madness, the mental maladies most often discussed in medieval and Renaissance medical works are *amor* (the lover's malady), lycanthropia (the wolf madness), hydrophobia, the falling sickness (epilepsy), and frenzy. The lover's malady and the wolf madness, as I shall show, are usually considered species of melancholy. Hydrophobia[108] and epilepsy[109] are sometimes characterized as melancholic diseases, and occasionally frenzy[110] is attributed to adust humors.

It looks somewhat as if melancholy embraces all irrationality, for there is hardly a mental disease which is not associated with melancholic humors by

---

105 One meets these classical examples very frequently in Renaissance works. Aristotle classifies Bellerophon, Heracles, and Ajax as melancholy men (*Problemata*, XXX, i). Concerning Timon, see Chap. IV, note 97. Concerning Democritus, see Chap. VIII, note 37.

106 Avicenna, *Canon*, p. 375; Ficino, *De Vita*, p. 15; Van der Velde, *De Cerebri Morbis*, pp. 223–26; Foreest, *Observationum*, pp. 341–42; Du Laurens, *Discourse*, p. 90. Some writers attribute mania not to adust melancholy, but to blood and choler.

107 Burton gives a list of authorities (including Galen) who consider melancholy and madness so closely allied as to be not clearly distinguishable (*Anatomy*, I, 160). Alexander's opinion is typical: "Nihil enim aliud est insania, quam Melancholiae ad maiorem feritatem intentio."—*Libri Duodecim*, fol. 32ʳ. Some writers say that melancholy is lesion of the imagination and that madness is lesion of the reason. This is the opinion of Tommaso Garzoni (*The Hospitall of Incurable Fooles* [London, 1600], p. 16), who cites various medical authorities. Bartholomaeus, citing Constantinus, says just the reverse (*Batman uppon Bartholome*, fol. 89ʳ).

108 See, for instance, Rufus, *Oeuvres*, p. 447; *Batman uppon Bartholome*, fol. 115ʳ.

109 See, for instance, Du Laurens, *Discourse*, p. 88; Wirtzung, *Praxis*, p. 131.

110 Frenzy is an inflammation of the brain due to an invasion of choler. Burton mentions "choler adust" among the causes of frenzy (*Anatomy*, I, 160–61), and Barrough mentions "burnt" choler in the same connection (*Phisick*, p. 22). The symptoms of frenzy seem to be identical with those of the wrathful and clamorous melancholy (the choleric melancholy). Frenzy, however, is continuous (Du Laurens, *Discourse*, p. 87; Burton, *Anatomy*, I, 160), while the choleric melancholy is cyclic.

one author or another. One can understand Burton's dismay as he sets out to "adventure through the midst of these perplexities," and one is ready to conclude with him "that all the world is mad, that it is melancholy, dotes. . . . For indeed who is not a fool, melancholy, mad?"[111] Yet in spite of this vague inclusiveness, the learned men of the Renaissance have a conception of melancholy with limits which, although hazy, are definable: melancholy is a psychosis caused by a black bilious humor and characterized by morbid depression, continuous or recurrent.

VI

A recapitulation at this point might be helpful. *Melancholy*, as it is used in Renaissance scientific literature, is a word of many meanings and implications. It means first of all a cold, dry humor which is normally present in the body. This is *natural melancholy*. The word may also designate blood, choler, salt phlegm, or natural melancholy depraved by unnatural heat, or by adustion. A humor corrupted and blackened by heat is known as *unnatural melancholy*, or *melancholy adust*. Natural melancholy has certain functions to perform in the body and is harmful only when it is superabundant. Unnatural melancholy is a noxious humor.

The term melancholy may denote, moreover, the physical and mental condition of the man in whose native temperament black bile is the dominant humor, the man of melancholy complexion. Since this man is cold and dry, he is subject to numerous physical infirmities and to various distressing passions, especially fear and sorrow. His condition, however, is not considered pathological.

There is, further, a genus of mental diseases called melancholy. This includes primarily a psychic disorder due to natural melancholy abounding beyond the rather vague limits of normality. This condition differs from the melancholy complexion more in degree than in kind. The principal symptoms are exaggerated griefs and fears, hallucinations, lethargy, unsociability, morbid love of darkness and seclusion, sometimes bitter misanthropy. The term covers also the multifarious mental disorders caused by adust melancholy. When it is hot, adust melancholy produces various mental aberrations, which are not clearly distinguishable in the old medical literature from madness. These are principally a hilarious melancholy arising from blood adust, a furious melancholy arising from choler adust, a stupid melancholy arising from phlegm adust, and a melancholy of violent terror and

---

[111] *Anatomy*, I, 202, 38–39.

despair arising from natural melancholy adust. When unnatural melancholy is cold, its effects are similar to those of natural melancholy in excess.

It might seem that, since there are so many and such diverse varieties of melancholy, the word could have no very definite significance as a psychiatric term. In the midst of this diversity, however, one finds the unifying idea of morbid fear and sorrow. Among the melancholic humors, the only ones which produce symptoms out of harmony with this central idea are blood adust and choler adust, and they do so only when they are hot. A typical definition of melancholy is: "a kinde of dotage without any feuer, hauing for his ordinarie companions, feare and sadnes, without any apparent occasion."[112]

VII

Atrabilious diseases "are rebellious, long and very hard to cure . . . for the melancholike humour is . . . contrarie to the two principles of our life, heate and moysture." Patients, moreover, resist "the meanes and remedies, neither giuing eare to good aduise, nor yet obeying the holesome precepts of Phisicke. And to be short, it is the very scourge and torment of Phisitions."[113] "It may be hard to cure, but not impossible, for him that is most grievously affected, if he be but willing to be helped."[114] The curative measures which the medical writers recommend[115] may be roughly divided into cures operating upon the body and cures operating upon the mind. Since the former classification has little bearing upon English literature, I shall treat it briefly.

Evacuation of the offending humor is the most obvious therapeutic measure. This may be accomplished by bloodletting. The medical writers name the specific veins to be opened for the evacuation of melancholy from the spleen, the liver, the head, etc. Phlebotomy, however, is usually regarded as a harsh measure to be avoided if possible. The most common method of evacuation is purgation. Black hellebore is the favorite purgative for melancholy. Clysters and emetics are sometimes recommended.

In addition to the drugs used for evacuation, there are various other pharmaceutical concoctions which the physician may employ. These include preparatives—medicines administered before purgation; alteratives—

---

112 Du Laurens, *Discourse*, pp. 86–87.
113 *Ibid.*, pp. 107–8.
114 Burton, *Anatomy*, II, 5.
115 The following section is an epitome of what I have found principally in Avicenna, *Canon*, pp. 377–79; Bernard, *Lilium Medicinae*, fols. 108–10; Elyot, *Castel of Helth*, fols. 67ᵛ, 73–74; Lemnius, *Touchstone*, fols. 152–57; Barrough, *Phisick*, pp. 46–47; Bright, *Treatise*, pp. 242 ff.; Wirtzung, *Praxis*, pp. 131–32; Du Laurens, *Discourse*, pp. 104–17, 134–40; Burton, *Anatomy*, vol. II.

medicines which render the melancholy humor less noxious by thinning, moistening, and warming it; comfortatives—medicines to "cheere vp the spirits"[116] so that they will warm and enliven the patient's sluggish blood. In hypochondriacal cases, physicians use carminative remedies and drugs designed to relieve and aid various abdominal organs. Some of the pharmaceutical recipes printed in the medical works are very elaborate and complicated.[117] It would take the physician or his apothecary many hours of labor to prepare them.

The medical writers have a great deal to say about the proper diet of the melancholic patient. He must, of course, avoid all foods that engender melancholy and eat foods which engender good blood, that is, warm and moist foods. (Adust melancholics should avoid hot and dry foods and eat cold and moist foods.) The dietary directions given by Du Laurens and Burton[118] are typical. The patient should eat plentifully of nourishing foods, for fattening is one means of cure. He should drink thin wines of light color and avoid dark wines, especially if they are old.

If possible the patient should expose himself only to warm, moist air. His surroundings should be light and cheerful. He should take exercise in moderation, and the physician must see that he does so in such a pleasant place as a garden or a meadow. He should bathe often in warm water to warm and moisten his system. Since insomnia is an aggravation as well as a symptom of melancholy, the physician often administers soporifics.

The psychological methods of curing melancholy include, first of all, mental diversion. The patient should never be allowed to indulge his taste for melancholy meditation or to brood over his fancies. Solitary meditation strengthens the hold that melancholy has upon him, and by brooding over his anxieties, he fixes them more firmly in his mind. He should never be left alone. He should always be busied at something which will keep his thoughts pleasantly engaged. He should hunt, fish, take part in athletic sports, make journeys, attend plays and pageants, frequent social gatherings.[119]

Perhaps the best medicine of all is gaiety (which is wholesome for any man). In Burton's judgment, nothing is so effective in curing melancholy "as a cup of strong drink, mirth, musick, and merry company."[120] For pleasure not only diverts the mind from melancholic broodings but also has its

---

[116] Du Laurens, *Discourse*, p. 112.

[117] For examples, see *ibid.*, pp. 108–11, 135–40.

[118] *Ibid.*, pp. 105–6; *Anatomy*, II, 24–30.

[119] The principle of cure through social diversion is set forth at length in Stefano Guazzo's *Civile Conversation* (translated by George Pettie and Bartholomew Young and published in English in 1581–86). This work consists of an extended conversation between a physician and a melancholy man.

[120] *Anatomy*, II, 132.

beneficial physiological effects. Joy is a warm, moist passion and consequently promotes the generation and dispersion of good blood and spirit to counteract the cold, dry melancholy humor. A merry tale is an excellent pill to purge melancholy. Gay melodies have great therapeutic value: "cheerefull musicke ... is to be sounded in the melancholicke eare," because music enlivens the vital spirit so that it may "stirre the bloud" and "attenuate the humours."[121]

The emotions of the patient must be controlled with great care. He should be kept from "all thynge that is greuouse to see, to smell, or to here, but most specially darkenesse."[122] He should be scrupulously protected from everything which might frighten or grieve him. If fear or sorrow has been the cause of his malady, he should by no means be allowed to see or hear anything which might remind him of his fear or sorrow. Anger and even excessive joy are harmful, for all immoderate passions cause "prodigall expence of the spirite."[123] The physician may sometimes find it expedient to divert the patient's thoughts from fear or sorrow by deliberately arousing another passion; "as one pinne is driuen out with another; so the later may expell the former."[124] This device, however, should be used with caution.

The melancholic should be urged to seek guidance and comfort in "the holsome counsayles founde in holy scripture, and in the bokes of morall doctrine,"[125] so that he may learn to regulate his passions, especially his sorrows. His friends should reason with him affably, counsel him, and encourage him. They should point out to him the unmanliness of allowing passion to rule reason and the danger therein to melancholy men in particular. They should offer him consolation for his sorrows, as Timothy Bright, in a prefatory letter, comforts the "Melancholicke friend: M." to whom his book is addressed.[126] Various writers attempt to do this friendly office for anyone who may care to read by offering consolation for all the common misfortunes which cause the griefs of mankind: loss of kindred or friends, poverty, disgrace, etc.[127]

The patient may do much toward his own cure. He must confide in his friends: "grief concealed strangles the soul," but when one's sorrow is imparted to a friend, "it is instantly removed, by his counsel haply, wisdom, persuasion, advice."[128] The patient must cooperate with his physician. He

---

[121] Bright, *Treatise*, pp. 247–48.
[122] Elyot, *Castel of Helth*, fol. 73ᵛ.
[123] Bright, *Treatise*, p. 251.
[124] *Ibid.*, p. 256. Cf. Burton, *Anatomy*, II, 131.
[125] Elyot, *Castel of Helth*, fol. 64ᵛ. Cf. Bright, *Treatise*, pp. 254–55.
[126] See also *Treatise*, pp. 207–42.
[127] For instance, Elyot, *Castel of Helth*, fols. 64–67; Burton, *Anatomy*, II, 145–236.
[128] Burton, *Anatomy*, II, 123.

must strive with all his power to rule his passions so that "alwayes there do remaine sufficient power in reasons hande to restraine."[129] Melancholy men, however, can hardly be expected to be sane and reasonable enough to cooperate in their own cure.

It is perhaps a little obvious to add that, if the malady has arisen from grief or fear, removing the cause of the grief or fear will be likely to effect a cure. "Many are instantly cured, when their minds are satisfied."[130] The physician or the patient's friends must take all possible steps to set the patient's mind at rest. Indeed he who wishes to aid a melancholy man cannot confine himself to pharmaceutical and dietary measures; he may have to intervene in the most intimate affairs of the patient's life.

---

[129] Bright, *Treatise*, p. 252.
[130] Burton, *Anatomy*, II, 126.

Chapter III. THE SCIENTIFIC THEORY OF MELAN-
CHOLY (*Continued*)

I

THE SUBJECT OF MELANCHOLIC HALLUCINATION deserves more attention than I have thus far given it. As I have said earlier, melancholy delusions are due primarily to the vitiation of the animal spirit and the substance of the brain by the melancholy humor or its vapors. Visual impressions are tinctured by the blackened spirit and appear as blackened images before the common sense and the imagination. Sense impressions of other sorts are falsified for reasons which are not so definitely stated by the authorities. Next to visual delusion, the type most frequently described is auditory. Some melancholy patients are conscious of a "ringing"[1] or a "hissing"[2] in the ears. They hear "bells"[3] or "a voyce sounding in [their] eares."[4] Authorities occasionally mention other fancied sensations: "I have known also a patient suffering from a melancholic lesion who declared that another person smelled of sulphur and pitch and believed that the food offered him tasted of pepper, although these things were clearly far from the truth. He asserted likewise that his privities were so corrupted by inflammation and decay that he greatly feared the development of gangrene, whereas all the while these parts were quite free of defect."[5]

A fancy which has found lodgment in a melancholy mind is very tenacious. The melancholy brain is dry and hard, and an impression upon it "suffereth not it selfe easily to be blotted out."[6] Melancholy men, therefore,

---

[1] Lemnius, *Touchstone*, fol. 143ʳ. This occurs in a passage on splenetic melancholy. Occasionally one finds the singing of the ears associated with melancholy flatulence (see Aëtius, *De Melancholia*, p. 701; Burton, *Anatomy*, I, 473), but just as often it is associated with no specific cause.

[2] Du Laurens, *Discourse*, p. 96.

[3] Burton, *Anatomy*, I, 491.

[4] Bright, *Treatise*, p. 195. Johann Weyer reports the case of a melancholy man "qui suis auribus semper obstrepere . . . quemcunque obuium, etiam coniunctissimum quereretur."—*De Praestigiis*, p. 228.

[5] "Scio quoque, ubi sulphur & picem redolere aliquem occlamaret melancholiae uitium patiens, & cibum oblatum piper resipere iudicaret: quae quam alienissima esse a rei ueritate, cognoscebantur. Partes item pudibundas inflammatione putoreque ita uitiatas asserebat, ut gangraenam suborituram pertimesceret, his interim locis ab omni uitio immunibus."—*Idem*.

[6] Du Laurens, *Discourse*, p. 97.

are peculiarly subject to hallucinatory obsessions and fixed ideas, usually of a sorrowful or fearful nature, and "haue in a maner all of them one speciall [delusion], from which they cannot be weined till time haue worne it out."[7] The medical writers of the Renaissance often pause in their more serious business to tell stories regarding the strange fancies of melancholy men, and stories of the same nature constitute perhaps the most readable parts of Renaissance books of jests and strange tales.[8] Many of these stories are repeated over and over. Some of them are derived ultimately from classical sources.[9]

Many melancholy men have absurd anxieties regarding their own persons. Some think that they are earthen pots and are continually afraid of being broken.[10] Some think that they are urinals. One believes that he is a brick and will not drink for fear of dissolving himself. Another is afraid to sit because he thinks that his buttocks are made of glass. Another thinks that he has no head; another that he has lost a leg; another that he has a serpent in his stomach; another, who has swallowed frogs' spawn, that he has live frogs in his belly. Another melancholy man believes himself with child. Another thinks that he has drunk poison; another that he has loathsome sores on his body; another that he is dead. Some melancholy persons find external causes for fear. One believes himself condemned to death and thinks that everyone who approaches him has come to arrest him and hale him to execution. Another fears that Atlas is weary of his burden and is about to let the sky fall. A certain melancholy man "did imagine that all the superficies of the world was very fine glasse, that the part vnder it was all full of Serpents, and that his bed was as it were in an Iland, from whence if hee did stirre, hee should breake the glasse and fall among the serpents."[11]

Melancholy persons sometimes imagine that they are birds or animals and imitate their voices and movements. "Some think they are beasts, wolves,

---

[7] *Ibid.*, p. 96. In saying that *all* melancholy men have fixed ideas, the doctor is clearly saying more than he means. Yet Aretaeus defines melancholy as a "lowness of spirits from a single phantasy."—*Works*, p. 298. Cf. Mercado, *Opera*, III, 89.

[8] There are a great many collections of tales about melancholic absurdities. Some examples: Lemnius, *Touchstone*, fols. 150–52; Du Laurens, *Discourse*, pp. 100–4; Garzoni, *Hospitall of Fooles*, pp. 17–18; Simon Goulart, *Admirable and Memorable Histories*, tr. Edward Grimeston (London, 1607), pp. 370 ff.; Walkington, *Optick Glasse*, pp. 134–40; Thomas Milles, *The Treasurie of Auncient and Moderne Times* (London, 1613), pp. 476–79; Burton, *Anatomy*, I, 462–65, 474; II, 131–32; Nathaniel Wanley, *The Wonders of the Little World* (London, 1678), pp. 94–96.

[9] When one looks up the ancient sources, one finds that some of these tales were not originally told of melancholy men. Melancholy seems to have attracted to itself many stories originally associated with other sorts of mental aberration.

[10] This is the melancholic delusion which Renaissance writers mention most frequently. They have read of such hallucinations in ancient sources. See Galen, *Opera*, VIII, 190; Aëtius, *De Melancholia*, p. 704 (from Rufus).

[11] Goulart, *Histories*, p. 376.

hogs, and cry like dogs, foxes, bray like asses, and low like kine."[12] The grimmest form of melancholia is lycanthropia, the wolf madness, which constitutes the subject matter of the most lurid chapters in classical, medieval, and Renaissance medical works. Among the

humours of melancholy, the Phisitions place a kinde of madnes by the Greeks called *Lycanthropia*, termed by the Latines *Insania Lupina;* or wolues furie: which bringeth a man to this point . . . that in Februarie he will goe out of the house in the night like a wolfe, hunting about the graues of the dead with great howling, and plucke the dead mens bones out of the sepulchers, carrying them about the streetes, to the great feare and astonishment of all them that meete him . . . melancholike persons of this kinde, haue pale faces, soaked and hollow eies, with a weake sight, neuer shedding one teare to the view of the worlde, a drie toong, extreme thirst, and they want spittle and moisture exceedingly.[13]

Startling tales are told of lycanthropes. Among them is the story of a farmer of Padua who, in the year 1541, conceived the idea that he was a wolf and sprang upon and killed many persons in the fields. When at length he was captured with great difficulty, he stoutly maintained that he was a true wolf, distinguished from others only by a skin with hair inverted. His cruel captors ("quidam omnem exuti humanitatem, uereque lupi truces, uoracesque") cut off his limbs with swords to seek the truth of the matter. When the man was found to be no wolf, they delivered him to surgeons, but after a few days he died.[14]

Some melancholic delusions, however, are not so grisly to the observer or so disagreeable to the patient. There is a story of an ancient Greek who sat in an empty theater under the impression that he was seeing plays, and there he laughed and clapped his hands and enjoyed himself immensely. A certain Athenian believed himself the owner of all the ships in the harbor of

---

[12] Burton, *Anatomy*, I, 462. Weyer refers to a Spanish nobleman ("nostro hoc seculo") who believed that he was a bear and roamed through the wilderness and mountains (*De Praestigiis*, p. 424). Melancholy beast hallucinations are mentioned in Aretaeus, *Works*, p. 300; Paulus Aegineta, *Seven Books*, I, 383; Avicenna, *Canon*, p. 377.

[13] Garzoni, *Hospitall of Fooles*, p. 19. This passage is representative of many such descriptions of lycanthropia which appear in Renaissance works. All of these seem to have been derived directly or indirectly from an ancient source: "Qui morbo lupino sive canino appellato corripiuntur, februario mense noctu exeunt, in omnibus imitantes lupos aut canes et adusque diem monumenta maxime aperiunt. Cognosces autem ita affectos ex his signis. Pallidi sunt et visu imbecilli et oculos siccos habent et non lacrymantur. Ipsos quoque cavos oculos habere cernes et linguam aridam, neque prorsus salivam profundunt. Sunt quoque siticulosi tibiasque exulceratas insanabiles habent propter assiduos casus et canum morsus; ac talia sunt signa. Nosse vero oportet melancholiae speciem esse hunc morbum."—Aëtius, *De Melancholia*, p. 719. The author of this often quoted description was Marcellus (late fourth century).

[14] Weyer, *De Praestigiis*, pp. 420–21.

Pyraeus, went daily to look over his property and to direct the mariners. These persons were greatly offended when the physicians cured them, for they had been living very pleasantly.[15]

There are melancholy men also who believe that they are kings, emperors, popes, cardinals. Milles mentions a melancholy man "who verily beleeued, that he was King of the *Gaules*."[16] Johann Weyer says that he has known a paranoiac ("melancholicum Italum") who claimed to be emperor of the whole world.[17] William Vaughan writes of a melancholy Venetian gentleman of his acquaintance who "would eyther be *aut Caesar, aut nihil*" and "wrote very learned letters and pathetical vnto the *Electours,* for his aduancement into the throne Emperiall."[18] Burton has collected other cases: "*Francisco Sansovino* records of a melancholy man in *Cremona*, that . . . would not be induced to believe but that he was *Pope*, gave pardons, made Cardinals, &c. *Christophorus à Vega* makes mention of another of his acquaintance, that thought he was a King driven from his Kingdom, and was very anxious to recover his estate."[19] There is a tale of a melancholy man who thought that he was a god; on the other hand there is a tale of one who thought that he was nothing.[20] In short, the Renaissance was inclined to attribute all tenacious delusions and irrational obsessions, fearful or pleasant, to melancholy: "hateful error" is "melancholy's child."[21]

It is not possible to find definite medical explanations for all these various hallucinations. The learned writers who tell the tales usually throw all cases together into the vague category of melancholic dotages and tell the stories, one suspects, more for the entertainment than for the instruction of their readers. A few types of delusion, however, are specifically explained. Du Laurens associates certain fancies with internal physical causes:

> Such as are of an extreme drie temperature, and haue the braine also very drie; if they happen cómmonly to looke vpon some pitcher or glasse . . . they will iudge themselues to be pitchers or glasses. Such as are troubled with wormes either in the stomacke or guts, will easily receiue, if they be melancholikely disposed, that they haue some serpent, viper, or other liuing thing in their bellies. Such as are

---

[15] Both of these stories are derived from classical sources. The first comes from the Aristotelian *De Mirabilibus Auscultationibus,* 31, and Horace, *Epistles,* II, ii, 128–40; the second from Athenaeus, *The Deipnosophists,* XII, 554. In the classical sources, the deluded persons are not described as melancholy men.

[16] *Treasurie,* p. 477ᵃ. The earliest reference to melancholy paranoiacs that I have found is in Avicenna, *Canon,* p. 377.

[17] *De Praestigiis,* p. 227.

[18] *Directions,* pp. 102–3.

[19] *Anatomy,* I, 464.

[20] Walkington, *Optick Glasse,* p. 138; Du Laurens, *Discourse,* p. 102.

[21] *Julius Caesar,* V, iii, 67.

troubled with very much windines, will oftentimes imagine themselues flying in the ayre, and to become birds. They that abound in seede, will runne a madding after women, hauing the same for continual obiects before their eyes.[22]

He connects other self-deceptions with the ordinary preoccupations of the patients: "If an ambitious man become melancholike, he straightway dreameth that he is a King, an Emperour, a Monarke. If he bee couetous, then all his foolish imaginations will runne vpon riches."[23]

In Burton's *Anatomy* one finds certain hallucinations attributed to particular humors. Melancholy men who believe that they are monarchs and those who fancy that they see pleasant spectacles are affected by blood adust; melancholics who see black men or devils, those who believe themselves dead, and those who think that they are beasts are troubled with natural melancholy adust.[24] Hypochondriacal flatulence, according to Burton, explains some melancholy fancies. Patients who think that there are frogs or serpents in their stomachs are deluded by "those ascending vapours and gripings rumbling beneath."[25]

If the patient is obsessed with an irrational fancy, it is part of the physician's task to dispel it. The mind must be eased before the body can be cured, and in some cases correcting the delusion is alone sufficient for the cure. Such a patient, however, is very obstinate and intractable. Any attempt to persuade him that his fancy is groundless only makes him cling to it more stubbornly, and anyone who tries to reason with him becomes the object of his sullen suspicion. The physician, therefore, must employ, in addition to medical therapy, a certain psychological strategy. First he must win the patient's confidence, and to do so he must humor him, agree with everything that he says, no matter how preposterous it may be: "*As they hate those, saith Alexander, that neglect or deride, so they will give ear to such as will sooth them up. If they say they have swallowed frogs, or a snake, by all means grant it, and tell them you can easily cure it, 'tis an ordinary thing.*"[26] Having established the proper relationship with the patient, the physician may then proceed to combat the delusion, but he must do so without betraying any skepticism concerning it. He usually employs "some feigned lie, strange news, witty device, artificial invention."[27]

To illustrate, a certain melancholy man believed that he had an enormous

---

[22] *Discourse*, p. 97. Cf. Aëtius, *De Melancholia*, p. 704 (from Rufus).
[23] *Discourse*, p. 98. Cf. Bright, *Treatise*, pp. 108–9; Burton, *Anatomy*, I, 464–65.
[24] I, 443, 460, 462.
[25] I, 474.
[26] *Ibid.*, II, 131. Burton repeats two case histories which Alexander uses to illustrate the technique which he recommends. See *Libri Duodecim*, fol. 34ʳ.
[27] Burton, *Anatomy*, II, 131.

nose, and no friend or physician could persuade him otherwise. Finally "a physician more expert in this humour than the rest" visited him. The doctor showed great astonishment at the size of the patient's nose and thus won his complete confidence. Two or three mock operations (performed while the patient was blindfolded) convinced him that his nose was reduced to normal proportions. Thereupon "the mans mind being satisfied, his greefe was eased, and his disease cured."[28] There is the strange tale of a Paris lawyer who thought that he was dead and therefore would not eat. His ingenious nephew dressed himself in a shroud and, garbed thus as a dead man, ate in the presence of his uncle. In this way the melancholy lawyer was persuaded that the dead took food like the living. He ate a hearty meal and his life was saved.[29] A certain gentleman believed that his bones were so soft that they would crumple if he stood upright. He would not leave his bed. A clever physician assured him that he could easily cure this infirmity and administered medicines to purge melancholy, representing them as remedies for softness of bone. Thus body and mind were cured at the same time.[30]

Sometimes, says Du Laurens, melancholy patients "must be chid for their foolish imaginations, as also reproached and made ashamed of their cowhardinesse."[31] There are authorities who recommend even threatening and terrifying in stubborn cases.[32] The milder methods, however, are generally considered the better.

II

With some hesitancy and some attempt to justify himself, Burton distinguishes a category which he calls *religious melancholy*. His hesitancy seems unnecessary, for his contemporaries were quite accustomed to the idea if not to the term. Thoughtful men of the Renaissance period realized that such phenomena as religious fanaticism and morbid fear of damnation (probably much more common then than now) might be symptoms of mental derangement. Scientific writers of the period frequently attributed the enthusiasms and despairs of the ardently devout to melancholy.

---

[28] The quotations are from the version in Reginald Scot's *The Discoverie of Witchcraft*, ed. Nicholson (London, 1886), pp. 41–42. The story appears in many Renaissance works.

[29] See Milles, *Treasurie*, pp. 477–78; Burton, *Anatomy*, I, 462, and II, 132. Foreest says that he has employed a similar stratagem in dealing with a melancholy theologian who would not eat because he believed himself dead (*Observationum*, p. 329).

[30] John Webster, *The Displaying of Supposed Witchcraft* (London, 1677), pp. 33–34.
[31] *Discourse*, p. 107.
[32] See Burton, *Anatomy*, II, 130–31.

Religious melancholy, if one accepts Burton's conception of it, comprises loosely all cases of melancholy in which the causes, the symptoms, or both are somehow connected with religion. Religious causes include the ascetic severities which fervid penitents practice. Bad diet, fasting, and self-inflicted physical torments produce black bile. The overzealous become quite "mortified and mad" through "penance, going woolward, whipping, alms, fasting, &c."[33] Fasting is especially likely to engender melancholy: "Monks, Anachorites, and the like, after much emptiness become melancholy, vertiginous, they think they hear strange noises, confer with Hobgoblins, Devils, rivell up their bodies."[34] Loneliness and intent meditation on questions of divinity often render pious persons melancholy: "Solitariness, much fasting, divine meditations, and contemplations of God's judgments . . . are main causes.[35] Anxiety for the future of their souls turns the wits of some. Pious persons brooding over the question of salvation may become persuaded that they are not among God's chosen and that at the Last Judgment they will be condemned to eternal torment. Such men often develop a dreadful melancholy which provokes them to commit monstrous crimes.[36]

Melancholy symptoms of a religious character include many rapturous fancies. Some devout patients see beatific visions: "Deos, & angelorum choros, & similia."[37] Others imagine themselves endowed with miraculous powers. Weyer writes of a melancholy man who claimed that he could compel Gabriel and Michael to appear and to give replies to questions concerning matters of high significance. When a certain cardinal requested that he do this, however, he replied that he could not unless he had previously prepared his body with much fasting and prayer and unless the welfare of the universal church were involved.[38] Louis Lavater has seen a melancholy man, "*Iohannes Leonardus Sertorius* by name," who firmly believed "that he coulde proue our Religion . . . to be true and catholicke, euen by a

---

[33] *Ibid.*, III, 392. To "go woolward" is to wear wool next to the skin.

[34] P. 394.

[35] P. 454.

[36] Some persons "se damnatos, Deo minime curae, nec praedistinatos esse, etsi religiosi et pij interim sint, sibi persuadent, & extremum iudicium, aeternumque supplicium metuunt." The melancholy which develops often impels such patients "ad blasphemiam erga Deum, ad multa horrenda perpetranda, ad manus violentas sibi inferendas, maritum, vxorem, liberos, vicinos, principem interficiendos, nulla zelotypia, nulla invidia erga illos."—Plater, *Praxeos*, pp. 98–99. "Videmus enim multos religiosos & in bona uita reuerendos, hanc passionem incidentes, ex dei timore, & futuri iudicij suspitione, & summi boni uiuendi cupiditate . . . sicut ebriosi fiunt, de nimia sua solicitudine, & sua quasi uanitate."—Constantinus, *Opera*, p. 283.

[37] Girolamo Fracastoro, *Opera Omnia* (Venice, 1555), fol. 199ᵛ. I find illustrative cases in Rhazes, *Continens* (Venice, 1529), fol. 6ᵛ; Burton, *Anatomy*, III, 425.

[38] *De Praestigiis*, p. 228.

miracle from heauen as somtime *Helias* did."[39] Some "thinke them selues inspired with the holy Ghost, and do prophecy vpon things to come."[40] Burton implies that the enthusiasm of the melancholy prophet is cyclic: "... he is inspired by the Holy Ghost, full of the spirit: one while he is saved, another while damned, or still troubled in mind for his sins, the Devil will surely have him, &c."[41]

A melancholy man's illusion of divine favor or prophetic power may be the work of the Devil or his minions. Because of their mental instability the Devil finds it easy to delude melancholy men. Melancholy is a humor into which the Devil readily slips ("cui uti aptae suis operationibus materiae non illibenter se insinuare solet daemonium").[42] Evil spirits "take all opportunities of humours decayed, or otherwise, to pervert the soul of man; and besides, the [melancholy] humour itself is *Balneum Diaboli*, the Devil's Bath, and, as *Agrippa* proves," invites demonic visitation.[43] The Devil works primarily upon the imagination, and "he moves the *phantasy* by mediation of humours."[44] Thus melancholy persons troubled "by the intercourse or medling of euill angels ... oftentimes ... foretell & forge very strange things in their imaginations."[45]

Never any strange illusions of devils amongst hermits, Anachorites, never any visions, phantasms, apparitions, Enthusiasms, Prophets, any revelations, but immoderate fasting, bad diet, sickness, melancholy, solitariness, or some such things were the precedent causes, the forerunners or concomitants of them. The best opportunity and sole occasion the Devil takes to delude them.[46]

The Devil, finding melancholy men easy prey, leads them to damnation by insinuating into their minds heretical notions or impious delusions of divine favor and divine revelation.

Two English writers whom I have consulted deny fervently that genuine prophetic powers are ever connected with melancholy. Henry Howard, Earl of Northampton, attempts to distinguish between false prophecies and

---

[39] *Of Ghostes and Spirites Walking by Nyght*, tr. R. H. (London, 1572); ed. J. Dover Wilson and May Yardley (Oxford, 1929), p. 11.
[40] Barrough, *Phisick*, p. 46. Greek physicians mention melancholy persons who fancy that they have prophetic powers; see Paulus Aegineta, *Seven Books*, I, 383; Alexander, *Libri Duodecim*, fol. 31ʳ. Bernard writes that to some melancholics "... videtur, quod sint prophetae, & quod sint inspirati a spiritu sancto, & incipiunt prophetare."—*Lilium Medicinae*, fol. 108ʳ. Burton gives many examples. See, for instance, *Anatomy*, III, 424–26.
[41] *Anatomy*, I, 465.
[42] Weyer, *De Praestigiis*, p. 531. Cf. Burton, *Anatomy*, I, 227–29.
[43] Burton, *Anatomy*, I, 493.
[44] *Ibid.*, p. 228. Cf. III, 490.
[45] Du Laurens, *Discourse*, p. 100.
[46] Burton, *Anatomy*, III, 393.

those truly inspired. Regarding melancholy prophets he is somewhat emphatic: "sooner shall a man finde out a pure virgin in Sodome, then a true Prophete in the caue of melancholy."[47] John Harvey, physician, grants that there may be something in "philosophicall, and astronomicall predictions," but the prophets who mislead the vulgar are ordinarily "Mad companions and mates of strange and monstrous disposition," among them "our common melancholique and *Saturnine* prophets, wherwith the world hath long space beene perilously seduced." He suggests, among other possibilities, that such persons may be "strangely deluded by some cogging diuell." He is not "so melancholique" as to believe, as some do, that melancholy engenders "*Delphicall,* or *Sybilline* properties."[48]

Yet many authorities believe that melancholy men sometimes really have miraculous knowledge of the future and of other matters. Commonly they attribute this to demonic possession. Melancholy persons possessed by evil spirits "prophesy, speak several languages, talk of Astronomy, & other unknown sciences to them, (of which they have been ever ignorant)."[49] Astonishing things are reported of "their actions, gestures, *contortions*, fasting, prophesying, speaking languages they were never taught, &c."[50] Renaissance authorities, however, do not always attribute the prophetic powers of melancholy men to infernal influences (see below, section v).

In other cases of religious melancholy, the principal symptom is despair of salvation. In these cases one finds, instead of fanatical enthusiasms and prophetic raptures, the excruciating despondency usually characteristic of melancholy. One finds also melancholic delusion, namely morbid exaggeration in the patient's mind of his guilt in the eyes of God accompanied by extravagant fear of damnation. "There are melancholics greatly tormented by the anxieties of a heavy conscience who, attaching great significance to trifles, imagine guilt where none exists. Distrusting divine mercy and believing themselves condemned to hell, they lament incessantly night and day."[51] The thought of hell-fire terrifies

47 *A Defensative Against the Poyson of Supposed Prophecies* (London, 1583), sig. Iiiir.

48 *A Discoursive Probleme Concerning Prophecies* (London, 1588), pp. 4, 6, 34–35.

49 Burton, *Anatomy*, I, 492. The association of melancholy and prophetic power appears in Aristotle, *Problemata*, XXX, i, and Rufus, *Oeuvres*, p. 456. Aretaeus says that madmen sometimes display knowledges which they have never learned (*Works*, p. 302).

50 Burton, *Anatomy*, I, 164. Cf. Plater, *Praxeos*, p. 102. For illustrative cases, see Weyer, *De Praestigiis*, pp. 531–32; Foreest, *Observationum*, p. 340; Burton, *Anatomy*, I, 461, 468.

51 "Sunt quos tam misere exercet plena scrupulis conscientia, qui nodos in laeui scirpo quaeritantes, culpam imaginantur ubi nulla est: & diuinae misericordiae diffidentes, se orco destinatos, lamentatione sedulo nocte duique deplorant."—Weyer, *De Praestigiis*, pp. 227–28. Cf. Van der Velde, *De Cerebri Morbis*, p. 271; Foreest, *Observationum*, p. 337. Illustrative instances appear in Burton, *Anatomy*, III, 464–66.

poor distressed souls, especially if their bodies be predisposed by melancholy, they religiously given, and have tender consciences, every small object affrights them, the very inconsiderate reading of Scripture itself, and misinterpretation of some places of it, as *Many are called, few are chosen. . . . They doubt of their Election, how shall they know it, by what signs. And so far forth, saith* Luther, *with such nice points, torture and crucify themselves, that they are almost mad, and all they get by it is this, they lay open a gap to the Devil by Desperation to carry them to Hell.* But the greatest harm of all proceeds from those thundering Ministers, a most frequent cause they are of this malady.[52]

"Fear takes away their content, and dries the blood, wasteth the marrow, alters their countenance."[53] Melancholy and fear of damnation aggravate each other in a vicious cycle.

Sometimes the patient sees phantasms, even smells odors, which make hell seem very real and near. Peter van Foreest describes the case of a patient of his, a divine of melancholy temperament whom fasting and study had driven to delirium. This gentleman believed himself damned; insisted that he was already in hell, that in fact he could smell it; saw demons in his bed chamber; believed that he himself, burning in the everlasting fire, was exhaling sulphur fumes. When the doctor attempted to reassure him on the latter point, the patient breathed in his face to prove it.[54]

"The principal agent and procurer of [despair] is the Devil," who, taking advantage of the melancholic's mental weakness, deludes him concerning his spiritual state and provokes him to commit the sin of distrusting God's mercy. "His ordinary engine by which he produceth this effect, is the melancholy humour itself . . . the Devil's bath . . . a shoeing-horn, a bait to allure" evil spirits.[55]

Pious writers of Elizabethan and early Stuart England distinguish carefully between melancholy despair and the true sense of sin. The despondent melancholic should realize that his state of mind is due to physical and pathological causes, or perhaps to the Devil's taking advantage of his weakness, not to any genuine intuition of God's disapproval. The avowed purpose of Timothy Bright's *Treatise of Melancholie*, which is as pietistic as it is scientific, is to clarify this significant distinction and a large part of the work is devoted to the subject. Bright addresses the book to an imaginary melancholic friend "M.," who, ill and despondent, has conceived the idea that he is the object of God's grave displeasure and has written to ask the doctor's

---

[52] Burton, *Anatomy*, III, 456.
[53] *Ibid.*, p. 463.
[54] *Observationum*, p. 329. Cf. Burton, *Anatomy*, III, 490.
[55] Burton, *Anatomy*, III, 452–53.

medical and spiritual advice.[56] Bright has responded by explaining the reciprocal influence of body and soul and the difference "betwixt natural melancholie, and that heauy hande of God vpon the afflicted conscience, tormented with remorse of sinne, & feare of his iudgement."[57] It is the doctor's opinion that his friend's mental condition is due both to God's "fatherly frowning"[58] and to melancholy. The symptoms of melancholy, the doctor notes, are abundantly present. The "feare & terror of God sent vpon man" falls "vpon you . . . more heauily, in so much as you are vnder the disaduantage of the melancholicke complexion: whose opportunity Sathan embraceth to vrge all terror against you to the fall."[59] It is of the utmost importance that the melancholy penitent should be able to recognize the symptoms of his malady, that he should know to what degree his despondency is due to his physical state, and that he should employ suitable curative measures. Bright accordingly offers instruction on the nature and cure of melancholy to anyone who may find himself in M.'s suppositious circumstances.

Certain early Stuart divines likewise emphasize the distinction between the true and the melancholy sense of sin. John Yates, in discussing the "*corporall inhabiting of Sathan.*" writes that the affrightments of the stricken soul may be "as well the operation of phansie from melancholie, as of conscience for sinne."[60] He devotes several pages to describing the two sorts of spiritual despondency, the one to be recognized by the physical and mental symptoms characteristic of melancholy, the other principally by their absence. The fact that the true affliction of conscience may produce melancholy, he notes, makes the distinction peculiarly difficult. He seems especially concerned lest the true sense of sin be mistaken for melancholy. Samuel Hieron writes that "There is a great likenesse in melancholike passions to a troubled conscience, but our best Diuines" agree that the melancholy person is troubled about sin "only in a confused manner" because of "some affrighted imagination." On the other hand, "the man afflicted in conscience, his trouble ariseth out of some certaine knowne corruption, and out of a true conceiuing of Gods wrath."[61] John Sedgwick, like Yates, is concerned lest the true "wound of conscience" be dismissed as mere melancholy: "melancholy prevailing in men doth come very neere to the trouble of conscience, but it is not the wound of conscience here spoken of; Satan

---

[56] See the prefatory letter "To His Melancholicke friend: M."

[57] Fol. iii^v. Cf. Burton, *Anatomy*, III, 453.

[58] Bright, *Treatise*, p. 191.

[59] P. 192.

[60] *Gods Arraignment of Hypocrites* (Cambridge, 1615), pp. 348–49. The entire discussion occupies pp. 348–59.

[61] *Davids Penitentiall Psalme Opened* (Cambridge, 1617), pp. 258–59.

makes it his bait, and man makes it his burden, but wee may not make it this wound."[62]

There are still other ways in which Satan may trouble the melancholy man. He may encourage impenitence. The Rev. Richard Greenham writes to a young friend on the subject of his blindness of mind and hardness of heart: ". . . partly Melancholie, partly Satan working therewith, make you do iniurie to your selfe, and to the graces of the spirit in you: which I beseech you take heed of."[63] The Devil also may interfere with pious thoughts and exercises:

A certain Student of a melancholick Constitution, distracted with grief for the death of a Sister, and wearied with lucubrations, did complain . . . of the Devil haunting of him: and did affirm that he felt the evil Spirit enter by his fundament with wind, and so did creep up his body until it possessed the head, lest he might attend his Prayers and Meditations with his accustomed devotion.[64]

Satan may even provoke blasphemous thoughts and utterances. "The Devil commonly suggests things opposite to nature, opposite to God and his word, impious, absurd, such as a man would never of himself, or could not conceive, they strike terror and horror into the party's own heart."[65]

The category of religious melancholy can be extended considerably further. Heresy is sometimes considered an effect of melancholy. Jerome Cardan classifies heretics with melancholy criminals and mentions superstition among the symptoms of melancholy.[66] Devils, says Jacques Du Bosc, often "serve themselves of this dull and sullen humour [melancholy] to entertaine superstition, despaire, or hipocrisy in a soule."[67] Burton includes among religious melancholics "*Mahometans, Jews, . . . Hereticks old and new, Schismaticks, Schoolmen, Prophets, Enthusiasts,* &c.,"[68] also "*Epicures, Atheists, Hypocrites, worldly secure, Carnalists, all impious persons, impenitent sinners, &c.*"[69]

The cure of religious melancholy is, of course, largely a task for the divine, who of all persons is best qualified to offer to the patient the proper

---

[62] *The Bearing and Burden of the Spirit* (London, 1640), p. 116. The entire discussion covers pp. 115–23.

[63] *Workes*, ed. H. H. (London, 1605), p. 257. Cf. Burton, *Anatomy*, III, 446.

[64] Webster, *Witchcraft*, p. 34.

[65] Burton, *Anatomy*, III, 478. Cf. 465.

[66] *De Rerum Varietate Libri XVII* (Basel, 1557), pp. 515–16.

[67] *The Compleat Woman*, tr. N. N. (London, 1639), p. 33.

[68] *Anatomy*, III, 397. Persons of these classes suffer from religious melancholy "In excess" (see *ibid.*, p. viii).

[69] *Ibid.*, p. 434. Such persons suffer from religious melancholy "In defect," as do those afflicted by melancholic despair.

counsel and comfort. Yet "There be those that prescribe Physick in such cases, 'tis God's instrument, and not unfit. The Devil works by mediation of humours, and mixt diseases must have mixt remedies."[70] The principles of evacuation, diet, and regimen which govern the treatment of melancholy in general are applicable in cases of religious melancholy. When the religious melancholic suffers from delusion, the strategy of deception may be employed. A certain nobleman, for example, was tormented by the "melancholy imagination" that he had sinned too greatly for God's pardon. His physician removed a tile from the roof over his chamber, dressed a man as an angel, and sent him by night, with a torch for illumination, to appear above the aperture. The angel announced to the patient that his sins were forgiven, and the patient recovered promptly.[71]

III

In learned works of the Renaissance one meets a theory concerning witchcraft which perhaps represents psychology's first attempt at humanitarian service. The principal proponent of this theory was the Lowlands physician Johann Weyer, who expounded it at considerable length in *De Praestigiis Daemonum, et Incantationibus ac Veneficiis Libri Sex*, first published in 1563.[72] In Weyer's book one finds a vitriolic indictment of persons who league themselves with the Devil and exercise infernal powers. From this class, however, the author excludes the beldams commonly condemned for witchcraft on their own confessions. These, he thinks, are harmless melancholy old women misled by the Devil. Because their imaginations have been corrupted by atrabilious vapors, he finds it easy to delude them. At his prompting, they have renounced God in return for supernatural powers which they fancy Satan has given them. They are firmly convinced and will stoutly maintain that by miraculous means they have perpetrated atrocious crimes of which they are utterly incapable. These supposed witches are

---

70 *Ibid.*, p. 490.

71 Wanley, *Wonders*, p. 94. Cf. Burton, *Anatomy*, III, 433.

72 I have used the augmented fourth edition of 1568. Gregory Zilboorg, in *The Medical Man and the Witch During the Renaissance* (Baltimore, 1935), gives an enthusiastic and interesting account of Weyer's personality and methods, of the social and intellectual milieu in which he worked, and of the purposes and content of this significant book. Zilboorg credits Weyer, however, with an intellectual independence—independence of medical tradition and of the popular beliefs of his period—which, it seems to me, is hardly substantiated by the content of the book itself.

feminine as regards sex, well advanced in years, melancholy by nature, feeble of intellect, rashly inclined to despair, weak in their faith in God. The Devil with pleasure seizes upon such women as instruments adapted to his uses and promptly creeps into them, confusing their minds with multifarious fancies. Bewitched by such deceits, they believe and confess that they have done things altogether impossible to them.[73]

Weyer is greatly distressed by the savage treatment of these feeble-minded old women, whom he has seen thrown heedlessly into dark and filthy prisons, dwelling places of specters and demons, to be haled thence to the place of execution and burned alive.[74]

Reginald Scot, in *The Discoverie of Witchcraft* (1584), sought to give these ideas currency in England. The startling confessions which supposed witches make when on trial, according to Scot, are merely the issue of melancholically disease imaginations. These women are

commonly old, lame, bleare-eied, pale, fowle, and full of wrinkles ... in [their] drousie minds the divell hath goten a fine seat; so as, what mischeefe, mischance, calamitie, or slaughter is brought to passe, they are easilie persuaded the same is doone by themselves; inprinting in their minds an earnest and constant imagination hereof. They are leane and deformed, shewing melancholie in their faces.... They are doting, scolds, mad, divelish ... so firme and stedfast in their opinions, as whosoever shall onelie have respect to the constancie of their words uttered, would easilie beleeve they were true indeed.[75]

Weyer's unorthodox theory of witchcraft was widely known and was the subject of warm controversy. Burton mentions three authors who supported him and eight who attacked him.[76] Of these, I have consulted only Jean Bodin, who refutes Weyer lengthily, "premierement pour l'honneur de Dieu, contre lequel il s'est armé."[77] Scot's *Discoverie* also was something of a storm center. The *Dictionary of National Biography* lists seven English writers who attacked Scot between 1587 and 1668 and two seventeenth-century Englishmen who defended his position. Among the former appears

---

[73] Sunt "sexu mulierculae, ut plurimum uetulae, natura melancholicae, mentis impotes, animum temere despondentes, exiguae in Deum fiduciae: ijs uelut idoneis organis libentius se diabolus adiungit, ac promptius insinuat, ut earum mentes uarijs conturbet formis: quarum ludibrijs effascinatae, se fecisse existimant, fatenturque id quod ab ipsis fuit alienissimum."—Weyer, *De Praestigiis*, p. 586.

[74] P. 18.

[75] Nicholson's edition, p. 5. Cf. p. 41.

[76] *Anatomy*, I, 240–41. Du Laurens refers to the controversy without taking sides (*Discourse*, pp. 98–99).

[77] *Le Fleau des Demons et Sorciers* (Niort, 1616), p. 476. Bodin's refutation appeared first in 1580.

King James,[78] who upon his accession to the English throne ordered the burning of all copies of Scot's book.

IV

An Elizabethan moralist writes that melancholy men "are more wickedly bente" than men of any other complexion, "the causes of mischiefe euery where."[79] However little this may harmonize with other current ideas concerning the melancholy man, one finds fairly general agreement among the learned authors that he is likely to be malevolent and prone to crime.

A clear and complete explanation of the melancholic's criminal bent is hard to find. Renaissance scientists apparently have not given the matter sufficient attention to work out anything very definite.[80] The concept of melancholic criminality seems to be due merely to a natural coalescence in learned minds of various abhorrent connotations of melancholy with a cumulative effect which is rather sinister. Since malevolence and evil are frequently associated with melancholy in Elizabethan literature, it seems worthwhile to gather together from scientific works the elements from which the concept of melancholic wickedness has been formed. Obviously these might include the influence which infernal spirits are supposed to exercise over the melancholy man. But when the authorities speak of the evil in the melancholic character, they seem usually to be thinking of natural rather than supernatural causes.

In the first place, the passions characteristic of the melancholy man include some which might impel him into evil courses. His chief passions, of course, are fear and sorrow. But there are others: Melancholy persons are "Enuious ... because of their owne false conceaued want. . . . Ielousie pricketh them, because they are not contented with any moderation, but thinke all too little for supply of their want. . . . They interpret readilie all to the worse part, suspitious . . . not indifferently weighing the case, but poysing

---

78 See James' *Daemonologie*, ed. G. B. Harrison (London, 1924), pp. 28–30. Robert H. West discusses the dispute concerning witchcraft and related controversies in *The Invisible World* (Athens, Ga., 1939), pp. 1–53.

79 Rogers, *Anatomie of the Minde*, fol. 79.

80 One finds disagreement and vagueness, for example, when he tries to ascertain which variety of melancholy humor causes melancholic criminality. Huarte attributes it to adust melancholy (see *Examen*, pp. 95, 147, 193), La Primaudaye to choler and melancholy "corrupte and mingled together" (*Academie*, p. 535). Most authors who touch upon the subject are less specific. The context usually indicates natural melancholy. With the possible exception of Walkington, all authors quoted in this section refer expressly or presumably to natural melancholy and its effects.

it by their fantasticall feare, and doubt at home."[81] They are "distrustful . . . envious, malicious . . . covetous . . . repining, discontent . . . *injuriarum tenaces*, prone to revenge."[82] Many melancholics become venomous misanthropes.

The passions of the melancholy man, moreover, are very persistent. For melancholy is a heavy and viscid humor, so thick and adhesive that physicians have great difficulty in qualifying or evacuating it, and the mental conditions which it engenders are accordingly highly tenacious. Melancholy men, therefore, are "Stiffe in opinions";[83] "stubborne, intractable, obstinate."[84] When the melancholic is "throughly heat" with passion, he "retaineth the feruency thereof farre longer time then anie other complexion: and more feruently boyleth therewith."[85] Melancholics harbor "hatred long in their breasts." They are "hardly incensed with anger," but if they become angry, it is "long ere this passion bee appeased and mitigated."[86] Thus rancor and malice thrive and persist in the minds of melancholy men: "if Serpents breed in standing waters, evill thoughts maintaine themselves in plodding humors, and if their spirit be apt to invent malice, their countenance is no lesse to cover it."[87] When black bile

exceeds Natures bounds, [it] is most fit to move us to any wickednesse. For men of this constitution conceive grievous and sharp passions, and that last long, for the contumacy of the humour, that will hardly melt and be dissolved. Whence it followes, that evill thoughts and apprehensions stay long in their minds, which sometimes break forth into action.[88]

There is, furthermore, the traditional association of melancholy with the malign planet Saturn. Saturnine men are melancholy; melancholy men are Saturnine. In the opinion of astrologers Saturnists are "false, envious, and full of debate . . . heavy, thoughtful, and malicious . . . they shall be full of law and vengeance, and will never forgive till they be revenged . . . and all evils shall grow in them."[89] They are "obstinate in opinion, laborious, of deepe cogitation[,] couetous, enuious, solitarie, mournfull, few woords,

[81] Bright, *Treatise*, p. 133.
[82] Burton, *Anatomy*, I, 451.
[83] Elyot, *Castel of Helth*, fol. 3ʳ.
[84] Lemnius, *Touchstone*, fol. 146ʳ.
[85] Bright, *Treatise*, p. 130.
[86] Walkington, *Optick Glasse*, pp. 130–31.
[87] Du Bosc, *Compleat Woman*, p. 33.
[88] Levinus Lemnius, *The Secret Miracles of Nature* (London, 1658), p. 63. This work was first published 1559–64.
[89] *The Kalendar & Compost of Shepherds*, pp. 141–42.

rauenous, deceiuers, superstitious, treasorers. . . . [Saturn] causeth imprison-ments, and secret enemies."[90]

Although melancholy men are taciturn persons who seem gloomily apa-thetic, their minds are continually busy. In the "exercise of their wittes . . . they be indefatigable."[91] This constant mental industry increases their power to do evil. The melancholy man "oftentimes . . . by his contemplative faculty, by his assiduity of sad and serious meditation, is a brocher of dan-gerous Matchiavellisme, an inventor of stratagems, quirkes, and policies."[92] Under some circumstances, moreover, melancholy may produce a high de-gree of mental ability. As I shall point out in the following section, Renais-sance writers credit melancholy minds with many achievements of worth and dignity. Mental powers due to melancholy, however, may be perverted to evil ends.

The melancholy man, then, is subject to evil passions which are stubbornly persistent and is under the malign influence of Saturn. When one adds a morose mental assiduity and a high degree of astuteness, the result is a very dangerous person, amply endowed with the qualifications of a villain. The swarthy ugliness of the melancholic's face is in keeping with the malignancy of his heart.

V

In previous sections I have made it clear, I am sure, that melancholy men are sluggish, dull, and blockish, that they are fearful and sorrowful without apparent cause and are subject to the most terrifying and ridiculous halluci-nations, that often they are wretched creatures who have fallen to the level of brutes, that they are more likely to be led by the Devil than by divine influence. This is the conception of melancholy which one finds in medical works in the tradition of Galen. I must now make it equally clear that "melancholy men of all others are most witty, [and their melancholy] causeth many times divine ravishment, and a kind of *enthusiasmus* . . . which stirreth them up to be excellent Philosophers, Poets, Prophets, &c."[93] For one discovers a second and very different conception of melancholy in learned works of the Renaissance, a conception of considerably greater dig-nity. This also has a classical source.

---

90 Dariot, *Judgement of the Starres,* sig. D2.
91 Bright, *Treatise,* p. 130.
92 Walkington, *Optick Glasse,* p. 129.
93 Burton, *Anatomy,* I, 461.

A problem of Aristotle's[94] which greatly interested Renaissance scholars begins with the question: "Why is it that all those who have become eminent in philosophy or politics or poetry or the arts are clearly of an atrabilious temperament . . . ?" Many of the ancient Greek heroes, says the writer, were melancholy. As examples he mentions Heracles, Ajax, and Bellerophon, all of whom went mad. The great thinkers Empedocles, Socrates, and Plato also were atrabilious.

In dealing with this question, Aristotle first propounds and answers another: Why does black bile, like wine, have such diverse effects upon behavior? This humor, he says, may become very hot or very cold and therefore produces, in one instance or another, all the various traits of personality which arise from internal heat or cold (as, in his opinion, most do). Cold melancholy causes torpidity and despondency; hot melancholy sometimes causes madness.

Many too, if this heat approaches the region of the intellect, are affected by diseases of frenzy and possession; and this is the origin of Sibyls and soothsayers and all inspired persons, when they are affected not by disease but by natural temperament. Maracus, the Syracusan, was actually a better poet when he was out of his mind. Those in whom the excessive heat dies down to a mean temperature are atrabilious, but they are cleverer and less eccentric and in many respects superior to others either in mental accomplishments or in the arts or in public life.

The writer suggests that black bile has detrimental effects when it is very hot, very cold, or very abundant. Yet atrabilious men whose melancholy is moderate in temperature and quantity—those who "possess a mixed temperament"—are likely to be "men of genius."

In the works of other ancient writers, Renaissance scholars find opinions concerning poetic creation which are vaguely similar to Aristotle's. Both Democritus and Plato assert that the true poet is touched with divine madness.[95] Although neither one specifically mentions melancholy, Renaissance authorities unhesitatingly assume that, like Aristotle, they attribute poetic inspiration to black bile.

Many Renaissance writers, fortified by ancient authority, declare that melancholy fosters intellectual and imaginative powers. Most of them see clearly how paradoxical it is to say this of the humor which, as they readily

---

[94] *Problemata*, XXX, i. I have used the translation of E. S. Forster in Vol. VII of *The Works of Aristotle*, ed. W. D. Ross (Oxford, 1908–31). There is considerable doubt concerning the authenticity of the *Problemata*. In classical times, however, the specific passage in question definitely was considered Aristotle's. See Cicero, *Tusculanae Disputationes*, I, xxxiii, and *De Divinatione*, I, xxxviii; Plutarch, *Lysander*, II.

[95] See Hermann Diels, *Die Fragmente der Vorsokratiker* (Berlin, 1934–35), II, 146 (fragments 17, 18); *Ion*, 533–34; *Phaedrus*, 245. Cf. Aristotle, *Poetics*, 1455a (XVII).

admit, commonly causes stupidity and absurdity. They consequently busy themselves with explanations (for Aristotle's explanation does not altogether explain), and they offer a diversity of opinions. They name this or that variety of black bile as the one which Aristotle must have meant. Many of them say that black bile must be qualified by intermixture with other humors. Frequently they call to their assistance an aphorism of Heraclitus': "Dry light is the wisest and best soul."[96] All melancholy is dry. It is supposed to shine when it is hot. Thus it is possible to assume that "Dry light" means hot melancholy. According to Renaissance psychology, dryness aids the intellect and heat aids the imagination.[97] Hot melancholy, therefore, should foster both intellectual and imaginative abilities. The learned writers seldom forget, however, that Aristotle seems to recommend moderate heat.[98]

Marsilio Ficino, Florentine humanist, philosopher, and physician, has a great deal to say about the relation between melancholy and the mental faculties in De Studiosorum Sanitate Tuenda, the first book of De Vita Libri Tres (1482–89).[99] Ficino believes, as all Renaissance physicians do, that the scholar's sedentary life and arduous mental endeavor breed the melancholic humor, which in turn engenders the various diseases of body and mind generally attributed to it. All men of letters are melancholy: "Musarum sacerdotes melancholici uel [sunt] ab initio, uel studio [fiunt]."[100] Yet this fact is not altogether unfortunate, says Ficino, for Aristotle, Plato, and Democritus attribute great excellence to melancholy minds. Adust melancholy causes mania. But natural melancholy, if it is properly mixed with warmer humors,[101] is kindled—without burning—and shines brilliantly. "Huc tendit illud Heracliti: Lux sicca, anima sapientissima."[102]

Ficino's sixth chapter is a lyric (physiological, astrological, and mystical) on this humor compounded of three. Its color is like that of gold, tinged

---

96 Heracleitus on the Universe, tr. W. H. S. Jones (London, 1931), p. 495.

97 See Huarte, Examen, pp. 59, 63–64, and Charron, Of Wisdome, p. 48.

98 If a writer specifies natural melancholy (normally very cold) as the beneficent humor, he usually explains that it must be heated by intermixture with blood or with blood and choler. Unnatural melancholy, of course, may be hot—even too hot—without intermixture with other humors.

99 According to Erwin Panofsky and Fritz Saxl (Dürers Kupferstich 'Melencolia I' [Leipzig-Berlin, 1923], pp. 32 ff.), this famous scholar was largely responsible for the popularity of the idea that melancholy and genius were allied. See also Erwin Panofsky, Albrecht Dürer (Princeton, 1945), pp. 165–67. Apparently there was little interest in the Aristotelian conception of melancholy before Ficino. Yet the Aristotelian problem was known and discussed during the Middle Ages (Panofsky and Saxl, op. cit., p. 20).

100 De Vita, p. 14. Ficino considered himself a Saturnine melancholic; see Panofsky, Dürer, pp. 165, 167, and Don Cameron Allen, The Star-Crossed Renaissance (Durham, N. C., 1941), p. 8. Dürer believed that he was atrabilious (Panofsky, Dürer, p. 171).

101 Ficino gives the exact proportions (p. 17): eight parts of blood, two of yellow bile, and two of black bile. Evidently he considers this a high proportion of melancholy.

102 Ibid., p. 18.

with purple. When it glows, it delivers colors varied like those of the rainbow from a flaming heart. The spirit which arises from it is the ideal instrument for thought—subtle, hot, lucent, agile, and yet stable and capable of long-continued and arduous service to the mind. With an instrument or a spur of this sort, which has affinity with the center of the world and concentrates the mind in its own center, the intellect continually seeks the fundamental natures of all things and penetrates their innermost recesses ("semper rerum omnium & centra petit, & penetralia penetrat"). It has affinity also with Saturn, highest of all the planets, and carries the searcher to the loftiest truths ("inuestigantem euehit ad altissima"). And why has he written so copiously of melancholy? So that the studious reader may realize fully how important it is that he foster the black bile of beneficent character ("atra bilis, imo candida bilis eiusmodi") and that he free himself of the noxious melancholy humor.[103] One of the chief purposes of *De Studiosorum Sanitate Tuenda* is to teach the scholar how to keep his melancholy happily tempered.

Juan Luis Vives believes that a proper combination of humors and heat promotes sharpness and soundness of mind ("acumen & sanitatem ingenij"). Black bile (apparently he means natural melancholy) is a dense and stable humor in which a high degree of persistent and penetrating heat may be generated. Mingled with other humors, especially with yellow bile, it greatly enhances the mental powers: "si subtilibus & claris spiritibus admixta sit nigra bilis, dexteritatem parit rationis, iudicij, prudentiae, sapientiae."[104] According to Philipp Melanchthon, natural melancholy, when it is abundant and suitably mixed with moderately warm blood, is a valuable aid to the intellectual faculties. "When Aristotle attributes intellectual superiority to melancholic men, it is clear that he is speaking of temperate complexions tending toward melancholy." In moderately melancholic blood, "the spirits are sharper, surer, and more eager in their movements."[105] Girolamo Fracastoro, the Italian physician whose poem on syphilis gave that disease its name, writes that artists, scholars, military leaders, and statesmen of the highest achievement are melancholy men. He draws a distinction, however, between melancholics of cold and dry constitution (these are likely to be

---

[103] *Ibid.*, pp. 18–20. Jason Van der Velde (*De Cerebri Morbis*, pp. 259–61), Baptista Porta (*De Humana Physiognomonia . . . Libri IV* [Oberusel, 1601], pp. 22–23), and François Valleriole (*Enarrationum Medicinalium Libri Sex*, pp. 426–30) have drawn freely from Ficino's sixth chapter.

[104] *De Anima et Vita Libri Tres* (Basel, 1543), pp. 115–16. Vives cites Plato, Democritus, and Aristotle as authorities (pp. 116–17).

[105] "Cum . . . Aristoteles tribuit ingenii praestantiam melancholicis, loqui eum de temperata crasi sciamus, declinante ad melancholicam . . . in tali sanguine spiritus efficiunt acriores, stabiliores et ardentiores motus."—*Opera*, XIII, 85–86.

timid, sluggish, and stupid) and persons who are considered melancholy because of abundance of unusually thick blood ("qui vero abundantia crassioris sanguinis melancholici dicuntur"). If this thick—or melancholic—blood is moderately warm, it endows its possessors with unusual powers of body and mind: "quos temperatior in omnibus habet melancholia, hi et ad animi excellentias et corporis bene nati sunt."[106] There follows a discussion of the physical qualities of the brain and spirits which this kind of melancholy produces.

According to Levinus Lemnius, a Dutch physician, adust melancholy, if properly qualified with "Bloud & other syncere Humors," produces "excellente good witts and sharpe iudgements." Its possessors sometimes seem divinely inspired.[107] The Spaniard Huarte says, without reservation, that adust melancholy makes men intelligent because "alwaies it is drie and of a very delicat substance" and because "it is cleere like the Agat stone, with which cleerenesse it giueth light within to the braine, and maketh the same to discerne well the figures."[108] In a commentary on the Aristotelian problem, Joannes Baptista Silvaticus, a physician of Milan, states that melancholy tempered with blood fosters wisdom. Adust melancholy (he assumes that it has cooled) does so much more effectively than natural melancholy.[109] The Spanish physician Luis Mercado, writing on the same subject, associates superior intellectual powers with one of the three kinds of natural melancholy which he distinguishes. The beneficent melancholy is a humor produced by the action of moderate heat upon natural humors. It verges upon the nature of *atra bilis*, a noxious humor produced by excessive heat.[110] André du Laurens, a French physician, says that melancholy (evidently he means the natural humor) "mixed with a certaine quantitie of blood . . . maketh men wittie, and causeth them to excell others."[111] This list of continental authorities could be considerably extended.

English writers also are interested in the influence of melancholy on the mental faculties. "The natural melancoly kepte in his temperance," says Sir Thomas Elyot, "profyteth moche to true iudgement of the wyt, but yet if it be to thicke, it darkeneth the spirites, maketh one timorous, and the wytte dulle."[112] Thomas Cogan believes that "the moste part of learned men" are

---

106 *De Intellectione Dialogus*, in *Opera*, fol. 202ᵛ.
107 *Touchstone*, fol. 149ʳ. It is burned blood or choler, according to Lemnius, that fosters the mental powers. He refers to Aristotle.
108 *Examen*, p. 85. Natural melancholy, says Huarte, is "not of any value for the wit, but maketh men blockish, sluggards, and grynnars" (p. 85). Huarte refers to Aristotle and Heraclitus.
109 *Controversiae Medicae Numero Centum*, p. 2.
110 *Opera*, I, 219; III, 89.
111 *Discourse*, p. 86. The author cites Aristotle and Heraclitus.
112 *Castel of Helth*, fol. 73ʳ. Elyot cites Ficino as authority.

melancholy, "especially those that be excellent, as *Aristotle* witnesseth."[113] Timothy Bright says that, though melancholics are usually dull, they are sometimes "verie wittie." Black bile, when it is somewhat heated, improves the quality of the spirits and provides "the drie light that Heraclitus approued."[114] If the humor "be attenuated with heate," it "deliuereth a drie, subtile and pearcing spirite, more constant and stable then anie other humour, which is a great helpe to this contemplation."[115] Natural melancholy, says Thomas Walkington, is called "the electuary and cordiall of the minde, a restorative conservice of the memory, the nurse of contemplation, the pretious balm of wit and policy: the enthusiasticall breath of poetry, the foyson of our phantasies, the sweet sleep of our senses, the fountain of sage advice and good purveyance."[116] Melancholy men, according to Burton, are "of a deep reach, excellent apprehension, judicious, wise, & witty."[117] In a passage which reveals the general interest in the Aristotelian problem and the general confusion of opinion, Burton reviews the statements of several authorities on the question of what kind of melancholy humor fosters wit.[118] He lets Fracastoro "decide the controversy."

The Galenic medical tradition represents the melancholy man as the most miserable of God's creatures. The Aristotelian tradition represents him otherwise. If men of letters, says Ficino, can avoid the diseases to which they are prone, they are the happiest of men.[119] Melancholy endows and distinguishes them with faculties far superior to those of the common man. The melancholic mind enjoys the contemplation of the innermost secrets of nature and the highest truths of heaven. Jacques Du Bosc writes that melancholy men bear the blows of fortune with equanimity. And no wonder, for

they alwayes reserve in themselves a privat roome, where to the tempests of Fortune cannot reach. There it is, where the soule retires, to maintaine her selfe in an eternall serenity; where she gaines an absolute command upon her judgements, and where she solitarily entertaines her self, even in the midst of companies, without interruption of the tumults of the world, to breake her rest or silence. . . . Here finally it is, where wee conserving the image of things delightfull, shall have meanes to have nought but goodly thoughts; . . . wee may . . . give contentment to our minde, while our senses are on the rack, and entertaine our Idea on beauty, at such time as foulnes shalbe the object of our eyes.

---

[113] *Haven of Health*, p. 20. Cogan specifies no variety of melancholy humor.
[114] *Treatise*, p. 130. Bright is speaking of natural melancholy.
[115] *Ibid.*, p. 200.
[116] *Optick Glasse*, pp. 131–32.
[117] *Anatomy*, I, 451.
[118] *Ibid.*, pp. 485–86. Burton mentions Aristotle and Heraclitus.
[119] *De Vita*, p. 11. To Ficino "Musarum sacerdotes" are all melancholy.

But who can praise enough this noble musing of the Melancholy, since by it the soule seemes to abandon when she list, the clamorous commerce of the senses.[120]

Robert Crofts, a Carolinian Englishman, believes that melancholy men,

if they adict themselves to seeke and follow Vertue and Piety (especially if their Melancholly bee with bloud and other good humours moderately humected and allay'd) commonly become of excellent wisedome, sharp Iudgements and seeme to doe many things so notably as if they were furthered by some divine Jnstinct or motion, Insomuch as oft-times even their Solitarinesse and melancholly dispositions become most profitable, sweet and pleasant to them.[121]

The scholarly and philosophical melancholy which these authors describe and commend is sober but not at all sorrowful or despondent.

According to the more ignoble conception of melancholy, the religious enthusiasms of melancholy men are manifestations of degrading mental disease and of the meddling of the Devil. Yet Ficino writes that, because of melancholy properly tempered, "philosophers in solitude ascend in spirit, for the mind, withdrawn from mundane disturbances and from the body itself and allied intimately with heavenly essences, becomes an instrument of the divine."[122] Jean Bodin has similar ideas:

And if it be so that the true purifying of the soule is by [God's] heauenly light, and by the force of contemplation in the most perfect subiect; without doubt they shall soonest attaine vnto it which haue their soules rauished vp into heauen; the which we see happen vnto melancholike men, which haue their spirits setled and giuen to contemplation, the which is called by the Hebrewes and Accademiks a pretious death, for that it drawes the soule out of this earthlie bodie vnto spirituall things.[123]

Edward Reynolds, a Carolinian divine, discusses the superiority of the dry mind:

it was the speech of the Philosopher *Heraclitus* . . . that *Anima sicca est sapientissima,* (which toucheth something upon that of *Aristotle,* That Melancholy complexions are usually the wisest, for that Temper is the driest of all the rest) That a Mind not steeped in the humours of carnall and grosse affections . . . but more

120 *Compleat Woman,* pp. 40–41.
121 *The Happie Mind* (London, 1640), pp. 104–5.
122 "Hinc philosophi singulares euadunt, praesertim quum animus sic ab externis motibus atque corpore proprio seuocatus, & quam proximus diuinis, diuinorum instrumentum efficiatur."–*De Vita,* p. 19.
123 *The Six Bookes of a Commonweale,* tr. Richard Knolles (London, 1606), p. 560.

raysed and soaring to its originall, by divine *contemplations*, is alwayes endued with the greater wisdome.[124]

In the minds of these writers, melancholy seems to be associated with mystic ecstasy.

Melancholy men may even become prophets through heavenly inspiration. Ficino believes that the melancholy mind becomes the instrument of divine spirits; and thus, "through heavenly influences and divinations inspired from on high, it forms ideas never before conceived and predicts events yet to come."[125] Cornelius Agrippa, citing Aristotle as authority,[126] declares that the rapture of divination is due to melancholy. The humor involved, however, is not *atra bilis* ("qui adeo praua horribilisque res est") but beneficent natural bile ("naturalis & candida bilis"). When the latter is heated it induces enthusiasm and endows one with marvelous powers. The person thus affected is under the influence of Saturn ("arcanae contemplationis autor"), a planet which inspires the loftiest thoughts and bestows knowledge of things to come. Celestial spirits, moreover, frequently enter the bodies and minds of such persons. Thus it happens that men become masters of arts that they have never studied, gain knowledge and wisdom beyond ordinary mortal capacity, and acquire the power of prophecy.[127] Jason Van der Velde writes that heavenly spirits insinuate themselves into the minds of atrabilious persons (if their melancholy is properly qualified) and dwell there happily

as if they were in the revolving sphere of the brightest stars. These spirits, when they are active, excite the mind and affect it marvelously, causing inspired frenzy. ... [Thus men become] contrivers of arts which they have not acquired through study, authors of the most sacred laws, explorers of natural phenomena, interpreters of heavenly mysteries, poets, prophets, seers.[128]

---

[124] *Passions*, p. 37.

[125] "Vnde diuinis influxibus oraculisque ex alto repletus, noua quaedam inusitataque semper excogitat, & futura praedicit."—*De Vita*, pp. 19–20.

[126] Agrippa refers not only to *Problemata*, XXX, i, but to passages in *De Divinitione per Somnum, Parva Naturalia*, 463[b], 464[a–b], in which the author attributes prophetic dreams to persons of unstable mind, among them atrabilious persons. Agrippa interprets these passages very freely. He cites Democritus and Plato as additional authorities.

[127] *De Occulta Philosophia Libri Tres* (Cologne, 1533), pp. lxxviii–lxxix. Agrippa distinguishes three degrees of celestial demons and three corresponding degrees of supernatural mental powers which melancholy men may enjoy.

[128] Coelestes daemones "ibi consident, ac deliciantur, tanquam in regione illa clarissimorum syderum uolubili: qui ubi sese commouerint, animum quoque commouent, & mirabiliter afficiunt, coguntque furere. . . . [Quidam fiunt] artium, quas nunquam didicere inuentores, legum sanctissimarum conditores, naturalium rerum perscrutatores, diuinorum mysteriorum interpretes, poetae, Prophetae, Vates."—*De Cerebri Morbis*, p. 262.

Fracastoro also believes in melancholic prophecy. Of all men, the person with the well-tempered melancholy constitution is most likely to receive inspiration from heavenly intelligences: "If God or an angel enters into us, it is reasonable that he should enter especially those who are pre-eminent for greatness of intellect or for praiseworthy accomplishments."[129] When melancholy properly mingled with blood grows hot, says Du Laurens, "it causeth as it were, a kinde of diuine rauishment, commonly called *Enthousiasma*, which stirreth men vp to plaie the Philosophers, Poets, and also to prophesie: in such maner, as it may seeme to containe in it some diuine parts."[130]

The Renaissance, then, held simultaneously two conceptions of melancholia. According to Galenic tradition, melancholy is a most ignominious and miserable condition of mind; according to the Aristotelian tradition, it is a most admirable and enviable condition of mind. Scholars in general denied the truth of neither; for behind the one was the authority of Galen and behind the other the authority of Aristotle. These two conceptions are hopelessly intertangled in Renaissance thought and literature. Sometimes they seem at least partially reconciled through the nice distinctions of the psychologists; sometimes they seem very much at war with each other.

There would have been no such duality, it may be noted, if there had been no Aristotelian problem, for this problem was the source of the idea that melancholy men are extraordinarily endowed. If Renaissance scholars knew of any other classical source for it, they were strangely silent about it.[131] Virtually the whole weight of classical and medieval medical opinion was against the idea. No less overpowering an authority than Aristotle's could have given it currency.

If there had been no Aristotelian problem, the melancholic attitude would never have won the popularity which it enjoyed during the Renaissance. No man would have cared to confess himself melancholy if that had been to confess himself blockish and silly. But Aristotle lent melancholia a philosophic and artistic glamor, and many men were more than willing to declare themselves affected. Thus the vogue of melancholy arose in Italy and in

---

129 Si "Deus, aut Angelus se admiscet nobis, rationabile est ijs maxime se miscere, qui ingenij magnitudine, et excellentia quadam actionum praestant."—*Opera*, fol. 203ʳ. Ficino, Agrippa, and Fracastoro believe that melancholy of noxious quality attracts infernal spirits.

130 *Discourse*, p. 86. Cf. Foreest, *Observationum*, p. 341ᵃ.

131 Plato and Democritus (see note 95) do not actually mention melancholy in connection with poetic genius. Cicero and Plutarch (see note 94) cite Aristotle as authority. The closest parallel to the Aristotelian theory that I have found in ancient sources is a statement by Rufus, preserved in Rhazes' *Continens:* "illi qui sunt subtilis ingenii et multae perspicationis de facili incidunt in melancolias, eo quod sunt velocis motus et multae praemeditationis et imaginationis."—Rufus, *Oeuvres*, p. 457. I have found no reference to this passage, however, in Renaissance works.

England. This vogue left a permanent record in Elizabethan and early Stuart literature. Aristotle's problem was the remote cause of the melancholy men in the English drama, satire, and character sketches of the late Renaissance period.

In the medical literature of the Renaissance, the Galenic conception of melancholy is dominant. The Aristotelian problem, however, is probably the most important document of all those which contributed to the complex and contradictory body of ideas which constituted the popular concept *melancholy* as it existed in sixteenth- and seventeenth-century Europe. Certainly it is the most significant to the student of literature.

VI

The phrase "Renaissance science,"[132] which we so often use in our studies of Renaissance ideas concerning the physical world and the physical nature of man, is subtly misleading. *Science,* to the twentieth-century mind, suggests order, consistency, definiteness, meticulous care regarding both data and reasoning. In science, moreover, we are accustomed to relative unanimity; when scientists disagree, they endeavor forthwith to resolve their disagreement by further investigation. Perhaps this description hardly fits contemporary psychology or the social sciences; but we think of these as "young sciences," and we confidently expect them to mature into something as systematic as physics. When we deal with Renaissance concepts under the heading of science, modern connotations set up troublesome expectations and may color or distort our thinking considerably. In "Renaissance science" there is no such order, consistency, and definiteness as there is in modern science, no such taking of pains, and above all no such unanimity.

Considered individually, Elizabethan treatises on psychology are often loosely reasoned and confusing. Writers make a great show of method without achieving much of the reality. One finds instances in which a writer leaves a topic half treated, instances in which a writer shifts without apparent consciousness of the fact from one meaning of a term to another, instances of classifications which illogically cut across one another, instances of simple muddiness of thought and expression. System, thoroughness, and logical consistency are qualities for which few psychological writers seem to have striven seriously and which few readers seem to have expected.

---

[132] In actual Renaissance usage, *science* had, of course, a far more inclusive meaning than it has in modern usage. Here and throughout this study, I use *science* in the modern sense.

Scientific writers more often seem to have striven for eloquence or grace of style.

Even more significant is the confusion of opinion in psychological works taken collectively. The physiological psychology of the Renaissance is a body of theory containing so many contradictions, semicontradictions, and disharmonies that any exposition of it is likely to misrepresent by introducing into it an orderliness which it does not really have. There is the question of the number of cells in the brain. Some writers say three, others four. Some writers distribute the mental faculties among these cells in one way, some in another. Some call the common sense *fancy;* others apply the term *fancy* to the imagination. Some present one list of passions, some another. Some distinguish three kinds of spirit, some only two.

This discord of opinion is nowhere more abundantly illustrated than among theories concerning melancholy. I have pointed out how diversely the term *melancholy* was used (in the psychiatric sense) and how vague its limits were. I have tried to suggest the heterogeneity of the body of opinion concerning the Aristotelian problem. There is considerable confusion also in what the authorities have to say concerning melancholic symptoms. One finds it a little difficult to keep the several melancholy symptoms associated in his mind with the proper melancholy humors. Precisely the symptoms which are attributed to unnatural melancholy in one work are attributed to natural melancholy in another. Very often a writer describes a particular form of melancholia without specifying the humor which causes it (Burton is much inclined to this kind of neglect). The curious reader must puzzle the matter out for himself or look elsewhere for information. There were probably not many lay readers so curious in the period in which these books were written.

It is astonishing to a twentieth-century reader to discover how much at home the Elizabethans could be with discrepancies and illogicalities. Their indifference to the contrarieties and inadequacies of their psychology does not mean, of course, that they were naïve. On the contrary one often gets an impression, as he reads psychological and medical material, of a civilized urbanity which one seldom finds in contemporary scientific writing. Yet the Elizabethans lacked the remorseless passion for exactitude, completeness, and logical perfection which (properly) distinguishes the modern scientific mind.

The principal reason for the lack of definiteness and unanimity in Renaissance scientific literature is, I believe, the Renaissance respect for authority. This medieval heritage had a much firmer hold on Renaissance thought than one would suppose from reading modern histories of science. The historians emphasize the new scientific movement which was born during the

Renaissance. They tell us a great deal about the Leonardos, the Keplers, the Bacons, and the Harveys, but neglect the crowd of lesser men who still turned to Aristotle, Galen, Ptolemy, Avicenna, and Aquinas for scientific knowledge. The new science, though it gave the late Renaissance many new ideas, especially in the field of astronomy, did not immediately affect habits of thinking. In Bacon's time the overwhelming majority of scientists still looked for the truth between the covers of books. The older the books, the better. If anyone doubts this, let him turn to virtually any early seventeenth-century medical work and note the marginal references.

Respect for authority meant that the Renaissance student of medicine had to read respectfully a great many works of very diverse character written in all periods from that of Hippocrates down to his own time, though of course the weight of authority was not always equal. The scholar did not question Aristotle's statement that all men of genius were melancholy; his task was simply to explain how this might be true. If he found Galen and Averroës in disagreement, he was likely to assume that both were right and attempt a reconciliation. Thus the task of Renaissance medical scholarship was to digest a heterogeneous body of opinion into a harmonious and systematic whole. Of necessity it failed.

It sometimes looks as if the Renaissance believed everything that it read in a book. This of course is not true. Critical scholars questioned the statements of even Aristotle and Galen. Yet a non-Baconian scholar would not lightly contradict the great authorities, and to such a scholar any book in print was something to be reckoned with. The Renaissance scholar could not, at least did not, ignore the Paracelsians, as modern medical writers ignore the spiritualists. The modern physician, moreover, enjoys a blessed privilege which was denied to his Renaissance predecessor: with few exceptions, he may disregard all works written more than a generation ago. The Renaissance physician had to deal with a body of medical literature which had been accumulating since ancient Greek times and was still growing. Science very badly needed the house cleaning which Bacon proposed.

The habit of learning from books rather than from nature may explain, furthermore, why Renaissance medicine accepted certain ideas that seem to violate common sense. How can it be that the character of one's dreams is determined by fumes rising from the abdominal organs to the head? During sleep, one's head is no higher than his abdomen. If dryness aids intelligence and heat aids imagination, why does not choler, rather than melancholy, foster genius? How can a humor be dry?[133] "Dry humor" is a con-

---

[133] Galen probably meant "dry" to be understood relatively. In a sense, molasses is drier than water. Some Renaissance writers, however, evidently consider black bile absolutely dry, "drie as ashes" (Du Laurens, *Discourse*, p. 95).

tradiction in terms. And surely a dry substance could not flow. It does not seem to have occurred to the medical writers that these matters call for explanation. Ancient authority was sufficient.

Although from the modern point of view the medicine and psychology of the Renaissance may have had their shortcomings, Elizabethan and early Stuart Englishmen found them more than adequate for their ethical purposes and were enthusiastically interested in them. The literature of the period contains abundant evidence of this fact. Authors frequently write of such matters as passion, youth and age, sickness, and death in phraseology derived from contemporary scientific theory. Much of this phraseology is so often repeated that it becomes conventional.[134] In representing human character and behavior, moreover, Elizabethan writers show unmistakably that the physiological psychology has affected their thinking. Probably no other group of psychological ideas made so deep an impression on the Elizabethan mind as those related to melancholy.

It is a fair assumption that, when the writers of the period make literary use of scientific material, they are offering their public something in which it is definitely interested. It is a fair assumption also that little of the scientific material appearing in literary works is beyond the comprehension of ordinary readers and playgoers. Authors, especially playwrights, do not commonly write above the heads of those to whom they address themselves. Some Elizabethan writers evidently have no difficulty in keeping within the bounds of popular understanding, for their own scientific information seems to be merely that which is common among educated laymen. Others seem to have a considerably greater fund of information, even a specialist's knowledge. (The distinction between layman and scientist was much less definite in the Renaissance period than it is now.) Yet no writer assumes a specialist's knowledge on the part of his public. Lodge has practiced medicine, but one would hardly suspect it from a reading of his literary works. Chapman seems to have had a thorough mastery of psychology. When he writes of Byron's "adust and melancholy choler,"[135] for example, he seems fully conscious of the physiological meaning and psychological implication of the phrase. His audience, however, can understand Byron's character and behavior perfectly well without understanding "adust and melancholy choler." Webster evidently has considerable physiological, pharmaceutical, and psychiatric learning. When he represents lycanthropia on the stage, however,

---

134 See Albert L. Walker, "Convention in Shakespeare's Description of Emotion," *Philological Quarterly*, XVII (1938), 26–66. Hardin Craig discusses the literary uses of Elizabethan psychology in *The Enchanted Glass* (New York, 1936), pp. 113–38. On the same subject, see Harry K. Russell, "Elizabethan Dramatic Poetry in the Light of Natural and Moral Philosophy," *Philological Quarterly*, XII (1933), 187–95.

135 *Plays*, ed. R. H. Shepherd (London, 1889), p. 224.

he does not assume that the audience will recognize the disease. He explains its nature fully through the mouth of the physician who attends the madman.[136]

As it appears in English Renaissance literature, melancholy represents the layman's ideas rather than the specialist's, and is consequently not just the same thing that is expounded in scientific works.[137] Scientific theory necessarily is simplified and modified during the process of popularization. In Renaissance scientific treatises taken collectively, moreover, the theory of melancholy is not altogether orderly, clear, and consistent. Logical distinctions are naturally even less precise in the lay mind. Under the circumstances, it would not be at all reasonable to expect the layman to carry in his head a collection of sharp, definite, and systematically interrelated ideas on the subject of melancholy. As I read the literary evidence, there is no clear distinction in the layman's mind between the melancholy temperament and the melancholic disease. There is no clear knowledge of the differentia which mark the various melancholic disorders. Yet the layman has heard enough about the odd varieties of melancholy to be prepared for any sort of eccentricity or extravagance from a melancholy man.

As one turns, then, from scientific accounts of melancholy to literary representations, he does not find an exact and detailed correspondency. He discovers nevertheless that many of the scientist's ideas have gained popular currency. The layman seems to know something of the causes of melancholy. Cold and dry passions, he realizes, are especially likely to cause it, for they cool and dry the blood and cause general physical debility. Intellectual labor, he knows, has the same effect. The melancholy man, as the layman thinks of him, is dark, lean, hollow-eyed, sluggish of movement, abstracted in manner, and very taciturn. He is subject to fears and sorrows without apparent cause. He is fretful, anxious, envious, suspicious, and highly extravagant in speech and actions. His imagination is continually busy with fancies, which sometimes develop into strange obsessions and hallucinations. He characteristically seeks solitude and darkness. Sometimes he has a criminal bias. Sometimes he is a bitter misanthrope. The layman understands that melancholy is ordinarily a most miserable condition, yet he has heard that

---

[136] *Works*, ed. F. L. Lucas (London, 1927), II, 106–7.

[137] Colloquially the word *melancholy* was often very loosely employed. Apparently it sometimes meant nothing more definite than "mental quirk." Recently *complex*, borrowed from psychological terminology, conveyed much the same idea in careless colloquial usage. In Jaques' speech on the respective melancholies of the scholar, the musician, the courtier, the soldier, the lawyer, the lady, and the lover (*As You Like It*, IV, i, 11–16), *melancholy* seems to have no more specific meaning than this. A character in Chapman's *May-Day* says that women are spoiled by men's adoration: "We are they that put a kind of wanton melancholy into 'em."—*Plays*, p. 278.

some melancholics derive deep pleasure from their solitary meditations. He understands that the melancholy man is likely to be ridiculously irrational, yet he realizes that melancholy often engenders intellectual and artistic powers of the highest order. He knows that the cures of melancholy include bloodletting, purgation, diet, and mental diversion, and he has heard stories of the ingenious psychological stratagems to which physicians sometimes resort in dealing with irrational patients.

A brief review cannot cover everything which melancholy meant or implied to the Elizabethan layman. Yet the foregoing, I believe, represents the popular ideas with reasonable accuracy. In literary works one occasionally finds odd bits of melancholic theory which could hardly have been generally understood. Yet the writers do not often go beyond the limits suggested.

The melancholy characters of Elizabethan literature tend to fall into types. Each of these has an adequate basis in scientific lore, and none of them would have existed if there had been no psychological theory. Yet they are definitely literary, not scientific, types. Some of them, as will appear in the next chapter, were based upon observation of Elizabethans who believed themselves melancholy, that is, of laymen who were behaving as they supposed a melancholy man should behave. Since melancholy was much in vogue in Elizabethan England, writers had ample opportunity for such observation. In any case, each literary type embodies a number of ideas ultimately from scientific sources which in one way or another have cohered and crystallized into a conventional pattern.

Chapter IV. THE MALCONTENT TYPES

I

THE VOGUE OF MELANCHOLY began to make its mark upon English literature about midway in the reign of Elizabeth. Melancholy had doubtless been a subject of lively interest among gentlemen and scholars for some time. Yet references to melancholy are rare in the literature of the earlier English Renaissance, and there is virtually no representation of melancholy persons.[1] In the 1580's, however, references to melancholy and representations of melancholy begin to appear with great frequency. Melancholia (especially love melancholy) is conspicuous in the works of John Lyly, whose example seems to have influenced his contemporaries and successors considerably.

The circulation of scientific works[2] during the first half of the sixteenth century indicates a general and probably increasing interest in physiology and psychology, but there is no indication that in this period melancholy was singled out for special notice. At some time during the first two decades of Elizabeth's reign, however, Englishmen began to develop an interest specifically in melancholy. The immediate reason seems to have been the imitation of the Italian affectation of melancholy by travelers returned from the Continent.

In Italy the Aristotelian conception of melancholy had been generally

---

[1] It is difficult to substantiate a statement like this, yet one should try. Between 1580 and 1642, the literary genre in which melancholy was most liberally represented was the drama. One would suppose, then, that if it appeared at all in English Renaissance literature before 1580, it would appear in the drama. I have read virtually all of the extant English plays written between 1500 and 1580 and have found only three occurrences of the word *melancholy: Calisto and Melibaea*, I, 84, and *Jack Juggler*, II, 17, in *A Select Collection of Old English Plays*, ed. Robert Dodsley and W. Carew Hazlitt (London, 1874–76); Richard Edwards, *Damon and Pithias*, l. 649. I have found no melancholic characters in this body of drama with the possible exception of certain lovesick persons. These, however, are never described as "melancholy." I shall return to the literary representation of lovesickness in Chap. VII.

I have not attempted to search pre-Renaissance English literature for melancholy. Yet I should point out in passing that Chaucer, who is notable for his interest in the sciences, shows considerable knowledge of theories related to melancholy, for instance in Partlet's commentary on dreams ("Nun's Priest's Tale," ll. 4113–29) and in the description of Arcite's lovesickness ("Knight's Tale," ll. 1361–79).

[2] E. g., Trevisa's translation of Bartholomaeus' *De Proprietatibus Rerum*; Paynell's translation of the *Regimen Sanitatis Salerni*; Elyot's *Castel of Helth*. It is noteworthy that the first work in English devoted entirely to melancholy was Bright's *Treatise*, 1586.

current among scholars and artists since the later years of the fifteenth century and had caused a great many of them to contract the malady. Erwin Panofsky and Fritz Saxl, in their monograph on the background of Dürer's *Melencolia*, attribute the popularity of Aristotelian melancholy in Italy largely to Marsilio Ficino and to his vindication of the melancholy temperament in *De Vita Libri Tres* (1482–89). They speak of an intimate circle of Saturnists among the Florentine intellectuals, with Ficino as the leading spirit,[3] and they credit his book with a very wide influence. They quote from an Italian letter of 1519 the revealing statement that Raphael is inclined toward melancholy like all men of such transcendent importance ("wie alle Männer von so überragender Bedeutung").[4] Clearly in Renaissance Italy melancholy was regarded as the malady of great minds. It is a fair assumption that it was affected by the would-be great.

Zera S. Fink has shown that various sixteenth-century observers noted the melancholy of the Italians and that English travelers who were prone to imitate foreign manners acquired the melancholic attitude in Italy and brought it home with them.[5] He has shown also that melancholy was definitely linked in the minds of Elizabethan Englishmen with Italy, with Englishmen who had traveled, and with the various vices which, according to Ascham and other indignant moralists, young Englishmen acquired in Italy. These vices, it should be noted, are altogether out of harmony with the conception of melancholy held by the Florentine humanists. Since the imitative travelers were ordinarily young gentlemen, melancholy for a time at least had aristocratic connotations in Elizabethan England, and these made the pose doubly attractive.

The Italianate traveler, then, was the principal immediate cause of the melancholia in English life and literature. Melancholic travelers evidently were so numerous in Elizabethan London as to constitute a social type, which was augmented by persons who took up the affectation even though they had never been abroad. Nashe called upon the Devil to do something, "take some order, that the streetes be not pestered with them so as they are."[6] Here was melancholy, not in a book, but walking the streets before one's eyes.

---

3 *Dürers 'Melencolia I,'* p. 47.

4 P. 31.

5 "Jaques and the Malcontent Traveler," *Philological Quarterly*, XIV (1935), 237–52. Some of the material on the malcontent quoted below serves to substantiate Fink's conclusions. Frenchmen as well as Italians, according to Fink, affected melancholy and encouraged the imitative English traveler to assume the pose. The French, however, copied the attitude from the Italians. See "Jaques," p. 242.

6 *Pierce Peniless*, in *Works*, ed. Ronald B. McKerrow (London, 1910), I, 170.

Men of this type were commonly called *malcontents*.[7] Their characteristic state of mind was known as *discontent,* and the adjectives *discontent* and *discontented* were often applied to them. There seem to have been two principal reasons for the term *malcontent:* First, melancholy travelers frequently were disappointed and disgruntled by their countrymen's failure to recognize and reward the talents and acquirements which they believed they had, and they were given to railing satirically at their unappreciative contemporaries. Second, this melancholy class included many seditious persons, men dissatisfied with the political *status quo* and eager to overthrow it. There must have been individuals to whom the term was appropriate for both reasons.

Apparently the disgruntled or seditious traveler had become well established as a social type by 1580.[8] Apparently he was the original melancholy malcontent. In the late sixteenth century the word *malcontent* is so often associated with foreign travel that one can hardly believe otherwise. In the literature of the period, however, the term is extended to melancholy types only tenuously connected with the returned traveler, sometimes even to the melancholy lover.[9] The species of the genus malcontent are rather dissimilar, yet some traits appear fairly consistently. The malcontent is usually black-suited and disheveled, unsociable, asperous, morosely meditative, taciturn yet prone to occasional railing. With the possible exception of the manner of dress, these traits are all symptoms of melancholy listed in the medical treatises. The malcontent's harsh, unpleasing, and eccentric ex-

---

[7] The malcontent type has received a good deal of attention from modern scholars. See especially E. E. Stoll, "Shakespere, Marston, and the Malcontent Type," *Modern Philology*, III (1906), 281–303; Fink, "Jaques"; O. J. Campbell, *Shakespeare's Satire* (New York, 1943), pp. 45–56, 142 ff.; Theodore Spencer, "The Elizabethan Malcontent," *Joseph Quincy Adams Memorial Studies* (Washington, 1948), pp. 523–35. The word *malcontent*, like the social type, seems to be of Italian origin, although *A New English Dictionary* derives it from Old French.

[8] Greene relates that, just after his continental travels, he affected malcontented melancholy (*The Repentance of Robert Greene,* in *Works,* ed. Grosart [London and Aylesbury, 1881–86], XII, 172). He returned from his continental tour probably in 1580. The disgruntled traveler type of malcontent, consequently, must have been well established by that time. Although the melancholy traveler was evidently the original malcontent, the term was already attached in the early 1580's to at least one other melancholic type, the melancholy scholar. In Lyly's *Sapho and Phao (c. 1582)* there appears a melancholy scholar, Pandion, who is called a malcontent (see below, section v). He is clearly not a disgruntled traveler.

[9] It is sometimes used also with no apparent implication of melancholy, usually in reference to politically disaffected persons. See *A New English Dictionary;* Peele's *Descensus Astraeae, Works,* ed. A. H. Bullen (London, 1888), I, 362, 366; Joseph Hall's character of "The malecontent," *Works,* ed. Philip Wynter (Oxford, 1863), VI, 111–13. When an Elizabethan or early Stuart writer refers to a character as a malcontent, he usually implies melancholy, but not always.

terior, then, is in the Galenic tradition. This unprepossessing exterior, however, is supposed to veil great interior excellence. The malcontent is—or thinks he is—a person of unusual intellectual or artistic talent. His melancholy is essentially Aristotelian. He represents a popular conception of melancholy in which the two melancholic traditions are fused.

I shall characterize four species of malcontent as I find them represented in Elizabethan and early Stuart literature. The primary malcontent type, which comprises the melancholy travelers and their imitators, is the melancholy man who resents the world's neglect of his superior abilities. The other three are derivative malcontent types appearing principally in the drama: the melancholy villain, the melancholy cynic, and the melancholy scholar. Although the melancholy lover is sometimes referred to as a malcontent or as a "discontented" person, I shall reserve him for a later chapter. Since nothing is to be gained by chronological arrangement of material, I have not attempted it. Classification of the various specimens sometimes does violence, for there is considerable overlapping among the types.

II

The primary malcontent type, the malcontent with the sense of neglected superiority, is a man who has persuaded himself that he is melancholy because melancholy signifies astuteness and profundity of mind. He snarls at the world because it has not perceived and rewarded his talents and self-improvements. He is likely to be a political troublemaker. Presumably his melancholy has been deepened by disappointment and frustration. He advertises his superiority and his tragic situation by various melancholic mannerisms.

Most Englishmen disliked him heartily. Elizabethan and Jacobean satirists howled in derision. Sometimes they made sport of him as a foolish attitudinizer; sometimes, apparently accepting him for a genuine melancholy man, they mocked his melancholy, regarding it not as a token of high endowment, but as a mark of churlish stupidity, mental derangement, or dangerous inclination to treachery. In any case, one can gain from their satiric sketches of him in verse, prose, and drama a rather clear idea of his appearance, behavior, and pretensions.

The malcontent's face is gloomy; his manner is surly and preoccupied. He "sits like *Mopsus* or *Corydon*, blockish, neuer laughing, neuer speaking, but so Bearishlie, as if he would deuour all the companie, which he doth to this end, that the guests might mutter, how this his deep Melancholy argueth great learning in him, & an intendment, to most weighty affaires and heauen-lie speculations."[10] He is "not affable in speech, or apt to vulgar compliment, but surly, dull, sad, austere, *cogitabundi* still, very intent, and, as *Albertus Durer* paints Melancholy, like a sad woman leaning on her arm with fixed looks, neglect habit, &c. held therefore by some proud, soft, sottish, or half-mad . . . and yet of a deep reach, excellent apprehension, judicious, wise, & witty."[11] The malcontent characteristically stands in a profoundly meditative attitude with his arms crossed and his hat pulled down over his eyes.[12] One reads in Nashe's *The Unfortunate Traveller* that among the foolish things which young men learn abroad is to "walke melancholy with their Armes folded."[13] A melancholy "Gull" whom Sir John Davies sketches sits alone "hoodwinck'd with his hat."[14] The hero of Samuel Rowlands' *The Melancholie Knight* soliloquizes:

> Like discontented *Tymon* in his Cell,
> My braines with *melancholy* humers swell,
> I crosse mine armes at crosses that arise,
> And scoffe blinde *Fortune*, with hat ore mine eyes:
> I bid the world take notice I abhorre it,
> Hauing great *melancholy* reason for it.[15]

On the title page of this work is a picture of the Melancholy Knight standing in a deep study, his arms folded, his hat over his eyes.

The malcontent is unsociable and inclined to seek solitude. Ordinary humanity cannot furnish fit companionship for him. The melancholy man in the Overbury characters "Is a strayer from the drove. . . . Impleasing to all, as all to him. . . . Hee'le seldome bee found without the shade of some grove in whose bottome a riuer dwels."[16] In company the malcontent stands apart from others. He is very taciturn, "one that can reproue the world but with a word, the follies of the people with a shrug, and sparing of his speech, giueth his answer with signs and dumb shews."[17]

One who is preoccupied with weighty or lofty matters can hardly be expected to attend to his personal appearance. The malcontent demonstrates that his life is a life of the mind through the neglectful disorder of his cloth-

---

[10] R. R:, *Questions, Concerning Conie-hood, and the Nature of the Conie* (London, 1595), sig. B3r.
[11] Burton, *Anatomy*, I, 451.
[12] The melancholy man "*loves darkness as life, & cannot endure the light*, or to sit in lightsome places; his hat still in his eyes, he will neither see nor be seen by his good will."—*Ibid.*, p. 445.
[13] *Works*, II, 300.
[14] *Poems*, ed. Clare Howard (New York, 1941), p. 57.
[15] *Works* (Glasgow, 1880), vol. II; p. 7.
[16] *The Overburian Characters*, ed. W. J. Paylor (Oxford, 1936), pp. 21–22.
[17] Barnaby Rich, *Faultes Faults, and Nothing Else but Faultes* (London, 1606), fol. 7r.

ing.[18] In Sir John Harington's *The Metamorphosis of Ajax* (1596), Ajax becomes "a perfect malcontent; *viz.* his hat without a band, his hose without garters, his waist without a girdle, his boots without spurs, his purse without coin, his head without wit."[19] John Earle writes of "A discontented Man": "His composure of himself is a studied carelesnesse with his armes a crosse, and a neglected hanging of his head and cloake, and he is as great an enemie to an hatband, as Fortune."[20] Often the malcontent goes in black. Bruto, the returned traveler of Marston's *Satires*, paces somberly with "discontented grace . . . 'Long Westminster" clothed in "sad colours."[21]

The manner and costume are intended to suggest to the beholder various superiorities, to any or all of which the malcontent pretends. For one thing, the malcontent pose suggests aristocracy. Melancholy is an attribute of young gallants. In Lyly's *King Midas* a page rebukes the barber for complaining of melancholy: "is melancholy a word for a barbars mouth? thou shouldst say heauie, dull and doltish: melancholy is the creast of Courtiers armes, and now euerie base companion . . . sayes he is melancholy."[22] Armado, of *Love's Labor's Lost*, regards the melancholy which he affects as a token of his superiority to the "rude multitude."[23] Sir John Davies' melancholy "Gull" wears a "long cloake" and a "great blacke feather, / By which each gull is now a gallant deemde."[24] In Jonson's *Every Man out of His Humour*, Carlo Buffone tells the lout Sogliardo how to be a gentleman: "You must endeuour to feede cleanly at your Ordinarie, sit melancholy, and picke your teeth when you cannot speake."[25] The melancholy pose also suggests literary ability. Rowlands' Melancholy Knight asserts that he has "a Muse hath beene at *Helicon*,"[26] and other such characters are versifiers.

---

18 Fink discovers that this negligence in dress was an affectation which the imitative traveler brought home from France. Apparently it was not associated with melancholy at first but soon became so. See "Jaques," p. 243.

19 Ed. C. Whittingham (Chiswick, 1814), pp. 1-2.

20 *Micro-Cosmographie*, ed. Arber (Westminster, 1895), p. 27. Sometimes the malcontent's clothing is shabby because of poverty.

21 *Works*, ed. A. H. Bullen (London, 1887), III, 274. Black was the Italian fashion (see Fink, "Jaques," pp. 241-42). A passage in *King John* indicates that young gentlemen of France also affected black (IV, i, 14-16). Black, of course, is highly appropriate for the garments of a melancholy man.

22 *Works*, ed. R. Warwick Bond (Oxford, 1902), III, 155.

23 V, i, 97. See I, i, 231-49; I, ii, 1-2; IV, i, 60-96. Armado must be included also among the love melancholics of Chap. VII.

24 *Poems*, p. 57.

25 *Ben Jonson*, ed. C. H. Herford, Percy Simpson, and Evelyn Simpson (Oxford, 1925-50), III, 445. See also *Every Man in His Humour, Jonson*, III, 314. The aristocratic connotations of melancholy must have died out toward the close of the Elizabethan reign. I find no suggestion of them in any work later than *Every Man out of His Humour*.

26 *Works*, vol. II; p. 35. Cf. p. 3 and *Every Man in His Humour, Jonson*, III, 340-41.

It suggests the sophistication and self-cultivation to be acquired by foreign travel. Malcontents

> walke with mumbling, and a grim neglect,
> As if each *stone* were bound to giue respect,
> With notice of their trauells.[27]

Above all the melancholy pose suggests wisdom and acumen. Malcontents affect a "wilful stillness"

> With purpose to be dress'd in an opinion
> Of wisdom, gravity, profound conceit;
> As who should say, "I am Sir Oracle,
> And when I ope my lips let no dog bark."[28]

A passage in Nashe's *Pierce Penilesse* furnishes a summary of the malcontent's pretensions:

All malcontent sits the greasie son of a Cloathier, & complaines (like a decaied Earle) of the ruin of ancient houses. . . . Sometimes (because Loue commonly weares the liuerey of Wit[29]) hee will be an *Inamorato Poeta*. . . . Al *Italionato* is his talke. . . . Hee will despise the barbarisme of his own Countrey, & tel a whole Legend of lyes of his trauiales vnto *Constantinople*. . . . [He] hath been but ouer to *Deepe*.

Some thinke to be counted rare Politicians and Statesmen, by being solitary: as who would say, I am a wise man, a braue man, *Secreta mea mihi: Frustra sapit, qui sibi non sapit:* and there is no man worthy of my companie or friendship. . . .[30]

Unless he happens to be a blabbing imposter like Nashe's "greasie son of a Cloathier," the malcontent is secure in his sense of merit and feels great contempt for spirits less lofty than his:

> The discontented *Money-scorning Knight,*
> I haue interiour excellence that shines
> Beyond your earthings gold and siluer mines.[31]

---

[27] Anton, *Satyrs*, p. 16.

[28] *The Merchant of Venice*, I, i, 90–94. Gratiano is making sport of Antonio's melancholy.

[29] That is, the melancholy lover deports himself in much the same manner as the malcontent. These two melancholy types overlap. In dress and manner they are indistinguishable. See Chap. VII.

[30] *Works*, I, 168–69.

[31] Rowlands, *The Melancholie Knight* (*Works*, vol. II), p. 35.

But since the obtuse Philistines who manage the world's affairs are incapable of recognizing excellence, the malcontent has not prospered. Advancement in the state has gone to undeserving dullards. Because the world has treated him ill, the malcontent occasionally breaks his characteristic silence to abuse the world in voluble and caustic commentary on its sins and follies. He is morbidly envious. Marston's Bruto, who is highly conscious of what he regards as self-improvement abroad, rails at the "corrupted age," which has slight regard for "men of sound carriage"—at the "ungrateful sots," the "oily snails," who are "respectless . . . Of my good parts."[32] Another malcontent walks with deliberate step and "sad and sowre countenance, as if hee would haue it saide; Lo, yonder goes the melancholy Gentleman, see there Vertue and Wisedome despised, this is the man, that dooth carry a whole commonwealth in his head, that can mannage the affaires of a State, and [is fit] to be of a *Princes priuy house counsaile.*"[33] In *Laugh and Lie Downe,* a prose satire possibly by Cyril Tourneur, a melancholy man who has "beene a trauailer" bewails his lot: "Tyre the bodie, spende the spirite, emptie the purse, weary friendes, waste the wittes, deserue well, desire little, and haue nothing: What comforte on the earth, but death? Fortune is such an enimie to vertue."[34] Robert Anton, in a satire directed against Saturnists, writes of those who, because of frivolous accomplishments acquired in travel (they have transformed themselves into *"Italionated* antick *shapes"*), profess themselves "deepe *politicians."* He commands them to "Packe to the *center"* and the "grosse and melancholly *caues"* where they belong and to leave state affairs to those better fitted.[35] Earle's discontented man "quarrels at the time, and vpstarts, and sighs at the neglect of men of Parts, that is, such as himselfe. His life is a perpetuall Satyre, and hee is still girding the ages vanity; when this very anger shewes he too much esteemes it."[36] Nashe considers it

a pitiful thing that a fellow that eates not a good meales meat in a weeke . . . should take vppe a scornfull melancholy in his gate and countenance, and talke as though our common welth were but a mockery of gouernment, and our Maiestrates fooles, who wronged him in not looking into his deserts, not imploying him in State matters, and that, if more regard were not had of him very shortly, the whole Realme should haue a misse of him, & he would go (I mary would he) where he should be more accounted of.[37]

---

32 *Works,* III, 274. The returned traveler especially is conscious of his acquirements and prone to think that the state owes him dignified employment. "Back of the pretensions of the traveler, of course, lay the Elizabethan theory that the purpose of foreign travel was to fit oneself for service to the state."—Fink, "Jaques," p. 244 (note 34).

33 Rich, *Faultes,* fol. 7ʳ. Cf. Sir John Davies' "Gull," *Poems,* p. 58.

34 *Works,* ed. Allardyce Nicoll (London, 1930), p. 279.

35 *Satyrs,* pp. 15–18.

36 *Micro-Cosmographie,* pp. 27–28.

37 *Pierce Penilesse, Works,* I, 170.

The malcontent is likely to be wretchedly poor. He "eates not a good meales meat in a weeke." Armado refuses to strip for combat: "The naked truth of it is, I have no shirt."[38] In Harington's *Metamorphosis* Ajax's purse is "without coin." Rowlands' Melancholy Knight is impecunious and debt ridden.[39]

The malcontent has a villainous reputation. In foreign parts (especially in Italy) he has acquired not such improving graces as he pretends to, but filthy vices and odious opinions. Robert Greene confesses that in his youth he traveled in "Italy, and Spaine, in which places I sawe and practizde such villainie as is abominable to declare. . . . At my return into England, I ruffeled out my silks, in the habit of *Malcontent*. . . ."[40] According to Marston, Bruto has given his time abroad to licentious indulgences. Lodge reviews the intel- ✗ lectual vices which the malcontent has picked up in travel: "well spoken he is, and hath some languages, and hath red ouer the coniuration of *Machiavel:* In beleife he is an Atheist, or a counterfait Catholicke. . . . He hath beene a long Traueller, and seene manie countries, but . . . from al those Prouinces he hath visited, bringeth home nothing but the corruptions, to disturbe the peace of his countrie, and destroy his owne bodie and soule."[41] Thus melancholy discontent is associated with libertinism, Machiavellian treachery, and devilish beliefs.

The malcontent's sense of injured merit makes him "the sparke that kindles the Commonwealth."[42] He is likely to be a furtive scoundrel,

his hat without a band, his hose vngartered, his Rapier *punto r'enuerso*, his lookes suspitious and heauie, his left hand continually on his dagger: if he walke Poules, he sculks in the backe Isles, and of all things loueth no societies. . . . [He hates his country, his king, and the royal counsellors] of meere innated and corrupt villanie; and vaine desire of Innouation. . . . [He] swears by no small bugs, that all the world is imprudent that imploies him not. . . . [He] delighteth in nought els but traiterous and deuillish stratagems[;] his daily companion in walke, bed, and bord, is rebellion and disobedience.[43]

John Davies of Hereford describes malcontents as proud and envious men, "Exclaiming on the *tymes*," complaining that "*Men* of woorth" are neglected and "*partlesse Spirits*" are rewarded. "These vnwise wittie *Mal-*

---

[38] *Love's Labor's Lost*, V, ii, 715–16.
[39] *Works*, vol. II; p. 60.
[40] *The Repentance of Robert Greene*, in *Works*, XII, 172. The fact that Greene mentions Spain may indicate that he picked up melancholy mannerisms there as well as in Italy. Shakespeare's Armado is a Spaniard.
[41] *Wits Miserie* (*Works* [London, 1883], vol. IV), p. 23.
[42] Earle, *Micro-Cosmographie*, p. 28. Cf. Fink, "Jaques," p. 244.
[43] Lodge, *Wits Miserie* (*Works*, vol. IV), pp. 23–24.

contents" are instigators of rebellion against royal authority.[44] In characterizing *"Saturn's* sullen *face,"* Robert Anton indirectly characterizes saturnine melancholics: Saturn is

> Pale, and of *ashie colour*, male content;
> A *Catelline*, to mortall *temperament:*
> That would blow vp the *Capitol* of *man*
> With *enuious influence;* melencholy, wan,
> And much resembling, a deepe plodding *pate*,
> Whose sallow *iawbones*, sinke with *wasting hate*
> At others *streames* of *fortunes* . . .
> Inspiring *Tragick plots*, of *death* and *hate;*
> Torturing our *inclinations* (like a *wrack*)
> To *dismal proiects*, ominous, and black
> *Prodigious thoughts*, and *deepe-fetcht treacheries*,
> Beating the *skul* with *sullen phantasies*.[45]

Satirists sometimes vilify persons who hold heterodox religious opinions—Catholic or Puritan—by accusing them of melancholy malcontentedness (see above, pp. 48–49, 53). Among the melancholy saturnists whom Robert Anton attacks are the Roman Catholics from the English universities: "discontented *Graduates"* leave their country and renounce its religion to seek preferment abroad and write *"scandalous volumes* gainst the *King* and *State."* These are *"Recusants* both in *faith* and *loyaltie,"* "deep *malecontent[s]."*[46] Apparently he refers to the same exodus of young academic converts to Catholicism recorded some years earlier in *The Return from Parnassus*.[47] Lodge personifies Sedition as a "malecontent" who, to escape the consequences of crime, has fled his country "vnder colour of Religion" and returned "with seditious bookes, false intelligences, and defamatorie Libels." Sedition works also, says Lodge, by fostering innovation in religion and slandering the clergy, notably the bishops. "Of this race was *Martine Marprelat*."[48] In William Strode's *The Floating Island* (performed in 1636) there appears a person called Melancholico, who is characterized in the *dramatis personae* as "a Malecontent turn'd Puritan." Another character, in trying to persuade him to join a conspiracy, flatters and tempts him:

---

[44] *Microcosmos*, (*Works*, vol. I), p. 72. Cf. Davies' *Against Murmurers, and Murmuring* (*Works*, vol. II), p. 7.

[45] *Satyrs*, p. 9.

[46] *Ibid.*, p. 10.

[47] *The Pilgrimage to Parnassus* . . . , ed. W. D. Macray (Oxford, 1886), pp. viii, 75, 90.

[48] *Wits Miserie* (*Works*, vol. IV), pp. 73–74. Melancholy is associated with Puritanism also in *An Almond for a Parrat* (Nashe, *Works*, III, 359) and in Spenser's *The Faerie Queene* (II, ii, 17).

Brother *Melancholy*, discreet you are,
But not expressive; unprefer'd you are,
Because precise; but say, would you with State
Infold your armes; look sad, and feele content;
Live careful over bags, retire your selfe
To solemn griefe in Temples of delight,
Sigh in a Sisters bosom, and complain
Of Persecution at a plenteous Feast?[49]

Melancholico joins the conspiracy.

The various specimens of the primary malcontent type do not, of course, agree with one another in every detail, and one detects subspecies within the species.[50] But the main features are clear enough: surly preoccupation, taciturnity, and unsociability; folded arms and hat pulled low; negligent disorder in dress; sense of superiority; tendency to rail enviously at an unappreciative world; inclination toward treachery and sedition.

When did this type die out? In *The Duchess of Malfi* Antonio accuses the malcontent Bosola of affecting an "out of [f]ashion mellancholly."[51] If Lucas is right in dating the play 1613–14,[52] it seems to me very likely that the pose had lost popularity when it was written. Some of the surviving sketches of the malcontent were written at about this time or later,[53] but these may represent literary rather than social convention. I do not mean that all melancholic mannerisms were out of style by 1614. A poem written apparently in the early 1630's represents John Ford as standing alone with "folded arms, and melancholy hat."[54] In his popular lyric "Melancholly," probably composed at about the same time, William Strode writes approvingly of "folded armes and fixed eyes."[55] When she met her husband-to-be in 1637, Lucy Apsley, evidently something of a blue stocking, was distinguished by "a melancholy negligence both of herself and others, as if she neither affected to please others, nor took notice of anything before her." The ladies of the neighborhood, with "witty spite," called the young man's attention to "the negligence of her dress and habit, and all womanish ornaments," due to her absorption in "study and writing."[56] Some of the

---

[49] *Works*, ed. Bertram Dobell (London, 1907), p. 157.
[50] See below, note 69.
[51] Webster, *Works*, II, 54.
[52] *Ibid.*, pp. 3–4.
[53] Anton's *Satyrs* was published in 1616; Earle's *Micro-Cosmographie* was published in 1628; Strode's *The Floating Island* was performed in 1636.
[54] Hemming's elegy on Randolph's finger; see J. J. Parry, "A Seventeenth Century Gallery of Poets," *Journal of English and Germanic Philology*, XIX (1920), 273.
[55] *Works*, p. 14.
[56] *Memoirs of the Life of Colonel Hutchinson*, by his widow Lucy (London, 1908), pp. 48, 50.

malcontent's manners, if not the malcontent himself, seem to have persisted into the Carolinian period.

III

The Elizabethans learned, both from scientific literature (see above, pp. 56–58) and from the malcontent's reputation for seditious activity, to associate melancholy with criminal violence and intrigue. Many passages in Elizabethan drama testify to this association. In *Titus Andronicus*, for example, Aaron is plotting iniquities. Saturn, he says, "is dominator over" his desires:

> What signifies my deadly-standing eye,
> My silence and my cloudy melancholy . . . ? (II, iii, 31–33)

Shakespeare's King John, on the point of instructing Hubert to murder young Arthur, makes a show of hesitation. He tells Hubert that he would speak plainly, however,

> if that surly spirit, melancholy,
> Had bak'd thy blood and made it heavy-thick. (III, iii, 42–43)

Lady Macbeth, as she determines to murder Duncan, calls upon supernatural powers to "make thick my blood" (I, v, 44). Thick blood is melancholic blood. The hero of Chettle's *The Tragedy of Hoffman*, living a savage and solitary life, nurses his rancor and devises his bloody schemes of revenge with a mind permeated by "Clouds of melancholy."[57] A character in Webster's *A Cure for a Cuckold*, in planning treachery, declares that "My melancholly and the devil shall fashion't."[58] In Nabbes' *Microcosmus* Melancholy (personified) boasts that he "could hatch a conspiracy . . . should cause posterity attribute all Matchiavillianisme to Melancholy."[59]

Elizabethan writers regard the melancholic's criminal bias as very dangerous because melancholy sometimes endows men with great acumen, which presumably may be turned to evil uses. Nathaniel Field takes the sympathetic view that melancholic villainies are due to the perversion of high mental endowments by adverse circumstances:

---

[57] Sig. B1r (Tudor Facsimile edition, 1913). Hoffman throws off his melancholy as he embarks upon his career of crime.

[58] *Works*, III, 76. The speaker is not a villain.

[59] *Works*, ed. A. H. Bullen (London, 1887), II, 181.

> Wit's a disease that fit employment wants;
> Therefore we see those happiest in best parts,
> And fortunes under-born unto their merits,
> Grow to a sullen envy, hate, and scorn
> Of their superiors; and at last, like winds,
> Break forth into rebellious civil wars
> Or private treasons: none so apt for these
> As melancholy wits, fetter'd with need.[60]

Others, however, are not so ready to make allowances. Robert Anton admits that melancholy saturnists are "most ingenious," but they

> long retaine their great *Italian-hate*,
> Wittie in nothing, but things desperate;
> To glut reuenge, with studious memorie
> Of shallow *wrongs*, or some slight *iniurie*.[61]

Several of the villainous characters of Elizabethan literature, as one would expect, are definitely characterized as melancholy men. Probably many others hazily suggested melancholy to readers or playgoers. These melancholy villains constitute the second of the malcontent types.

At least two members of this class, both dramatic characters, correspond closely to the primary malcontent type, the melancholy man who bears a grudge against the world for its neglect. Both of them, to use a phrase of E. E. Stoll's,[62] are tool-villains, that is, cat's-paws for villains of higher social rank. To the Elizabethan audience it would seem quite natural that a malcontent should easily be induced to play such a role. A great man who needed an instrument for criminal service would be likely to look for just such a person. The malcontent is shrewd and ambitious, but frustrated, poverty-stricken, and embittered. One would suppose that he could be bribed, either with money or with promise of preferment, to perform the greatest iniquities. His bitterness and his melancholy have smothered all his scruples; his needs are urgent; he has little to lose and everything to gain.

In *The First Part of Jeronimo*, Lorenzo, son of the Duke of Castile, wishes to hire a man to commit a murder. He interviews a certain Lazarotto,

> A melancholy, discontented courtier,
> Whose famisht iawes look like the chap of death;

---

[60] *A Woman Is a Weathercock*, in *Old Plays*, ed. Dodsley and Hazlitt, XI, 63.
[61] *Satyrs*, p. 9.
[62] *John Webster* (Cambridge, Mass., 1905), pp. 96, 104, 118, etc. Stoll alludes to the connection between tool-villainy and melancholy (see notes on pp. 125, 126).

> Vpon whose eie browes hangs damnation;
> Whose hands are washt in rape, and murders bould.[63]

Lazarotto tells Lorenzo that he is rotting for lack of employment, that he has more mischief in him than he can hold. He delivers an acrid little speech concerning the paths to hell which is a typical bit of malcontented satire:

> from vserers doores
> There goes one pathe: from friers that nurse whores
> There goes another path: from brokers stals,
> From rich that die and build no hospitals,
> Two other paths . . . .

Lorenzo finds him "a slaue iust a the stampe I wish"[64] and hires him. Lazarotto, however, proves deficient in melancholic shrewdness, and his career in crime is brief and ignominious.

Bosola, of Webster's *The Duchess of Malfi*, is also a melancholy tool-villain. Probably somewhat melancholy by nature, he has been rendered bitterly malcontent by the Cardinal's failure to reward him for past services, apparently criminal services.[65] He is a witty and acid railer, "The onely Court-Gall."[66] His "foule mellancholly," says Antonio,

> Will poyson all his goodnesse . . .
> . . . . want of action
> Breeds all blacke male-contents.[67]

The Cardinal and Ferdinand, the two major villains of the play, see in Bosola the ideal instrument for their cruel practices upon their sister. He accepts the offer of this ignoble employment with no illusions regarding the foulness of it and is the brothers' agent throughout most of the play. Toward the close, however, he is touched by pity for his victims and repentance for his crimes. His melancholy is no longer discontented melancholy but the melancholy of remorse.

The idea of melancholy tool-villainy appears also in certain episodes of the drama in which a man of high rank blunders in selecting his tool. He chooses a man who is (or appears to be) a melancholy malcontent. The Elizabethan audience, realizing that melancholy discontent is an excellent

---

63 Kyd, *Works*, ed. Frederick S. Boas (Oxford, 1901), p. 301. The play is probably not by Kyd.
64 P. 305.
65 *Works*, II, 38.
66 P. 37.
67 P. 39.

recommendation for criminal employment, would consider the patron's selection a very natural one. The tool, however, takes advantage of his position of trust to carry out his own designs instead of his master's.

In Marston's *The Malcontent* Mendoza needs an instrument to commit murder and act as pander. He chooses "Malevole" (Duke Altofronto, the hero of the play, in disguise) simply because he is (or seems to be) a poverty-stricken malcontent. Mendoza sounds Malevole out: ". . . thou art an arrant knave. . . . Thou art very poore."[68] Malevole endeavors to give the impression that he is a desperate villain who will do anything for money, accepts the criminal employment which is offered him, and pleases his new patron immensely both by his alacrity and by his ingenious suggestions. He makes good use of his advantageous situation in thwarting Mendoza and in pursuing his own righteous ends.

Chapman's Bussy D'Ambois is a soldier[69] to whom Fortune has been unkind,

> A man of spirit beyond the reach of fear,
> Who (discontent with his neglected worth)
> Neglects the light, and loves obscure abodes
> . . . .
> None loathes the world so much, nor loves to scoff it.[70]

He is very poor; his clothing is threadbare.[71] All in all, he has such promise of value as a tool that Monsieur seeks him out and takes him into his service. Bussy proves to be a very unmanageable instrument, but undoubtedly, during the first act, the Elizabethan audience was as much deceived by appearances as was Monsieur.

In Tourneur's *The Revenger's Tragedy* a villain of high rank twice makes this kind of mistake. Lussurioso feels the need of a pander, preferably

---

68 *Plays*, ed. H. Harvey Wood (Edinburgh, 1934–39), I, 181.

69 *Bussy D'Ambois*, in *Plays*, p. 143. Before they rose in the world, the D'Ambois brothers were "A ragged couple of decay'd commanders."—*The Revenge of Bussy D'Ambois*, in *Plays*, p. 182. The hazy outline of a malcontent type consisting of discharged soldiers appears in the literature of the period. See Nashe, *Summers Last Will and Testament*, in *Works*, III, 275; Anton, *Satyrs*, p. 20. Belgarde, an unemployed captain in Massinger's *The Unnatural Combat*, complains bitterly of society's ingratitude in time of peace toward its defenders. (*Plays*, ed. Gifford [London, 1813], I, 181–84). He is called "The malcontent Belgarde" (p. 205). Bosola, of Webster's *The Duchess of Malfi*, has likewise seen military service and likewise complains of neglect (*Works*, II, 38). Another example is Benatzi, of Ford's *The Lady's Trial* (*Works*, ed. Gifford and Dyce [London, 1869], III, 18, 47, 84).

70 Chapman, *Plays*, p. 141.

71 Pp. 140, 142.

> some strange digested fellow . . .
> Of ill-contented nature, either disgracst
> In former times, or by new groomes displacst.[72]

Vendice, who has undertaken the revenge murder of Lussurioso and his entire family, presents himself disguised as "Piato." Lussurioso examines Piato, discovers that he is as shrewd, blunt, and satiric as a malcontent could be expected to be, and hires him.[73] Piato uses his position to carry out designs of his own and then disappears. Later Lussurioso once more needs a tool. Vendice has an accomplice at court, his own brother. The brother suggests Vendice for the place, characterizing him as a man "full of want and discontent," one "in whom much melancholy dwels." Lussurioso is interested: ". . . discontent and want / Is the best clay to mould a villaine off"; "hope of preferment / Will grinde him to an Edge."[74] Prepared to simulate melancholy, Vendice presents himself for the usual interview, this time in his own person, and endeavors to impress Lussurioso with his satiric cleverness. Lussurioso is pleased: "A parlous melancholy, has wit enough / To murder any man."[75] Once more for politic reasons Vendice plays the role of malcontent—a role apparently not altogether foreign to his real nature[76]—and once more Lussurioso makes the mistake of hiring the man who is seeking his life.

There are, of course, several melancholy villains in Elizabethan literature who are not tool-villains. The denomination *malcontent* is perhaps less appropriate to these than to Lazarotto and Bosola, for they do not exhibit the poverty-stricken frustration which the word might seem to imply. Some of them are men of high station. Yet the writers sometimes characterize them as "discontented" persons and probably would not hesitate to call them malcontents. All of them are dangerous intriguers.

I have found two melancholy villains in Elizabethan novels. In Greene's *Planetomachia* one reads the story of Duke Valdracko, who, "being stricken in age," is of "a melancholicke disposition,"[77] tyrannical, cruel, froward, distrustful, wily, deceitful, avaricious. He treacherously murders his enemy and his enemy's son, even though the latter is the beloved of his daughter.

---

[72] *Works*, p. 81.

[73] Pp. 90–91.

[74] Pp. 130–31.

[75] P. 134.

[76] Vendice is hard to classify. Although the playwright never calls him "melancholy" or "malcontent," his asperity, his railing, his cleverness, his brooding sense of wrong indicate that he is actually a melancholy malcontent (see Stoll, *Webster*, pp. 108–11). If so, he is merely exaggerating characteristics which he really possesses during his interviews with Lussurioso.

[77] *Works*, V, 51.

The story of Valdracko is told to illustrate the malignant influence of Saturn. Another melancholy tyrant appears in Sidney's *Arcadia*. This is the King of Phrygia, "a Prince of a melancholy constitution both of bodie and mind; wickedly sad, ever musing of horrible matters," suspicious, fearful, secret, bloody.[78] Both Pyrocles and Musidorus narrowly escape death at his hands.

Examples are more numerous in the drama. The villain of *Lust's Dominion* is Eleazar the Moor, a sinister person who stands "with crost arms . . . malecontent."[79] He shrewdly plans and daringly executes a series of cruel and bloody intrigues. Don John, whose cunning and malevolent devices cause the nearly tragic complications in *Much Ado About Nothing*, is a person "of a very melancholy disposition" (II, i, 6), "compos'd and fram'd of treachery" (V, i, 261). He is a very silent gentleman with a tart expression (II, i, 3–10). His tool, Conrade, speaks of Don John's "discontent" (I, iii, 40). Conrade himself was "born under Saturn" (I, iii, 12). The Cardinal in Webster's *The Duchess of Malfi*, archvillain of the play, is "a mellancholly Churchman" who "laies [wicked] plots." Toward the close he is touched, like Bosola, by remorse and grows "wondrous mellancholly."[80] In Fletcher's *The Faithful Shepherdess* there appears a "Melancholy Swain" whose evil practices cause distressing complications among the rustic characters. He is "More sullen Discontent than *Saturns* Brow."[81] The villain of Jonson's *The Sad Shepherd* is the witch Maudlin, a "fearfull, and melancholique" creature.[82] In Shirley's *The Politician*, the subtle villain Gotharus speaks of his own machinations as the issue of "mutinous thoughts" and "witty melancholy."[83]

Revenge as well as villainy is associated with melancholy in Elizabethan literature. Several revengers and villain-revengers of the drama were certainly or probably intended by their creators as melancholy men. Among them are Hieronimo of Kyd's *The Spanish Tragedy*, Hamlet, Malevole of Marston's *The Malcontent*, Vendice of Tourneur's *The Revenger's Trag-*

---

[78] *Works*, ed. Albert Feuillerat (Cambridge, 1922–26), I, 196.

[79] Ed. J. Le Gay Brereton, *Materials for the Study of the Old English Drama*, V (Louvain, 1931), 19. Although Eleazar's principal motive in crime is revenge for the death of his father, I classify him as a villain in accordance with Fredson T. Bowers' theory that, in Elizabethan eyes, the revenger becomes a villain when he becomes a Machiavellian intriguer (*Elizabethan Revenge Tragedy: 1587–1642* [Princeton, 1940], pp. 89–90). Certainly Eleazar relishes his bloody intrigues too much to win the sympathy of any audience.

[80] *Works*, II, 41, 111. The Cardinal's iniquitous brother Ferdinand becomes the victim of a melancholy madness (pp. 106–7).

[81] *The Works of Francis Beaumont and John Fletcher*, ed. Arnold Glover and A. R. Waller (Cambridge, 1905–12), II, 419, 380.

[82] *Jonson*, VII, 40. See also p. 39.

[83] *Works*, ed. Gifford and Dyce (London, 1833), V, 100.

edy, Francisco de Medici of Webster's *The White Devil*, all of whom are discussed elsewhere. In Lodge's novel *A Margarite of America* there appears a melancholy revenger, Arsinous, whose situation is very similar to Hieronimo's.[84] Few of the melancholy revengers could be classified as malcontents.

Before leaving the subject of melancholy intrigue, I should like to discuss briefly a curious dramatic convention connected with it. *The Duchess of Malfi* furnishes illustration. Ferdinand, as he engages Bosola for criminal services, instructs him to continue his customary melancholic manner:

> This will gaine
> Accesse, to private lodgings, where your selfe
> May (like a pollitique dormouse—[85]

The melancholy intriguer has a ready-made disguise of which Ferdinand wishes Bosola to take advantage. Since a melancholy man may be supposed to be somewhere near the borderline of sanity, others are inclined to regard him as a harmless eccentric, interesting but not to be taken too seriously. A melancholic, then, without changing his customary manner (except perhaps to exaggerate it), may act as spy and plotter without arousing suspicion. If it seems strange that melancholy is at the same time associated with both cunning evil and harmless eccentricity, there are stranger contradictions in the Elizabethan mind.

In the Elizabethan drama, an intriguing villain or revenger who is in any degree abnormal mentally is very likely to utilize his abnormality, even to exaggerate it, for the purpose of convincing others that he is helpless and harmless. His principal motive may be to insure his safety, or it may be to gain opportunity to make his observations and devise and execute his plots.[86] This convention is due primarily, I think, to the influence of Kyd's *The Spanish Tragedy*. In this play, the murder of his son drives Hieronimo mad. Yet he is cannily shrewd in his madness, shrewd enough to use his distraction to allay suspicion and shrewd enough to plan his murders perfectly. He is contemptuous toward his enemies for underestimating him. They

---

84 *Works*, vol. III; pp. 5, 43–44, 82.

85 Webster, *Works*, II, 44–45.

86 Various modern commentators have noted the literary convention of madness or melancholy assumed for politic reasons. Bowers (*op. cit.*, p. 90, note 27) and G. L. Kittredge (*Hamlet* [Boston, 1939], p. ix) observe that the story of David (I Samuel, 21:10–15) and the story of Brutus (Livy, i, 56; Ovid, *Fasti*, ii, 717–18) furnish precedent for this convention. No modern commentator, however, seems to be conscious of the frequency with which the madman plays the politic madman in the Elizabethan drama. Elizabethan dramatists like to pile madness upon madness.

rated me for brainsicke lunacie,
With *God amende that mad Hieronimo!*[87]

The mad Titus Andronicus exaggerates his madness and capitalizes upon his enemies' low opinion of him:

I know them all, though they suppose me mad;
And will o'er-reach them in their own devices. (V, ii, 142–43)

If *Fratricide Punished* truly represents the *Ur-Hamlet,* the hero of the latter was a melancholic playing the madman.[88] We have seen that in Renaissance science the distinction between melancholy and madness is rather one of degree than of kind. To the Elizabethan audience, the hero of the *Ur-Hamlet* would be simply exaggerating his actual mental abnormality. Shakespeare's Hamlet, for politic reasons, chooses "To put an antic disposition on" (I, v, 172). In Marston's *The Malcontent* the melancholy Duke Altofronto, for similar motives, assumes the role of a highly eccentric malcontent.

The behavior of the melancholy intriguer, whether he is a villain or a man of good will, is likely to be doubly melancholy, even mad.

IV

The portraits of the melancholy malcontent thus far considered are not sympathetic. There are other malcontent characters in the drama, however, who lack the more odious traits of the primary type. Among these are the melancholy cynics, who, though they may be eccentrics, are not regarded as posers, and who, though they may be intriguers, are not villains.

The malcontent of this type appeals to other characters of the play in which he appears—and presumably also to the audience—as a person of interesting and amusing peculiarities. He is shaggy and disheveled; he is gruff and bearish; he is prone to taciturn moping in corners; if spoken to, he is likely to break out into misanthropic railings against human nature and human sin and vanity. He is indeed a psychopathological "antic," exhibiting many of the symptoms of melancholy described in medical treatises. The Elizabethans and Jacobeans were fascinated by the vagaries of the mentally

---

[87] *Works,* p. 93. I am speaking here of Hieronimo as he is represented in the early (Kydian) version of the play.

[88] The same is true in Belleforest's *Hamblet.* The melancholy antecedents of *Hamlet* are discussed in Chap. V, note 25.

diseased. The drama of the period is full of psychopathic monstrosities.[89] The malcontent cynic, then, is regarded with tolerant amusement. Since he is on the borderline of sanity, he is granted the license which is naturally given to irresponsible persons. He has privileges somewhat like those of the court jester. He may be as sour and surly as he pleases, as acidly satiric, even as offensive, as he pleases. Those about him often question him, prod him, to bring forth his satire, just as one uses provocative devices to make an animal show its tricks.

Although the Elizabethans and Jacobeans are very impatient with melancholy posers, they are prepared to expect wit and wisdom in a genuine melancholy man. The melancholy cynic is something of a philosopher, some one well worth heeding, although his thinking is deeply colored by pessimism and misanthropy. His wit and wisdom in combination with his vituperative asperity and his contempt for the world make him a telling satirist. He is, furthermore, a virtuous and honest man. He hates stupidity, affectation, and vice. He speaks his mind candidly and volubly without reference to either good manners or self-interest. Other characters place a high value on his blunt frankness. The malcontent will not flatter.

In presenting a character of this kind, the dramatist sometimes makes it clear that he has sufficient cause for his melancholy. He has suffered great misfortunes, which have been due to the sins and stupidities of mankind. He has been disappointed, disillusioned, embittered. His case elicits sympathy, for his quarrel with the world is a just quarrel.

Bohan, the churlish and satiric Scot appearing in the induction to Greene's *James IV*, is an early example.[90] Bohan has fled from human society because he hates it, and he dwells lugubriously in a tomb (his own). The play proper, which shows how great men are ruled by their appetites and misled by parasites and flatterers, illustrates the ways of the world which have aroused such loathing in Bohan.

In *As You Like It* one meets "the melancholy Jaques" (II, i, 26, 41). Although Shakespeare never reveals the cause of Jaques' melancholy,[91] he depicts its results rather fully. Jaques is morose, cynical, and rude. He hates "th' infected world" (II, vii, 60). He nurses his melancholy, apparently finding great pleasure in it (II, v). He has difficulty in sleeping (II, v, 60).

---

[89] Edgar Allison Peers, in *Elizabethan Drama and Its Mad Folk* (Cambridge, 1914), has assembled a great many examples.

[90] Thomas H. Dickinson, in the introduction to the Mermaid edition of Greene's plays, writes that "Bohan is an early 'malcontent'" (p. lxv) and that he "is a prototype of Jaques" (p. lxi).

[91] Possibly his melancholy has originated in the same manner as that of the Italianate malcontent. Like the latter, Jaques has been a traveler (IV, i, 19, 22) and a libertine (II, vii, 65–66). Fink believes that Jaques is a modification of the traveler malcontent.

He loves solitude and at the close of the play elects a lonely and contemplative life as the other characters prepare to return to the ducal court. He
asks to have such liberty as a jester has "To blow on whom I please" (II, vii,
49). This request seems unnecessary, for he is already privileged. His discourse is salted with satiric wisdom. The banished Duke, in any case, seems
to think so, although his attitude toward Jaques has something of amused
condescension in it:

> I love to cope him in these sullen fits,
> For then he's full of matter. (II, i, 67–68)

Many generations of readers have agreed with the Duke. Jaques moralizes
sympathetically and fittingly upon the wounded deer (II, i), and it is he who
delivers the speech upon the seven ages of man (II, vii, 139–66), one of the
most frequently quoted passages in English literature. The ages of man is
a favorite theme of Renaissance moralists. To the Elizabethan audience this
speech would have seemed a thing of considerable worth and dignity.

Jaques is the best example in the drama of the malcontent in the role of
philosophic critic. He is, moreover, humane, for he is sorry for the deer
and weeps over it. Shakespeare does not ask his audience to take Jaques
altogether seriously—he is too much the surly eccentric for that, nor does
he ask it to admire him, for Jaques has "been a libertine, / As sensual as the
brutish sting itself" (II, vii, 65–66). Yet in *As You Like It* one finds probably the kindliest portrait of the melancholy malcontent in Elizabethan and
early Stuart literature.[92]

Giovanni Altofronto, the deposed Duke of Genoa who appears in Marston's *The Malcontent* under the alias "Malevole," has been rendered a melancholy malcontent by misfortune. He has lost his dukedom to the usurper
Pietro. He suffered deep disillusionment concerning human nature when
his people leagued with the usurper to depose him. He soliloquizes:

> I cannot sleepe . . . .
> . . . . in night all creatures sleepe,
> Onely the Malecontent that gainst his fate,
> Repines and quarrels, alas hees goodman tell-clocke;
> His sallow jaw-bones sincke with wasting mone.[93]

This indicates his state of mind as he lives disguised, in semisolitude, in the
place where he should be master. He is seeking revenge on Pietro and await-

---

[92] There has been considerable discussion of Jaques' melancholy: e.g., Fink, "Jaques";
O. J. Campbell, "Jaques," *Huntington Library Bulletin*, No. 8 (October, 1935), 71–102;
E. E. Stoll, "Jaques, and the Antiquaries," *Modern Language Notes*, LIV (1939), 79–85.
[93] *Plays*, I, 178.

ing the opportunity to regain the ducal crown. The revenge which he plans is relatively civilized, for he wishes to inflict mental, not physical, pain upon his enemy.

He has disguised himself physically, and he greatly exaggerates his melancholic traits because they enable him to pursue his designs under the guise of a harmless eccentric. This "affected straine," moreover, gives him something which few men enjoy, an opportunity to speak his mind freely; his tongue is "fetterlesse as is an Emperours."[94] Duke Pietro assumes an attitude of amused patronization toward him and questions him indulgently to elicit his snarling satire. He is, says Pietro, "rather a monster" than a man, "more discontent than Lucifer . . . his speach is halter-worthy at all howers: I like him faith, he gives good intelligence to my spirit, makes me understand those weakenesses which others flattery palliates . . . he is as free as ayre: he blowes over every man."[95] Malevole is the licensed critic of those about him. He is insolently and scurrilously offensive to the sycophantic courtiers who surround the Duke. He addresses an elderly timeserver: "And how do's my olde Muckill overspread with fresh snow: thou halfe a man, halfe a Goate, al a Beast: how do's thy young wife, old huddle? . . . thou hugely hornd olde Dukes Oxe, good Maister Make-pleece."[96] He plays his role exceedingly well. Yet since he really feels the contempt for fools and the hatred for knaves which he expresses, he should have no great difficulty with his part.

Fundamentally Altofronto is a wise and benevolent person, and it seems quite proper that his political adventures should have a happy ending. Possibly the happy ending cures his melancholy.

The Shakespearean *Timon of Athens* dramatizes the story of a character very frequently named by Renaissance writers as the embodiment of melancholy cynicism and misanthropy.[97] Timon lives splendidly and happily amid a crowd of supposed friends, persons attracted by his wealth and lavish generosity. Suddenly he finds himself penniless and therefore friendless. His fall from high to low estate and the desertion of his fair-weather friends

94 P. 150. It is easy to confuse the real man (Altofronto) with the assumed character (Malevole). The difference is one of degree, not of kind, yet the difference is a very real one. When he is alone with his confidant Celso, Altofronto drops his fantastic manner and becomes sober and sensible; when some else enters, he "shifteth his speach" (p. 152).

95 P. 146.

96 P. 147.

97 See, for example, Lemnius, *Touchstone*, fol. 143ʳ; Coeffeteau, *Passions*, p. 193; Burton, *Anatomy*, I, 286, 323, 497. Timon is not characterized as a melancholy man, however, in the classical sources (Plutarch, *Antonius*, LXIX–LXX; Strabo, *Geography*, XVII, i, 19; Lucian, *Timon*) or in William Painter's *Palace of Pleasure* (novel 28). The author of the play known as the "academic" *Timon* does not seem to have thought of the hero as a melancholic, although there is some incidental mention of melancholy in it.

render Timon acidly melancholy. Bitterly disillusioned, he develops a deep hatred for his former friends, for his fellow citizens of Athens, and for mankind in general. He leaves Athens to dwell in solitude and to nurse his misanthropy. All men, he says in soliloquy, are deceitful flatterers:

> all is oblique;
> There's nothing level in our cursed natures
> But direct villany. Therefore, be abhorr'd
> All feasts, societies, and throngs of men!
> His semblable, yea, himself, Timon disdains:
> Destruction fang mankind! (IV, iii, 18–23)

In his retirement Timon is unwilling host to a series of visitors at whom he rails corrosively. They comment, most of them somewhat sympathetically, on his mental condition and its causes.[98] A longing for death grows upon Timon. He writes a surly epitaph for himself, prepares a rude sepulchre, and apparently kills himself. It would not be accurate to say that *Timon of Athens* presents a kindly portrait of its hero. The writer is more interested in his vagaries than sympathetic with them. His psychic disorder, however, is due to a mistaken faith in human nature; his quarrel with the world is valid. The author's attitude is not satiric.

In the same play there appears another malcontent, Apemantus, who is characterized in the *dramatis personae* as "a churlish Philosopher." Apemantus apparently is a malcontent by nature, not by accident. He deeply distrusts and hates all mankind, and he snarls and rails accordingly. While Timon is still in his prosperity, he receives Apemantus in his house and seems to find it amusing to provoke his growling misanthropy (I, i, 177 ff.). As Timon and his friends enter with fanfare to a banquet, Apemantus follows "*dropping after all . . . discontentedly, like himself*" (I, ii). When Timon himself becomes a melancholy malcontent, Apemantus scolds him for usurping his personality: "Do not assume my likeness" (IV, iii, 219). Timon's new character, he says, is "A poor unmanly melancholy sprung / From change of fortune" (IV, iii, 204–5). The two malcontents spiritedly express their disgust with each other. Apemantus, in spite of his eccentricities, is an intelligent, candid, and honest man. In Timon's gala days, Apemantus alone tells him the truth about the bloodsuckers who surround him and about the foolish course he is taking (I, ii, 39 ff.).

Two additional examples of the honest and satirical malcontent appear in

---

[98] See IV, iii, 88–89, 203–5, 403–5; V, i, 127–28, 229–30. Timon and other melancholy persons of Shakespeare's plays are discussed in Draper, *The Humors & Shakespeare's Characters*, pp. 62–80, 109–14. See also O. J. Campbell's chapter on Timon (*Shakespeare's Satire*, pp. 168–97).

the plays of John Ford.[99] One of these is Rhetias of *The Lover's Melancholy*, "a reduced courtier."[100] He appears "*carelessly attired*" and in soliloquy contemns "the madness of the times" and "the riots" of "Our wanton gentry."[101] It soon appears that this malcontent is a benevolent intriguer who, for politic reasons, has assumed "poor disguises . . . that play in rudeness."[102] In other words the malcontent is playing the role of malcontent. In the Cyprian court, he has developed a reputation for acrimonious railing and outspoken honesty. He devotes his ready wit to abusing the courtiers. They are not angered, however, for he has, it seems, "a patent to abuse."[103] Evidently he believes that, by playing this role, he can better serve his friends Eroclea and Prince Palador. The Prince, at any rate, thinks so, for he directs Rhetias to "Continue still thy discontented fashion, / Humour the lords."[104] Yet Palador and Eroclea do not seem to need him; they have no apparent enemies. Ford is inclined to repeat his predecessors (in this case Marston) rather unthinkingly. Benatzi, of Ford's *The Lady's Trial*, is perhaps the latest malcontent of the drama. He is shaggy, tattered, wild-looking; he is very poor; he has suffered many misfortunes and disappointments; he rails in the vein of caustic disillusionment characteristic of the malcontent.[105] A gallant finds his "humour . . . pretty, odd"[106] and takes him into his service. The play has a happy ending for Benatzi, and he is apparently on the way to recovering his lost humanity.

V

A fourth malcontent type is the melancholy scholar. As in the case of the melancholy cynic, literary representation of the type seems to be confined to the drama. Evidently the melancholy scholar of the stage corresponded more or less closely to an actual social type of Elizabethan London, Oxford, and Cambridge. Several English writers of the late Renaissance, a period in

---

[99] Romanello, of Ford's *The Fancies Chaste and Noble*, also has some of the traits of this type. He has been rendered sour and abusive by the ill success of his wooing and other misfortunes. For the purpose of spying on his beloved, this malcontent disguises himself as a malcontent, transforms himself "Into the beast itself he does resemble" (*Works*, II, 268; see further, pp. 265–67, 276 ff.). He is not at all sympathetically characterized.

[100] *Ibid.*, I, 5 (*dramatis personae*). He refers to his "sunk fortunes" (p. 18).

[101] P. 17.

[102] P. 74.

[103] P. 19.

[104] P. 37.

[105] *Ibid.*, III, 47–49.

[106] P. 49.

which writers were commonly scholars, belonged to this class (see Chap. VIII).

In a preceding chapter (pp. 24–26) I have given the medical reasons for the scholar's melancholy: The scholar is poor and ill nourished; his sedentary life is unhealthful; he is neglected and frustrated. Above all, his arduous mental labor consumes the heat and moisture of his body. It would be unusual indeed for a scholar to escape melancholy. Ficino says that all literati are atrabilious. Yet the scholar need not deplore his melancholy, for melancholy, according to the Aristotelian conception, is a cause and a token of intellectual and imaginative capability. It is the attribute of his profession and bears witness to his intellectual labors and achievements.

"Your greatest students," Burton writes, "are commonly . . . silly, soft fellows in their outward behaviour, absurd, ridiculous to others, and no whit experienced in worldly business." Because they lack the social graces, they are scorned "by our gallants. Yea, many times, such is their misery, they deserve it: a mere scholar, a mere ass."[107] The melancholy scholar of the stage in large measure corresponds to this characterization. He is ordinarily ill kempt, meanly clothed in black, socially clumsy, and morosely taciturn. When he speaks it is usually to rail satirically. The dramatists nevertheless sometimes treat him sympathetically and usually give him intellectual qualities worthy of respect. For the playwrights themselves are servants of the Muses. The fundamental trait of the melancholy scholar, as they usually represent him, is a despondent, disillusioned lassitude, a sense of weariness and futility. In much wisdom is much grief; and he that increaseth wisdom increaseth sorrow.

Probably the earliest representative of the type is Pandion, of Lyly's *Sapho and Phao*. The courtier Trachinus has drawn Pandion from his university studies and brought him to the court of Sapho to introduce him to the pleasures and splendors of the world. Pandion, however, is too philosophic a person to be interested, and his reaction is caustic disgust.[108] He offends a lady with his asperity. She urges him to purge his melancholy and surmises that he is "a male content."[109] Trachinus does not succeed in mitigating his friend's "deepe Melancholy."[110] It is worth noting that Pandion is brought into the play entirely for his own sake, for he contributes nothing to the action.

Macilente, the malcontent of Jonson's *Every Man out of His Humour*, is "A Man well parted, a sufficient Scholler, and trauail'd; who (wanting that

---

107 *Anatomy*, I, 352–53.
108 *Works*, II, 375–77.
109 P. 392.
110 P. 393.

place in the worlds account, which he thinks his merit capable of) falls into
. . . an enuious apoplexie."[111] His scholarship is considerably emphasized in
the play. At the same time he has many of the traits which distinguish
the primary malcontent type. He is "a lanke raw-bon'd anatomie," "a leane
mungrell," who "lookes as if he were chap-falne, with barking at other
mens good fortunes."[112] He dresses in black.[113] He is wretchedly poverty-
stricken, a "poore seame-rent" fellow,[114] and he rails continually at the fools
who have fared better in life than he. Evidently he is a satiric author, for
he "carries oile and fire in his pen."[115] Jonson has not painted an amiable
picture of him, yet he is, after all, the most intelligent character in the play
and serves as the scourge with which the author lashes the others for their
sins and follies.

The most elaborate treatment of scholar's melancholy in the Elizabethan
drama is that in the Parnassus trilogy. The unknown author, evidently a
scholar writing for an academic audience, has very feelingly depicted the
wretched existence to which the servants of the Muses are condemned.
When he wrote *The Pilgrimage to Parnassus,* the first of the three plays, he
was apparently convinced that learning was worth all the sacrifices which
it demanded. But even here one learns that study

> Is wonte to eate mens marrowes, drye there bloude,
> And make them seem leane shadowles pale ghostes.[116]

Before the author wrote the two parts of *The Return from Parnassus,* he
had become sadly disillusioned. His theme in both parts is the poverty and
misery of scholars. References to their hard lot and their "discontent" are
frequent. The various academic characters, in attempting to live by their
academic acquirements, react differently to their misfortunes according to
their natures. Philomusus, the scholar-artist, becomes deeply melancholy.
He is so consistently dogged by poverty and humiliation that he habitually
bears the "characters of Melancholy in his face."[117] He contemplates suicide.[118] He continues to lead an irksome existence, however, and at the end
of the play is about to retire to a solitary pastoral life with his friend Stu-

---

111 *Jonson,* III, 423. There are further references to Macilente's scholarship on pp.
450–51, 491.
112 Pp. 540, 450–51.
113 P. 450. Black was apparently the conventional color of the scholar's garments
whether or not he was melancholy.
114 P. 491.
115 P. 451.
116 Parnassus plays, ed. Macray, p. 10.
117 P. 66.
118 P. 127.

dioso. They plan to chant their "woes vpon an oaten reede" and "shun the company of men, / That growes more hatefull as the world growes old."[119] *The Return from Parnassus* seems to be a warning to young men against "Spending the marrow of their flowring age" in scholarship.[120]

In *What You Will* Marston presents Lampatho, a scholar who has been rendered melancholy not by material misfortune but by laborious study and by intellectual confusion and frustration. Lampatho is a caustic railer determined "with a frightlesse resolution" to "Rip up and launce our times impieties."[121] Quadratus, a blithe epicure who condescendingly accepts Lampatho as a companion because he finds him amusing, characterizes him as an "envy-starved Curre," "a ragg'd *Satyrist*, / A skrubbing railer."[122] Lampatho dresses in black. In social gatherings he is awkward, morose, and sarcastic.[123] He is characteristically dispirited and pessimistic:

> In heavens handiwork ther's naught
> None more vile, accursed, reprobate to blisse
> Then man, and mong men a scholler most.[124]

He relates his intellectual history: For seven years, he says, he studied conflicting opinions regarding the nature of the human soul and stuffed his notebooks with quotations from the philosophers.

> The more I learnt the more I learnt to doubt,
> Knowledge and wit, faithes foes, turne fayth about.
> . . . .
>
> *Delight* my spaniell slept, whilst I bausd leaves,
> Tossd ore the dunces, por'd on the old print
> Of titled wordes, and stil my spaniell slept.
> . . . .
>
> At length he wakt and yawned, and by yon sky,
> For aught I know he knew as much as I.

After a wasted youth he "crept abroad," and "Finding my numnesse in this nimble age, / I fell a railing."[125]

---

[119] P. 152.

[120] P. 142. Cf.: study poisons "The nimble spirits in the arteries," *Love's Labor's Lost*, IV, iii, 306; "lean and wasteful learning," *As You Like It*, III, ii, 344–45; "I am not ... lean enough to be thought a good student," *Twelfth Night*, IV, ii, 7–9.

[121] *Plays*, II, 265. Apparently he writes satires (see p. 248).

[122] Pp. 248–49.

[123] See pp. 277–80.

[124] P. 257.

[125] Pp. 257–58.

Dowsecer, in Chapman's *An Humorous Day's Mirth*, is melancholy to such a degree that other characters consider him half mad. The play does not reveal the cause of Dowsecer's melancholy, but its character is highly scholarly. The King of France has heard of his "humour": "they say the young Lord Dowsecer is rarely learned, and nothing lunatic as men suppose, but hateth company, and worldly trash." The King wishes to see and hear him. With others, he conceals himself where he may listen to Dowsecer's discourse (for Dowsecer "will brook no company"). As he enters "contemplating," Dowsecer's first words are a quotation from Cicero. He subsequently moralizes satirically on human vices and on the things which men commonly value. He believes that "men were like giants [once], but pigmies now, yet full of villanies as their skin can hold." The King is deeply impressed by Dowsecer's melancholy eloquence: "Nay, he's more humane than all we are"; Dowsecer's "humour" is "a holy fury, not a frenzy."[126] Dowsecer is a learned and thoughtful man who has been brooding over the spectacle of human frailty.

So strong is the association between melancholy and learning that not only do the scholars of the drama tend to be melancholy but melancholics tend to be scholarly. Bussy D'Ambois, Bosola, and Benatzi are supposed to be scholars.[127] Hamlet is a scholar. Melancholy men so often come upon the stage reading a book that reading almost seems to be a conventional dramatic symptom of melancholy.

VI

In the drama there appears another type-character which, like the malcontent (of whatever variety), is prone to satiric criticism of humanity. Since this type resembles the malcontent rather closely, the difference between the two should be noted. Crites, of Jonson's *Cythia's Revels*, is a sharp-tongued social critic who is nevertheless not a melancholy man. He is "A creature of a most perfect and diuine temper. One, in whom the humours and elements are peaceably met, without emulation of precedencie: he is neyther to phantastikely melancholy, too slowly phlegmaticke, too lightly sanguine, or too rashly cholericke. . . . [Nature] did more then make a man,

---

[126] *Plays*, pp. 31–33. During this scene, Dowsecer's friend Lavel attempts to cure his melancholy. Lavel places before the patient's eyes certain objects calculated to divert his mind from its morbid brooding by reminding him of the normal interests of man (see p. 32). The treatment is unsuccessful. Dowsecer is finally cured by falling in love.

[127] *Ibid.*, p. 143; Webster, *Works*, II, 81; Ford, *Works*, III, 48.

when she made him."[128] In other words, Crites enjoys the perfect temperament, the complexion of the golden mean. I believe that Jonson thought of Asper, the presenter in *Every Man out of His Humour*, as a person of this nature. In the same category I should place Feliche, of Marston's *Antonio and Mellida*, a man "amply suted, with all full content."[129] These are men of sane and penetrating minds and wholesome personalities. They have been roused to virtuous indignation by the spectacle of human sin and folly. In the melancholy character, there is almost always a morbidity.

---

[128] *Jonson*, IV, 74. Cf. "the elements / So mix'd in him that Nature might stand up / And say to all the world, 'This was a man!' "—*Julius Caesar*, V, v, 73-75.

[129] *Plays*, I, 36.

I

THE MALCONTENT CHARACTERS are cut to patterns which are more literary
than scientific. They represent conventions which arose ultimately from
scientific theories regarding melancholy but which are somewhat remote
from their scientific origins. As it appears in the malcontent types, scientific
theory has been considerably modified by unscientific minds. I shall next
endeavor to show a more direct influence of the melancholic theories on
Elizabethan literature—their influence upon the dramatic representation of
grief. In speaking of a more direct influence, I do not mean to imply that
all Elizabethan playwrights pored over scientific treatises. Some probably
read such works; others undoubtedly did not. Those who did not would
have had opportunity to pick up bits of scientific lore from the literary work
or the conversation of men who were better informed.

In the following discussion of pathological grief, I am including shame
and remorse as species in the general category of sorrow. In this I am following the example of Elizabethan psychologists. All of the examples that
I use come from the drama. I find few pertinent passages in prose fiction,
and most of these few are rather indefinitely scientific.[1] The reason may
be that the novels are relatively early. The scientific conception of sorrow
does not appear frequently in any genre until about 1600. At about this
time, apparently, assimilation of scientific theory among the intellectuals
had reached the point at which they felt sufficiently at home with it to make
literary use of it. Few of the plays from which I quote in the following
pages were written earlier.

II

Elizabethan playwrights often use phraseology which shows that they are
thinking in terms of the contemporary physiology of grief. Evidently they
expect what they write to mean something to at least the better educated

---

[1] There are, of course, exceptions. Two passages in *Pandosto*, for instance, show that
Greene had a specific knowledge of the pathology of grief (*Works*, IV, 253, 261). In
the same novel, the hero kills himself in a "melancholy fit" (p. 317).

part of the audience. The Renaissance physiologist believes that immoderate sorrow deprives the body of the natural heat and moisture which reside in the vital spirit of the blood (see above, pp. 12–14). The constriction of the grief-stricken heart prevents generation and distribution of spirit. Through loss of spirit, the blood degenerates into cold, dry melancholy. Grief, furthermore, stimulates the spleen to emit melancholy, which chills and dries the vital spirit and the heart. Grief means loss of blood and increase of melancholy. Since cold and dryness, the qualities of melancholy, are inimical to life, the grief-stricken person becomes thin and ill. He may die. Immoderate sorrow is a disease.[2]

Several examples of phraseology showing the influence of these ideas occur in Shakespeare's plays. At their final parting, Romeo says to Juliet, "Dry sorrow drinks our blood" (III, v, 59). In *The Merchant of Venice* Antonio declares that

> These griefs and losses have so bated me,
> That I shall hardly spare a pound of flesh. (III, iii, 32–33)

In *Pericles* Dionyza counsels Marina not to "Consume" her blood with grieving: "Lord! how your favour's chang'd / With this unprofitable woe" (IV, i, 22–25). Christopher Sly, in *The Taming of the Shrew*, is told that

> too much sadness hath congeal'd your blood,
> And melancholy is the nurse of frenzy.[3]

In *Much Ado About Nothing* Hero swoons when falsely accused of immoral conduct. "These things come thus to light," says Don John, "Smother her spirits up" (IV, i, 112–13). Her too credulous father hopes that her dishonor will kill her, that her "spirits" will not prove "stronger than [her] shames" (IV, i, 127). In *Cymbeline* the remorseful Iachimo feels his spirits "Quail" as he recalls his misdeeds: "Give me leave; I faint" (V, v, 150). Imogen, of the same play, sickens as a result of grief (IV, ii, 1–60). Her friends attribute her apparent death to "melancholy" (IV, ii, 203, 208). In *Antony and Cleopatra* Enobarbus says that his heart is "dried with grief" (IV, ix, 17).

---

[2] Grief may have noxious effects other than those mentioned, such as suffocation of the heart, burning of the heart, and breaking of the heart (see Chap. I, notes 49, 60, 62). There are many references to these in the Elizabethan drama, but since they are not melancholic phenomena, I shall disregard them in the sections which follow.

[3] Induction, ii, 134–35. Physicians have directed that he see a play for the sake of "mirth and merriment, / Which bars a thousand harms and lengthens life."—induction, ii, 137–38. Cf. "life-harming heaviness," *Richard II*, II, ii, 3; "care's an enemy to life," *Twelfth Night*, I, iii, 3; "excessive grief [is] the enemy to the living," *All's Well That Ends Well*, I, i, 66.

Similar evidence of scientific influence appears in the language of other playwrights. In Jonson's *The Case Is Altered* an unhappy lady explains her sober demeanor:

> as my lookes appeare, such is my spirit,
> Drown'd vp with confluence of griefe, and melancholy,
> That like to riuers run through all my vaines,
> Quenching the pride and feruour of my bloud.[4]

In Marston's *Antonio and Mellida* Andrugio attempts to comfort Antonio: "Son, heat thy bloode, be not frose up with grief."[5] The central character of Marston's *The Malcontent* hopes to see his enemy Pietro afflicted by grief: "Leane thoughtfulnes . . . Sucke thy veines drie, distemperance rob thy sleepe." His hopes are fulfilled; Pietro later fears that he will die of sorrow, which

> sucks veines drye,
> Rivels the skinne, casts ashes in mens faces,
> Be-duls the eye, unstrengthens all the blood.[6]

Bussy D'Ambois observes that "grief's a natural sickness of the blood."[7] In *Four Plays in One* there is mention of a grief which "feeds within upon [the] spirits."[8] Vitelli, of Massinger's *The Renegado*, wishes that his grief would kill him "By choaking up at once [his] vital spirits."[9]

Many dramatic characters die of grief. Shirley, in *The Politician*, suggests the physiological process by which such a death occurs. Haraldus, a sensitive youth, hears a tale which grieves him deeply. He feels it "strike upon [his] spirits," develops "a melancholy," and becomes dangerously ill. Attending physicians diagnose the case accurately. His mother succeeds in cheering and reviving him somewhat; but when his mind returns to his distress, his "spirits faint" and he dies.[10]

III

The mental states and the behavior of dramatic characters stricken with grief likewise show the influence of scientific theory. In some cases, of

---

[4] *Jonson*, III, 121.
[5] *Plays*, I, 51.
[6] *Ibid.*, I, 150, 167.
[7] Chapman, *Plays*, p. 162.
[8] *Beaumont and Fletcher*, X, 348.
[9] *Plays*, II, 227. Cf. *The Bondman, ibid.*, p. 113.
[10] *Works*, V, 132, 147–50.

course, the influence is clearer than in others. It is a fair assumption that when an Elizabethan dramatist refers to a character as "melancholy," he has black bile and its symptoms in mind. In many cases, however, the symptoms do not appear plainly in the lines of the play. In *Soliman and Perseda*, for instance, the playwright makes much of the fact that affliction has rendered Erastus melancholy, but the only definite symptom is Erastus' black clothing.[11] Webster makes it very clear, in *The Duchess of Malfi*, that the unfortunate heroine is melancholy but furnishes no symptomatic details unless her premonition of madness may be considered such.[12] In choosing illustrations, I have confined myself to cases in which the scientific influence is clearer and more specific.

A great sorrow, because it engenders the melancholy humor, leads to lethargic misery. A passage from La Primaudaye's *Academie* will serve as reminder of what has been said earlier on this subject (pp. 31–33):

this blacke melancholy humour ... will make the spirit & mind darkish, whereby it groweth to be blockish, & the heart loseth al his cheerefulnes. And because the braine is cooled therby, it waxeth very heauy & drowsie. Now when griefe is in great measure, it bringeth withall a kinde of loathing & tediousnes, which causeth a man to hate & to be weary of all things, euen of the light & of a mans selfe so that he shal take pleasure in nothing but in his melancholy ... refusing all ioy & consolation. To conclude, some grow so far as to hate themselues, & so fall to despaire, yea many kil & destroy themselues.[13]

Because it cools and deadens the spirits, melancholy produces a physical torpor; a sensory and mental dullness, which sometimes suspends the powers of hearing and speech; and a heavy, despondent lassitude in which the patient finds the world and his own life wearisome and distasteful, contemns himself, and has suicidal impulses.

Lyly's King Midas, understandably grieved by Apollo's gift of an ass's ears, develops just such a heaviness and drowsiness, just such a loathing and tediousness. He sits in "a traunce ... where nature cannot moue, nor counsaile, nor musick, nor phisicke, nor daunger, nor death, nor all." His daughter wonders why "musick (a methridat for melancholy) should make him mad."[14] He will admit no one but his barber to his presence. He has become testy and suspicious and is irresolute in handling the affairs of the kingdom. He is cured when Apollo relieves him of his ass's ears. In the Shakespearean *Pericles* the central character, having heard a false report of

---

[11] Kyd, *Works*, pp. 201, 205–6.
[12] *Works*, II, 94.
[13] P. 467.
[14] *Midas*, in *Works*, III, 150.

his daughter's death, sits dully brooding in a similar melancholic lethargy. He hears nothing; he has not spoken for three months. His attendants despair of his cure.[15]

The Count St. Anne, of Chapman's *Monsieur D'Olive*, has become melancholy as a consequence of his wife's death. He spends his days in seclusion and darkness mourning over the body, which he has had preserved against corruption and refuses to bury. Clad "like a mortified hermit," he sits at her feet "weeping out his life."[16] In yielding to his grief, he says, he has experienced

> A kind of false, sluggish, and rotting sweetness
> Mix'd with an humour where all things in life
> Lie drown'd in sour, wretched, and horrid thoughts.

He has lain "Whole days and nights" contemplating suicide.[17] Another case of torpid despondency occurs in *A Wife for a Month*. Alphonso, grieving over his father's death, has sunk into a "sad and silent melancholy."[18] He has not spoken since the hour in which his father died.[19] He cares for nothing apparently but weeping over his father's tomb. He is growing worse daily, and the affairs of his kingdom meanwhile cry out for his attention.

IV

In Shakespeare's Hamlet the wretched lethargy characteristic of the melancholy man appears once more. In this case, however, the physical and sensory symptoms are lacking. Hamlet's melancholic lassitude is a purely intellectual phenomenon.

To Hamlet all the uses of this world have become "weary, stale, flat, and unprofitable" (I, ii, 133), and he feels an apathetic indifference toward everything which once pleased or inspired him:

I have of late . . . lost all my mirth, forgone all custom of exercises; and indeed it goes so heavily with my disposition that this goodly frame, the earth, seems to me a sterile promontory; this most excellent canopy, the air, look you, this brave

---

[15] V, i, 24, 47, 53. Pericles' condition is referred to as a "melancholy state" (V, i, 222). He has previously suffered from melancholy (see below, note 91).

[16] *Plays*, p. 115.

[17] P. 126. Under similar circumstances, Hippolito, of Dekker's *The Honest Whore (I)*, acts much as St. Anne does (*Works* [London, 1873], II, 32, 54).

[18] *Beaumont and Fletcher*, V, 9.

[19] P. 27.

o'erhanging firmament, this majestical roof fretted with golden fire, why, it appears no other thing to me but a foul and pestilent congregation of vapours. (II, ii, 313–22)

He is wearily disillusioned. His satirical outbursts, which resemble the railing of the malcontent, reveal a deep cynicism. His self-castigations reveal a deep disgust with himself. He finds life a loathsome and tedious business which he would like to be done with: "O! that this too too solid flesh would melt...." (I, ii, 129); "To be, or not to be...." (III, i, 56). Ophelia's characterization of the Hamlet of former days (III, i, 159–70) indicates that this state of mind is a recent development, the result of recent griefs and frustrations.

The subject of Hamlet's melancholy has been bewritten to the point of appalling confusion.[20] I shall not greatly confound the confusion, I hope, if I consider two rather significant questions. First, is Hamlet, as Shakespeare conceives him, suffering merely from a vague depression of spirit like Antonio's melancholy at the opening of *The Merchant of Venice*, or is Hamlet's psychic condition definitely pathological? Second, if the latter is true, to what extent is the Elizabethan concept of melancholy useful in the interpretation of the character?

As for the first of these questions, both Claudius and Hamlet himself refer to Hamlet's condition as "melancholy" in contexts which indicate that the playwright is using the word with full consciousness of its medical and psychiatric implications. Claudius believes that there is something in Hamlet's soul

> O'er which his melancholy sits on brood . . .
> [A] something-settled matter in his heart,
> Whereon his brains still beating puts him thus
> From fashion of himself. (III, i, 174–84)

This is the moody preoccupation with the single idea which is characteristic of the melancholy man (see Chap. III, note 7). A voyage to England, says the King, should give Hamlet diversion of therapeutic value (see above, p. 39).

Perhaps what Claudius says is pertinent only to Hamlet's assumed character (yet Claudius does not seem altogether deceived by Hamlet's antic disposition). This could hardly be true, however, of Hamlet's own state-

---

[20] It would be impossible to list all the literature on the subject, not to speak of attempting evaluation of the innumerable items. A. C. Bradley (*Shakespearean Tragedy* [London, 1905], pp. 108–28) is, in my opinion, substantially right. All of the melancholic traits appearing in Hamlet, it should be noted, were traditional and commonplace. It is not necessary to assume that Shakespeare had read a book about melancholy.

ment in soliloquy. Hamlet wishes to assure himself that the Ghost is an "honest ghost." The spirit that he has seen "May be the devil," who perhaps

> Out of my weakness and my melancholy—
> As he is very potent with such spirits—
> Abuses me to damn me. (II, ii, 636–40)

Behind this passage lies the idea, so voluminously discussed in psychiatric and pious works (see above, pp. 49–53), of the Devil's practice of victimizing melancholy men.[21] These lines had a cogent and sinister meaning to the Elizabethans.

If one could define the conception of Hamlet which the Globe audience formed, he would have the answer to the question concerning Shakespeare's intention, for Shakespeare was too completely master of his craft and too intimately acquainted with his audience ever to present a hero who would be misunderstood. The Globe spectator, I believe, would quickly and confidently have recognized Hamlet as a melancholy man (not a madman). The Elizabethans were very ready to expect melancholy in anyone suffering from grief and frustration. Hamlet's black clothing and moody unsociability in the second scene would have been taken as significant indications. His morose brooding, his weary despondency, his suicidal impulses, his cynical satire, his sudden changes of mood and unpredictable fits and starts of rash activity[22] are all in keeping with the Elizabethan idea of the melancholic. The melancholy man, moreover, is traditionally a person who reflects rather than acts, who is painfully circumspect and very much inclined to "thinking too precisely on the event."[23]

---

[21] Cf. John E. Hankins, *The Character of Hamlet and Other Essays* (Chapel Hill, N. C., 1941), pp. 166–71.

[22] "*Humorous* they are beyond all measure, sometimes profusely laughing, extraordinary merry, and then again weeping without a cause."—Burton, *Anatomy*, I, 452. "*Inconstant* they are in all their actions, vertiginous, restless, unapt to resolve of any business, they will and will not, persuaded to and fro. . . ."—*Ibid.*, p. 450. The reason for the melancholic's traditional inconstancy of mood appears above, p. 35.

[23] IV, iv, 41. Melancholy men "be studious . . . they thinke nothing sure," *Regimen Sanitatis Salerni*, fol. cxliii; the melancholy man is "Suspitious," has "A wary wit" and "a spirit little daring," *The School of Salernum*, tr. Sir John Harington, ed. Packard (New York, 1920), p. 140; the melancholic is "doubtfull before, and long in deliberation: suspicious, painefull in studie, and circumspect," Bright, *Treatise*, p. 124; "melancholy breedeth a ielousie of doubt . . . and causeth [melancholics] to be the more exact & curious in pondering the very moments of things," *ibid.*, p. 130; melancholics "be not so apt for action," *ibid.*, p. 200; "in delayes" melancholy Saturnists surpass "*Scipio*, and *Fabius*," Greene, *Planetomachia*, in *Works*, V, 50; the melancholy man "thinks busines, but never does any: he is all contemplation no action," *Overburian Characters*, p. 22; melancholy men's "irresolution, inconstancy . . . care, jealousy, suspicion, &c. continues, and they cannot be relieved," Burton, *Anatomy*, I, 448; they are "*cogitabundi* still, very intent," *ibid.*, p. 451.

If, then, Hamlet's creator thought of him as definitely melancholy in the usual Elizabethan sense, how useful is the Elizabethan concept of melancholy in interpretation?[24] There may be subtleties in Hamlet's personality and behavior which this concept cannot explain. It may be that a knowledge of human nature is more necessary to the understanding of Hamlet than a knowledge of Elizabethan melancholy. Yet it would be patently absurd to ignore commonplace ideas of which Shakespeare was certainly conscious and which Hamlet's speech and deportment certainly suggested to the spectators in the Globe.

To Elizabethan playgoers Hamlet's melancholy would seem quite sufficient explanation for his procrastination. To them the play would be no mystery. In their eyes Hamlet would be a tragic character because he had become passion's slave, because he had failed to master his grief. This failure in self-mastery, they would perceive, had resulted in the atrophy of powers which were urgently necessary to the solution of his problem.

A word also concerning the relationship between Shakespeare's *Hamlet* and the older play on which it was based. The melancholy of the uncouth hero of the earlier drama[25] would have suggested to Shakespeare that his own protagonist should be melancholy and might have led some playgoers to expect melancholy in Shakespeare's Hamlet. The elder hero's melancholy, however, has no real dramatic meaning. Its function is merely to make of him such a psychopathological oddity as appealed to the Elizabethan taste. He is prevented from killing the King not by his condition of mind, but by a tangible difficulty—the royal guards. As various commentators have noted, Shakespeare has minimized the guards. The mental state of the hero, which I believe Shakespeare would have called "melancholy," becomes dramatically significant as the impediment to action. The conflict is now subjective rather than objective; the interest has shifted from circumstance to character; the grotesque eccentric of the older play has become a dignified and human tragic hero.

The apathetic and cynical disillusionment which appears in Hamlet is

---

[24] J. Q. Adams has utilized descriptions of melancholia in modern psychiatric works. See his edition of *Hamlet* (Boston, 1929), pp. 195–298.

[25] I am assuming that *Der Bestrafte Brudermord* truly represents the *Ur-Hamlet*. In the German play Hamlet's "Melancholie" is referred to four times. See the reprint in W. Creizenach's *Die Schauspiele der Englischen Komödianten* (Berlin-Stuttgart, 1899), pp. 158, 159, 170, 183. In the first two cases the word clearly refers to Hamlet's condition before his feigned madness. Because Hamlet is "melancholish," the King offers to summon physicians (p. 159). Hamlet is a melancholy man also in Belleforest's version of the tale. Belleforest attributes Hamlet's powers of divination (exhibited at the English court) to melancholy and the Devil (*The Sources of* Hamlet, ed. Israel Gollancz [London, 1926], pp. 236–39). There is no perceptible melancholy in the Hamlet of Saxo Grammaticus' version.

evident in many other melancholy characters. Hamlet is the most perfect example of a type which cuts across types. Philomusus of the Parnassus trilogy, Dowsecer of Chapman's *An Humorous Day's Mirth*, Lampatho of Marston's *What You Will*, Jaques of *As You Like It*, Malevole of *The Malcontent*, and others are pessimists of the Hamlet type. In such characters as these the despondency of the late English Renaissance seems to become articulate. Like Hamlet, also, many other melancholy persons become weary of their lives and feel the impulse to kill themselves. The melancholy man is inclined to seek death, for he finds life a wretchedly tedious affair:

> Death fears me, for in troth I seek him out.
> The sun is stale to me; to-morrow morn,
> As this, 'twill rise: I see no difference.
> The night doth visit me but in one robe,
> She brings as many thoughts as she wears stars,
> When she is pleasant, but no rest at all.
> For what new strange thing should I covet life, then?[26]

V

A frequent result of melancholy, according to medical authorities, is halluci-nation—usually fearful—due to the corruption of the physical instruments of the mind, especially the animal spirit, by the melancholy humor or its vapors (see above, pp. 42 ff.). Several melancholic characters of the drama suffer from hallucination.

Melancholic optical delusion, which is frequently mentioned in scientific works, occurs in Webster's *The White Devil*. Francisco de Medici, brood-ing over the murder of his sister, closes his eyes and sees her image "in a melancholicke thought." The figment of his imagination is so vivid that it might, he thinks, be a specter. He reminds himself, however, that its cause is "Common as sickenesse. 'Tis my melancholy."[27] In *The Duchess of Malfi*, the melancholy Bosola is troubled by visions of the Duchess, whom he has murdered: "Still me thinkes the Dutchesse / Haunts me: there, there! ... 'tis nothing but my mellancholy."[28] In *The Witch of Edmonton*, by Dekker and Ford, Frank Thorney lies seriously ill as a result of a wound and of remorse for the murder of his wife. He sleeps badly, eats little, and reflects

---

[26] Field, *A Woman Is a Weathercock*, in *Old Plays*, ed. Dodsley and Hazlitt, XI, 61. This speech is uttered by Scudmore, who has been rendered melancholy by the perfidy of his love (see especially p. 31).

[27] *Works*, I, 152.

[28] *Ibid.*, II, 116.

on death, which he half desires.[29] Standing at his bedside, he sees *"The spirit of* Susan," which he explains as "my fancy; / Some windmill in my brains for want of sleep."[30] The hero of Glapthorne's *Albertus Wallenstein,* stricken by remorse for the killing of his son and his son's sweetheart, likewise sees ghastly apparitions. He is shaken with "Strange horrors"; his mind, he thinks, is diseased "past cure"; his sleep is troubled with fearful dreams.[31] Just before he is murdered he sees a vision of the dead lovers

> in their shrowds,
> Pale and as meager, as they had convers'd
> A yeere with the inhabitants of the earth.

They seem to be inviting him to "visit them in their cold Urnes."[32]

In Massinger's *A Very Woman,* Almira, distracted by grief, has auditory illusions. Laying her ear to the ground, she hears the cries of a man whom she believes to be suffering torment in hell.[33] A lady in Webster's *The Devil's Law-Case,* melancholically disordered by news of her lover's death, also hears strange things:

> Ha, ha, what say you?
> I doe talke to somewhat, me thinks; it may be
> My evill Genius. Doe not the Bells ring?
> I have a strange noyse in my head.[34]

Since melancholy is supposed to disorder the imagination greatly, many characters of the drama, including some already mentioned, go insane as a result of grief or remorse.[35] Their irrationality is manifested in mad fancies (sometimes the single fixed idea so often associated with melancholy) and in extravagant conduct of various sorts which corresponds more or less closely with the symptoms of melancholy described by the scientists.

In Webster's *The Duchess of Malfi,* Duke Ferdinand, deranged by re-

---

[29] Ford, *Works,* III, 247–49.

[30] Pp. 250–51.

[31] *Plays and Poems* (London, 1874), II, 63, 66, 67.

[32] Pp. 78–79. Wallenstein refers to his "sad distemper," his "melancholy" (p. 76). A "sullen humour" possesses his "much distemper'd faculties" (p. 74). Premonitory fear seems to contribute to Wallenstein's melancholy.

[33] *Plays,* IV, 268–69.

[34] *Works,* II, 281–82. "The melancholly humour flowes in [her] face" (p. 287). The hearing of "Bells" is a peculiarly definite symptom. See above, p. 42.

[35] An early dramatic passage associating melancholy with insanity occurs in *A Comedy of Errors.* The Abbess considers Antipholus' apparent madness a "moody moping, and dull melancholy" (V, i, 79). She explains it as due to his wife's nagging, which has hindered his sleep and digestion.

morse for the murder of his sister, imagines that he is a wolf. The attending physician explains that the Duke's malady is called lycanthropia (see above, p. 44), that it is due to an excess of the melancholy humor, and that it prompts men to visit churchyards by night and dig dead bodies from their graves:

> two nights since
> One met the Duke, 'bout midnight in a lane
> Behind St. *Markes* Church, with the leg of a man
> Upon his shoulder; and he howl'd fearefully:
> Said he was a Woolffe: onely the difference
> Was, a Woolffes skinne was hairy on the out-side,
> His on the In-side: bad them take their swords,
> Rip up his flesh, and trie.[36]

When Ferdinand enters he reveals a distaste for company, throws himself on his own shadow and tries to throttle it, and talks most irrationally. The doctor makes futile therapeutic efforts. Ferdinand is still mad when, near the close of the play, he is killed.

The fixed idea (see above, pp. 42–47) appears in Massinger's *The Duke of Milan.* Sforza has killed his wife in a fit of jealousy. He grieves so passionately that the attending physicians, to prevent his doing violence, cry out that her wound has not been mortal. From this time forward, having fallen into a "melancholy . . . ending in distraction,"[37] Sforza firmly believes that the beautiful corpse is a living body. He hovers continually over the body and thinks of nothing but his wife's expected recovery. The doctors fear that "He's past hope."[38] Still out of his mind, he is horribly poisoned by an enemy.

Aeglamour, of Jonson's *The Sad Shepherd,* has various chimerical notions. He has "falne into a deepe Melancholy"[39] at the false report that his sweetheart Earine has drowned. He avoids company and sometimes "sits, and thinkes all day, then walkes, / Then thinkes againe; and sighes, weeps, laughs, and talkes."[40] His wits are gone. He imagines that river nymphs have pulled his beloved into the water and plans revenge upon them. To his "deepe hurt Phant'sie," it seems that nature has sickened since her death.[41]

---

[36] *Works,* II, 106–7. Weyer tells the story of a man who stoutly asserted that he differed from a wolf only "in pelle cum pilis inuersa."—*De Praestigiis,* p. 420.

[37] *Plays,* I, 334.

[38] P. 339. In Massinger's *A Very Woman,* Almira, disordered by grief (see *Plays,* IV, 267) develops the delusion that her lover is dead (p. 268).

[39] *Jonson,* VII, 8.

[40] P. 17.

[41] P. 18.

He declares that in heaven Earine is instructing the planets in harmony.[42] And he has other fancies. His sympathetic companions fear that he will die and do their best to help him. They endeavor to soothe him by humoring his fancies ("You should not crosse him") and by music.[43] Apparently Jonson meant to cure him by reunion with his beloved, but the play is unfinished.

Ford's *The Lover's Melancholy*, a play avowedly indebted to Burton,[44] contains two studies in psychopathology. In Prince Palador, Ford presents a study of love melancholy, to be discussed later. In Meleander he presents a study in the pathology of grief. Meleander has been deprived of wealth and dignities by the late Prince of Cyprus and has been forced, because of unspecified dangers, to part with his beloved daughter Eroclea, whom he has sent abroad. As a result of these afflictions, the old man suffers from a melancholy verging on insanity. He is hairy and unkempt; he is very lean, for he neglects to eat; he suffers from insomnia; throngs of perturbing thoughts ("rude divisions") trouble his peace and sleep; his dreams are funereal.[45] He has fits when he chafes, fumes, roars, thunders; he once comes upon the stage waving a poleax dangerously.[46] He rails at visitors from the court in the fashion of the malcontent.[47] Meleander's mind runs on death. Three times he speaks as though his own were not far away.[48] He has thoughts of suicide: "The hangman is a rare physician."[49]

The list of melancholy madmen could be considerably extended by including all the characters in the Elizabethan drama who are crazed by grief—characters such as Hieronimo, his wife Isabella, Titus Andronicus, Constance of Shakespeare's *King John* (see IV, ii, 122), Ophelia, Lear, Lucibella of Chettle's *Hoffman*, Cornelia of Webster's *The White Devil*, the "Tyrant" of *The Second Maiden's Tragedy*, etc. The Elizabethan audience doubtless

---

[42] Pp. 45–46.

[43] Pp. 17, 19–20.

[44] Ford acknowledges his debt to Burton in a marginal note ("Vide *Democritus Junior*") opposite a passage on the nature of melancholy (*Works*, I, 52). Many details in *The Lover's Melancholy* can be traced to Burton. Indeed the *Anatomy* seems to have been the inspiration of the entire play, which is little more than a study in melancholic abnormalities and cures. G. F. Sensabaugh (*The Tragic Muse of John Ford* [Stanford, Cal., 1944], pp. 36–42, 47–50, 63–64, 75–78) and S. Blaine Ewing (*Burtonian Melancholy in the Plays of John Ford* [Princeton, 1940], pp. 32–46) have studied the relation between this play and Burton's *Anatomy* in some detail. See also Mary Edith Cochnower, "John Ford," in *Seventeenth Century Studies*, ed. Robert Shafer (Princeton, 1933), pp. 121–275.

[45] *Works*, I, 43–44, 77–78. See above, pp. 29–33.

[46] Pp. 73–75.

[47] Pp. 45–46. See also p. 76.

[48] Pp. 46, 75, 79.

[49] P. 76.

thought vaguely of any madness due to grief as melancholy madness. With one exception,[50] however, the word *melancholy* is never used in connection with any of the persons just named, and their symptoms are only very vaguely melancholic. It seems best to confine this discussion to cases in which the playwright very clearly intended to represent melancholy as the Renaissance physician understood the term.

VI

In the plays of Massinger there occur two cases of melancholy distraction which are evidently related to the concept of religious melancholy expounded in scientific works (see above, pp. 50–52). In *The Renegado* reversals of fortune and remorse for his sins have unsettled the wits of the pirate Grimaldi. He becomes convinced that he is damned.[51] He is especially repentant for a blasphemy committed at the altar of a certain cathedral and consequently never hears mention of "The church, or the high altar, but his melancholy / Grows and increases on him."[52] Cardenes, of *A Very Woman*, dishonorably provokes a duel, in which he is severely wounded. As he lies abed, he reflects on his disgraceful conduct and is overcome with shame. The attending physician reports that, although the wound is healing,

> melancholy,
> And at the height, too, near akin to madness,
> Possesses him; his senses are distracted,
> Not one, but all.[53]

His discourse, which reveals that he is something of a scholar and thinker, is darkly despondent. He is obsessed with the idea that he has proved himself irredeemably vile: "I am a beast. . . . And like a beast I make my blood my master."[54] He has lost the will to live.[55]

VII

The Elizabethan drama is notable for the number of its psychopathic characters. It is notable also for the number of physicians who appear on the

---

50 Hieronimo's madness is once referred to as "melanchollie" (Kyd, *Works*, p. 64).
51 *Plays*, II, 174–76.
52 P. 189. Grimaldi is said to have gone mad (p. 217).
53 *Ibid.*, IV, 265. The doctor seems to be referring to the internal senses: common sense, imagination, and memory (see Burton, *Anatomy*, I, 180).
54 Massinger, *Plays*, IV, 292.
55 P. 308.

stage to give psychiatric treatment and for the frequency with which such treatment is represented. I shall review some cases in which the cure of melancholy, by such therapeutic methods as the medical writers recommend (see above, pp. 38–41, 54), is dramatized in Elizabethan plays.

Obviously melancholy may sometimes be cured by eliminating the cause of grief. "Many are instantly cured, when their minds are satisfied."[56] Lyly's Midas recovers when Apollo relieves him of his ass's ears, and other melancholy characters are similarly cured by a fortunate turn of events. When the cure is as simple as this, the writer seldom draws upon medical lore. Yet I have found two cases in which the playwright attempts to make a cure of this kind a matter of some scientific interest—the cases of Pericles and Meleander.

In *Pericles* the hero is restored to health by the artful ministrations of his daughter Marina (V, i, 64–201). Pericles' melancholy is due to his belief that Marina is dead. It might seem that she would need merely to present herself before her father to cure him. But since Pericles has sunk into a coma in which he neither sees, hears, nor speaks, the cure is not so easy. Before Marina can convince him that she is alive, she must make him see and hear her. First she sings to him. Physicians recommend cheerful music for melancholy patients because it enlivens the vital spirit and thus animates the entire system. Although Pericles seems to pay no heed, the music evidently stirs his spirit to the extent that he can hear what she subsequently says. She tells the story of her own misfortunes and compares them with his own. Her purpose evidently is to awaken his interest and to inspire fellow feeling and confidence. Medical writers emphasize the importance of winning the patient's confidence. Her story produces a decided reaction. Pericles rouses himself, speaks at first brokenly, then more fluently, notices Marina's resemblance to her mother, questions her, discovers that she is his supposedly dead daughter. The cure is soon complete.

In Ford's *The Lover's Melancholy*, Meleander's melancholy is due to the loss of his wealth and dignities and to his separation from his daughter Eroclea. The learned physician Corax, who has been summoned from the university to attend the lovesick Prince Palador, undertakes the treatment of Meleander also. Corax displays some rather hazy Burtonian lore in a brief discourse on melancholy for the benefit of two inquisitive courtiers and in a "Masque of Melancholy," an instructive entertainment which he arranges for the court.[57] Two scenes of the play show the doctor at work in his treatment of Meleander. In the earlier one,[58] he puts on a hideous

---

[56] Burton, *Anatomy*, II, 126.
[57] *Works*, I, 52–53, 63–68. The masque is discussed below.
[58] Pp. 75–79.

mask and replies to the patient's insane storming in kind, apparently following the theory that, in dealing with a demented patient, one should intimidate him by simulating a madness as violent as his own.[59] Meleander becomes milder. Corax, adapting his method to the patient's mood,[60] begins to humor him, agrees with everything that he says, even feigns melancholy in order to inspire sympathetic confidence. At the close of the scene, the patient does not seem greatly improved. It happens to be possible to return to Meleander his dignities and his daughter. Corax arranges a dramatic restoration. He administers a sleeping potion (good medical practice), and after a restful slumber, the patient is awakened by music. Then Meleander's various former titles and his long-absent daughter (Corax refers to these as "physic" and "cordial"[61]) are presented to him in rapid succession. The patient recovers. Corax, incidentally, is not necessary to Meleander's cure, for good fortune would have come to him anyway.

In Chapman's *Monsieur D'Olive* the Count St. Anne is cured of his melancholy torpor by the orthodox device of diverting the patient's mind from sorrow by arousing another passion; "as one pinne is driuen out with another, so the later may expell the former."[62] The Count's brother-in-law, Vandome, a skillful psychologist, undertakes to "dissolve / His settled melancholy . . . fire his heavy spirits."[63] Realizing that one should comfort, "persuade," and "advise" a melancholy man,[64] he first does what he can with cheerful discourse and good counsel. He succeeds in talking St. Anne into a more sanguine and more rational state of mind and prevails upon him to bury the body of his dead wife, thus removing a reminder of grief. Vandome then contrives to make the Count fall in love, and love effects a complete cure.[65]

Grimaldi, of Massinger's *The Renegado*, and Cardenes, of Massinger's *A Very Woman*, are cured of their melancholy despair by the strategy of

[59] Cf. "I'll buffet his madnesse out of him. . . . I must do mad trickes with him, / For that's the onely way on't. . . . Now he begins / To feare me . . . ," Webster, *The Duchess of Malfi*, in *Works*, II, 107–8; "a Bedlam cannot cure him," Ford, *Perkin Warbeck*, in *Works*, II, 211. I find a disapproving reference to this method in Burton, *Anatomy*, II, 127.

[60] See Du Laurens, *Discourse*, pp. 106–7; Burton, *Anatomy*, II, 130–31. Corax (or Ford) violates a rule of mental therapy in reminding Meleander of the loss of his daughter (p. 77).

[61] Ford, *Works*, I, 98, 99. Elizabethan physicians would not approve of such great emotional disturbance as that to which Corax subjects his patient in this scene. See Bright, *Treatise*, p. 252.

[62] Bright, *Treatise*, p. 256.

[63] *Plays*, p. 121.

[64] Burton, *Anatomy*, II, 129.

[65] See Chapman, *Plays*, pp. 126–27, 130–31. Dowsecer, of Chapman's *An Humorous Day's Mirth*, and Almira, of Massinger's *A Very Woman*, are likewise cured by falling in love.

deception which medical writers recommend for the treatment of patients suffering from hallucination or obsession ("some feigned lie, strange news, witty device, artificial invention"[66]). Grimaldi's melancholy is due largely to remorse for a blasphemy committed at a cathedral altar. He has conceived the idea that only the bishop in whose presence he sinned can absolve him. A benevolent Jesuit undertakes to cure his "wounded conscience."[67] He impersonates the bishop and tells Grimaldi that the sin is pardoned.[68] Grimaldi is restored to spiritual and mental health. Cardenes is obsessed with the idea that he is vile beyond redemption and wishes to die. He is attended by the ingenious physician Paulo, whose task is to encourage hope and counteract despair. According to his own account, Paulo does so by presenting before the patient a series of moral lessons in the form of dramatic spectacles. His equipment for this, it seems, is very elaborate; he has fitted Cardenes' chamber

> With trapdoors, and descents; sometimes presenting
> Good spirits of the air, bad of the earth.[69]

Cardenes' disordered mind scarcely distinguishes the doctor's fantastic inventions from realities. Toward the end of the play, the spectator sees the doctor at work. Paulo appears disguised successively as a friar, a soldier, and a philosopher to offer encouragement, good example, and instruction.[70] His strategy is wholly successful.

Although his case seems hopeless, Alphonso, of *A Wife for a Month*, is cured by a pharmaceutical accident. A villain comes to the sick man's attendants with a deadly poison, representing it as a medicine which "will in half a day dissolve his melancholy."[71] The effect of the poison is to torture Alphonso with unendurable internal heat.[72] Instead of dying, however, he recovers perfect health of body and mind. The heat generated by the poison and the cold melancholy humor have neutralized each other. The poison

---

[66] Burton, *Anatomy*, II, 131.
[67] *Plays*, II, 176.
[68] Pp. 192–94.
[69] *Ibid.*, IV, 307.
[70] Pp. 308–15. Paulo's procedure is orthodox throughout. He protects the patient from reminders of his grief (p. 265) and will not allow attending surgeons to shut him in a dark room (p. 291). Locking demented persons in dark rooms was common practice in Elizabethan England. According to medical writers, however, a melancholy patient should be kept in lightsome surroundings as much as possible. Strangely, the Jesuit who cures Grimaldi directs that he be kept in solitude and darkness (*ibid.*, II, 191). In *The Two Noble Kinsmen*, the physician attending the jailer's daughter, victim of a melancholy madness due to disappointed love, prescribes a dark room (*Beaumont and Fletcher*, IX, 357).
[71] *Beaumont and Fletcher*, V, 41.
[72] P. 54.

> wrought upon the dull cold misty parts,
> That clog'd his soul, which was another poison
> . . . . . . had the malitious villain
> Given him a cooling poison, he had paid him.[73]

Accidental bloodletting effects a cure in *The Nice Valour, or the Passionate Madman*. In this play there appears an anonymous "passionate Lord" distracted by an unspecified cause. He goes repeatedly through a cycle of four distinct forms of dementia:[74] lovesickness, morosely meditative melancholy, insane anger, and crazy mirth. The first two clearly are forms of melancholia; the last two may be intended respectively as the forms of melancholy arising from choler and blood adust. The passionate madman's compound insanity is obviously unscientific. Evidently the playwright has afflicted one character with four mental maladies simply to make a more abundant and more diversified psychopathological display on the stage. Toward the end of the play, the madman offends a soldier, is severely wounded in the fight which ensues, and loses much blood. When he has recovered from his wound, he has recovered his wits.[75]

VIII

The types of physical and mental degeneration which I have discussed would not have appeared in the drama if the playwrights had not been influenced, directly or indirectly, by the pathology of grief expounded in scientific works. The exact extent of the scientific influence would be very hard to determine, for it is often subtle and elusive. But the foregoing pages have shown, I believe, that most of the principal dramatists give at least occasional evidence of acquaintanceship with scientific theories regarding grief. Evidently they assume that the audience has scientific interests like their own.

My collection of dramatic case histories includes several which illustrate the tendency among Elizabethan playwrights to dramatize psychological conflict. In *Pericles*, *A Wife for a Month*, and *Monsieur D'Olive*, for instance, the potentially tragic force is not a personal antagonist, not a set of circumstances, but simply the sorrow in the central character's own mind. The drama, whether or not it is good drama, is fundamentally subjective.

In psychological conflicts such as these, thoughtful Elizabethans must

---

[73] P. 59.
[74] See *ibid.*, X, 145–46, 149–51, 154–58, 170–72, 173, 185–88.
[75] Pp. 188–89, 196.

have seen an ethical significance. A primary function of the drama, they believed, was moral instruction.[76] Many of the dramatists themselves expressed this opinion.[77] According to Renaissance moralists, man's passions are likely to be his powerful and dangerous enemies. If he is to live virtuously, successfully, and happily, he must subdue and direct them by the exercise of reason and will. The cases of pathological grief which I have reviewed illustrate very clearly the power of the passions and the danger which lies in them.

The dramatists fail to suggest, however, the possibility of mastering them. Not one of the grief-stricken characters mentioned above is able to cope with the passion which threatens to ruin him. Some of them die without relief from their melancholy. Those who recover are cured not by their own efforts, but by a fortunate turn of events or by the ministrations of a friend or a physician. The dramatists appear to believe that grief may be too strong for the regulative powers of reason.

IX

In *A Looking-Glass for London and England*, by Greene and Lodge, the King of Paphlagonia, who has suffered a great calamity and a great wrong, enters "*Male-content.*"[78] The word is clearly inapplicable to Paphlagonia's character; he does not belong to any of the malcontent types. Since it occurs in a stage direction, it is evidently intended to specify the appearance and demeanor of the actor. It seems to direct him to appear in disordered clothing (possibly black) and to stand with folded arms, hat pulled low, and eyes morosely fixed.[79] Evidently the superficial attributes of the malcontent, who constituted the most familiar form in which Elizabethan Londoners knew melancholy, have been put to use as symbols of grief and despondency.

There is further evidence. According to a stage direction, the "Tyrant" of *The Second Maiden's Tragedy*, just after the suicide of the woman whom

---

[76] See Campbell, *Shakespeare's Tragic Heroes*, pp. 3–43.

[77] See David Klein, *Literary Criticism from the Elizabethan Dramatists* (New York, 1910), pp. 3–10, 100–4, 163–66. Dramatists occasionally refer to the morally degrading effect of grief (e.g., *Romeo and Juliet*, III, iii, 108–12).

[78] Greene, *Plays and Poems*, ed. J. Churton Collins (Oxford, 1905), I, 169.

[79] A passage in *The Nice Valour* helps one to visualize the pose. The "Passionate Madman" enters "*rudely, and carelesly apparrell'd, unbrac'd, and untruss'd*" (*Beaumont and Fletcher*, X, 170). He sings a lyric on melancholy in which he refers to "folded Arms," "fixed Eyes," a piercing sigh, "A look that's fast'ned to the ground," "A tongue chain'd up" (p. 172). For further information on this lyric, see Chap. VIII, note 2.

he loves, enters *"wondrous discont[ent]edly."*[80] The hero of Greene's *Alphonsus, King of Aragon,* after hearing the unhappy history of his family, hangs his "head as malcontent."[81] In *Alphonsus, Emperor of Germany,* Prince Edward, affected by his uncle's misfortunes, "standeth melancholy."[82] Titus Andronicus asks his brother Marcus to

> unknit that sorrow-wreathen knot:
> Thy niece and I, poor creatures, want our hands,
> And cannot passionate our ten-fold grief
> With folded arms. (III, ii, 4–7)

When news comes that Macbeth has murdered his wife and children, Macduff stands overwhelmed with grief. Malcolm tries to hearten him: "What! man; ne'er pull your hat upon your brows; / Give sorrow words" (IV, iii, 208–9). Feminine characters also may indicate sorrow by "discontented" appearance and conduct. The grief-stricken Constance, in *The Troublesome Reign of King John,* enters "All malecontent."[83] According to a stage direction in Massinger's *A Very Woman,* Almira, distracted by grief, enters *"in black, carelessly habited."*[84]

The adjective *melancholy* sometimes occurs in a stage direction at the entrance of a grief-stricken character. It can hardly be meant to refer to anything besides the actor's appearance and deportment, and its implications are probably similar to those of *malcontent.* There are two instances in Lodge's *The Wounds of Civil War.* Marius, after the city of Minturnum has refused him sanctuary, enters *"very melancholie."*[85] Young Marius, his son, making the last defense of a lost cause, walks upon the walls of Praeneste *"all in blacke and wonderfull mellancoly."*[86] In Webster's *The Devil's Law-Case,* Romelio, in the midst of calamity, enters *"very melancholly."*[87] A clown in Webster's *Appius and Virginia* enters *"melancholy."*[88]

The foregoing supports Alfred Harbage's argument for "formal" as op-

---

80 P. 52 (Malone Society Reprints).

81 *Plays,* I, 82.

82 Chapman, *Plays,* p. 388. The play is probably not Chapman's.

83 *Shakespeare's Library,* ed. W. Carew Hazlitt (London, 1875), V, 260. Cf. Shakespeare, *The Rape of Lucrece,* l. 793; Spenser, *The Visions of Bellay,* X, 2.

84 *Plays,* IV, 268.

85 P. 20 (in *Works,* vol. III).

86 P. 62. The fact that he is in armor precludes some of the characteristic details.

87 *Works,* II, 312.

88 *Ibid.,* III, 197. Marlowe's Tamburlaine makes an entry *"all in blacke, and verie melancholy"* (*Works,* ed. Tucker Brooke [Oxford, 1910], p. 58). Here, however, the melancholic attitude seems intended to indicate glowering or threatening anger rather than grief.

posed to "natural" acting on the Elizabethan stage.[89] Evidently sorrow was represented formally. The folded arms and melancholy hat probably appeared frequently on the Elizabethan stage, much more frequently than the slender evidence can demonstrate. In the second scene of *Hamlet*, for example, the actor in the title role may have advertised his state of mind not only by his "inky cloak," but also by standing apart with arms crossed, hat pulled down, and eyes morosely fixed, a figure in marked contrast with the gayly dressed courtiers.

X

Most of the melancholy in the Elizabethan drama is due to sorrow of one kind or another. Even the melancholy lovers, to be discussed later, are distracted by sorrow, for love melancholy is due to disappointment in love. Yet there are some cases of melancholy arising from other causes.

Sometimes fear is the cause. Mosbie, the criminal intriguer in *Arden of Feversham*, is deeply troubled by anxiety:

> Disturbed thoughts dryues me from company
> And dryes my marrow with their watchfulnes;
> Continuall trouble of my moody braine
> Feebles my body . . .[90]

In the early part of *Pericles*, the central character suffers from "dull-ey'd melancholy," the result of his fear of Antiochus. His apprehensions, he says, have drawn "sleep out of mine eyes, blood from my cheeks."[91] In *The Lover's Progress*, Cleander has premonitions of death (based on the appearances of a ghost, apparently a real one). A "dulness / Invades [him] all over."[92] Soon he has no wish to live:

---

[89] "Elizabethan Acting," *Publications of the Modern Language Association*, LIV (1939), 685–708. See also Robert H. Bowers, "Gesticulation in Elizabethan Acting," *Southern Folklore Quarterly*, XII (1948), 267–77.

[90] *The Shakespeare Apochrypha*, ed. Tucker Brooke (Oxford, 1908), p. 18. The Elizabethan drama abounds in passages which, like this one, suggest the physiological effects of fear.

[91] I, ii, 2, 96. Later Pericles' melancholy seems to be deepened by his falling in love (II, iii). In after years, believing his daughter dead, he falls into the melancholy torpor already discussed. Pericles is a very melancholy character.

[92] *Beaumont and Fletcher*, V, 122. His brother speaks of his recent sadness and his "melancholy" (p. 122).

> I cannot sleep, strange visions
> Make this poor life, I fear'd of late to lose,
> A toy that I grow weary of.[93]

Cleander is murdered.

Intent cogitation engenders black bile by consuming spirit. In the man involved in dangerous conspiracy, continual activity of mind may combine with anxiety to produce melancholy. Shortly before the assassination in *Julius Caesar*, Brutus walks "Musing and sighing, with [his] arms across" (II, i, 240). He cannot "eat, nor talk, nor sleep" (II, i, 52). In *1 Henry IV*, Hotspur, as he plots rebellion, is the victim of "thick-eyed musing and curst melancholy" (II, iii, 51). It takes from him his "stomach, pleasure, and [his] golden sleep" (II, iii, 46). Intent brooding on something greatly desired likewise may result in melancholy. Appius, of Webster's *Appius and Virginia*, speaks of his ambition to become a *decemvir:*

> 'twas my sleeps disturber,
> My dyets ill digestion, my melancholy
> Past physicks cure.[94]

Long and intense preoccupation with the alluring idea of greatness may produce the melancholic illusion of greatness. The lowborn hero of Ford's *Perkin Warbeck* claims to be the rightful King of England with such earnest persistence that even King Henry, whom he seeks to supplant, is convinced of his sincerity. In Henry's opinion, the Duchess of Burgundy, his own enemy and Perkin's patroness, has so thoroughly drilled Perkin for his role of pretender that he has come to believe his claim really a just one.[95] Perkin, says the King, has been "distracted" by "vain ambition."

> The custom, sure, of being styl'd a king
> Hath fasten'd in his thought that he is such.[96]

Perkin does not falter even when he is about to be hanged for his presumption. An observer comments:

---

[93] P. 127. It is a temptation to add Macbeth to the list of melancholics because of his hallucinations due to fear (II, i, 33–49; II, ii, 36–44; III, iv, 39–108). Macbeth himself, however, attributes the dagger illusion to a "heat-oppressed brain" (II, i, 39). I think it very likely that Shakespeare thought of Lady Macbeth's distraction (V, i) as a melancholy arising from fear and remorse.

[94] *Works*, III, 157.

[95] *Works*, II, 204. Bacon, whose *History of the Reign of King Henry VII* was probably Ford's source, characterizes Perkin as a dissembling scoundrel. By making Perkin a psychopathic case, Ford has given him the sincerity requisite to a tragic hero.

[96] P. 206.

> Thus witches,
> Possess'd, even [to] their deaths deluded, say
> They have been wolves and dogs, and sail'd in egg-shells
> Over the sea, and rid on fiery dragons,
> Pass'd in the air more than a thousand miles,
> All in a night:—the enemy of mankind
> Is powerful, but false, and falsehood confident.[97]

This is the only trace of Weyer's and Scot's theory of witchcraft (see above, pp. 54–56) that I have found in Elizabethan literature. Perkin is never referred to as a melancholy man. Yet there is little doubt that in writing the play Ford had in mind the melancholy kings, emperors, and popes of whom one reads so often in scientific works and in collections of strange tales.

The hero of Brome's *The Antipodes* is another young man who has thought too much on one subject. Perigrine has been unbalanced by his intense interest in strange and distant countries. Even when he was a boy he read travelers' tales constantly while other boys were engaging in sports and restoring "their spirits" with food and sleep.[98] Now he talks continually and irrationally of the strange beasts and men that he believes he would see in distant lands. His disorder is thought to be "a most deepe melancholy."[99] His father, hoping that marriage would divert his mind from his obsession, has procured for him a wife, but marriage has made no difference. Dr. Hughball, who is skilled in "medicine of the minde,"[100] undertakes his case and cures him by an elaborate course of treatment which occupies the greater part of the play. *The Antipodes*, like Ford's *The Lover's Melancholy*, is little more than an attempt at the dramatization of psychiatric therapy. Dr. Hughball humors the patient and arranges elaborate dramatic performances designed to inveigle him into thinking and doing what is for his good. Otherwise the doctor's methods have little resemblance to anything that I have found in medical writings. Brome was more intent on being entertaining than on being scientific.

Other dramatic cases of melancholy are due to vexation or resentment. Young Lassenbergh, of *The Wisdome of Doctor Dodypoll*, becomes pettishly melancholy because he is forced to marry.[101] Marcellina, in Chapman's *Monsieur D'Olive*, is so angry and resentful at her husband's jealousies

---

[97] P. 212.

[98] *Works* (London, 1873), III, 238.

[99] P. 237.

[100] P. 234. The doctor has two other mental patients, Joyless, Perigrine's father, and Martha, Perigrine's wife. Both are mentioned under other headings.

[101] *Old Plays*, ed. A. H. Bullen (London, 1882–85), III, 113, 123–24.

that she shuts herself up in seclusion and darkness and swears never to emerge. Her "perfect judgment" is "drown'd in humour."[102] In *A York-shire Tragedy*, the vicious "Husband," having spent beyond his means in licentious pleasures, broods over his precarious financial state: "He sits and sullenly lockes vp his Armes ... Walks heauyly ... A fearefull mellancholie, vngodly sorrow."[103]

XI

The Elizabethan drama includes many frankly instructive plays and masques, most of them allegories in the morality tradition and most of them apparently intended for the more cultivated audiences.[104] Because of its ethical significance, psychology is a favorite theme in drama of this type. Thus melancholy is a subject which, among various other psychological subjects, appears fairly frequently.

Lyly's *The Woman in the Moon* is a semiserious lesson on the influence which the various planets have on feminine personality (nearly all of it bad influence). Pandora, the heroine, is ruled in turn by each of the seven. Saturn's turn comes first. He engenders in her a "melancholy moode ... by corrupting of her purest bloud"; he clouds her brain "with sullen sorrowes" and surrounds her heart "with froward care."[105] Saturn is supposed to have begun the corruption of Pandora's character which continues throughout the play.

In Tomkis' *Lingua* the human senses and various other faculties are personified. There is no character to represent melancholy, yet the playwright finds occasion to display his knowledge of the subject. Tactus feigns melancholy. He tells Olfactus that, coming lately from the house of Phantastes (imagination), he became aware of the fact that he was made entirely of glass. Then it seemed to him that he was a urinal; he is afraid of being broken and does not wish Olfactus to come near him. Olfactus comments:

---

[102] *Plays,* p. 119. She is referred to as "melancholy" (p. 136). She is cured by the benevolent machinations of Vandome, the amateur psychiatrist who cures St. Anne.

[103] *Shakespeare Apocrypha,* p. 252.

[104] Harry K. Russell reviews most of the extant plays of this type in "Tudor and Stuart Dramatizations of the Doctrines of Natural and Moral Philosophy," *Studies in Philology,* XXXI (1934), 1–27.

[105] *Works,* III, 246. Greene's *Planetomachia* also contains instruction concerning the influence of Saturn. See *Works,* V, 40–100. The emphasis is upon the evil caused by Saturn and melancholy.

See the strange working of dull melancholy!
Whose drossy thoughts, drying the feeble brain,
Corrupts the sense, deludes the intellect,
And in the soul's fair table falsely graves
Whole squadrons of fantastical chimeras
And thousand vain imaginations,
Making some think their heads as big as horses,
Some that th'are dead, some that th'are turn'd to wolves,
As now it makes him think himself all glass.[106]

The *dramatis personae* of *The Floating Island*, a psychological and moral allegory by William Strode, is made up altogether of the faculties of the soul. The floating island itself is the microcosm. The play tells the story of a rebellion of the passions against Prudentius, the king. Among the rebellious passions is Melancholico. This person is a character of illogical complexity. He represents the passion sorrow; he is a satire directed against the Puritans;[107] he displays many of the traits of the melancholy malcontent type; he has a liking for "men of Arts"[108] which seems surprising in a Puritan. In two other allegories, Barton Holiday's *Technogamia; or the Marriage of the Arts* (published 1630) and Thomas Nabbes' *Microcosmus* (published 1637), one finds personifications of melancholy.

In Jonson's masque *Hymenaei*, "*the foure* Humors, *and foure* Affections" emerge from "*a* Microcosme, *or* Globe, *(figuring Man).*" Their appearance prompts Hymen to cry out, "Saue, saue the *virgins.*" He fears the influence of "The foure vntemp'red *Humors*" and "their wild *affections.*"[109] Reason curbs the humors and passions. *The Sun's Darling*, by Dekker and Ford, contains a masque (a masque within a masque) in which the characters are the four elements and the four complexions, including of course Melancholy.[110] Brome's *The Antipodes* closes with a masque in which Discord, attended by Folly, Jealousy, Melancholy, and Madness, is overcome by Harmony, attended by Mercury, Cupid, Bacchus, and Apollo. Bacchus is the specific adversary of Melancholy.[111]

The most curious of all these instructional dramas is the "Masque of Mel-

---

[106] *Old Plays*, ed. Dodsley and Hazlitt, IX, 351. Phantastes, in Spenser's House of Temperance, is melancholy (*Faerie Queene*, II, ix, 52).

[107] Strode's Melancholico has been mentioned previously (p. 82) in connection with Puritanism.

[108] *Works*, p. 174.

[109] *Jonson*, VII, 213.

[110] Ford, *Works*, III, 165.

[111] *Works*, III, 336–38.

ancholy" in Ford's *The Lover's Melancholy*.[112] This has none of the qualities which one expects in a masque. It resembles rather the madhouse scenes and madmen's dances included in various early Stuart plays for the entertainment of audiences which were always delighted by the antics of demented persons. It is presented before the Cyprian court by the physician Corax to illustrate his assertion that "Melancholy is / The root of every apish frenzy,"[113] and it gives the dramatist the opportunity to exhibit some rather ill-digested psychiatric learning. Characters representing lycanthropia, hydrophobia, delirium ("mere dotage"), frenzy, hypochondriacal melancholy, and "the Wanton Melancholy" appear successively to deliver speeches about themselves. Corax makes a comment on each one, and at the close all six join in a dance.

The principal source of the masque is that part of the *Anatomy* in which Burton defines and distinguishes the diseases of the head.[114] Here one discovers that *dotage*, or *delirium*, is a generic term, "a common name" for all the various mental diseases which Burton describes. Delirium is not a species of melancholy as Ford seems to believe; melancholy is a species of delirium. Reading farther, one finds discussions of lycanthropia, hydrophobia, frenzy, and "the Wanton Melancholy" (St. Vitus' dance). Burton excludes all of these from the category of melancholy. (Most authorities, however, regard lycanthropia as a melancholic disease, and some regard hydrophobia as such.) Hypochondriacal melancholy is treated elsewhere in the *Anatomy*.[115] In representing lycanthropia and hydrophobia, Ford follows his source fairly well, although unaccountably he associates hydrophobia with jealousy. The character "Delirium" seems to be a satiric embodiment of the miseries and intellectual vices of the scholar. In Ford's representations of frenzy and hypochondriacal melancholy, one finds little more than the fatuous absurdity of the conventional stage madman. The passage on "the Wanton Melancholy" best of all illustrates the carelessness of Ford's use of scientific material. This malady is represented by "*a* Sea-Nymph *big-bellied, singing and dancing*," who makes wanton advances to the male madmen. Details in this passage and in Corax's subsequent comment are traceable to Burton's account of St. Vitus dance: "the lascivious dance, *Paracelsus* calls it, because they that are taken with it, can do nothing but dance till they be dead, or cured . . . even great-bellied women sometimes . . . will dance so long that they can stir neither hand nor foot. . . ."[116] Ford has misinterpreted

---

112 *Works*, I, 63–68.
113 P. 63.
114 I, 158–64.
115 Especially I, 436–38, 472–75.
116 *Anatomy*, I, 163.

"lascivious dance," by which Burton and Paracelsus mean "sportive dance" (Latin *lascivus*),[117] and has distorted St. Vitus' dance into something rather unpleasant.

---

[117] Paracelsus' term is *chorea lasciva*. See *Paracelsi . . . Opera* (Strassburg, 1603), Part I, pp. 491–92. Cf. Plater, *Praxeos*, pp. 103–4; Plater, *Observationum . . . Libri Tres* (Basel, 1614), p. 85. The disease to which Burton, Paracelsus, and Plater refer is not the chorea, or St. Vitus' dance, described in modern medical works, but a peculiar form of hysteria which swept through Western Europe in the fifteenth century. Howard W. Haggard, in *The Lame, the Halt, and the Blind* (New York, 1932), devotes a highly readable chapter to it (pp. 206–15).

Chapter VI. THE LOVER'S MALADY IN MEDICAL THEORY

I

The word *love* has many meanings, which ordinarily are very hazily distinguished from one another. This chapter deals with erotic love, which is, in Renaissance psychology, a species of the passion desire. All passions, to the Renaissance psychologist, are physical conditions, or physical processes. Erotic love is "*a Motion of the blood . . . through the hope of pleasure.*"[1] It may or may not be accompanied by corresponding admirations on the intellectual plane. It is, moreover, commonly regarded very unromantically as a disease. (Any immoderate passion may be so regarded.) "They that are in love are likewise sick," says Burton,[2] and he is expressing an idea of great antiquity, widely current in his own day. Common names for the malady are *erotic love, heroical love*, and *love melancholy*. Both sexes are susceptible, although in the following I shall refer to the lover in the masculine gender.

The Renaissance conception of the love malady, like virtually all of its medical lore, is drawn from classical sources and from medieval treatises, Arabian and European, which are based upon classical sources. The earliest work in which I have found a separate chapter on love is the medical compendium of Oribasius (fourth century).[3] Galen, however, refers several times to love as a disease,[4] and there are indications in Galen's works that the lover's malady had long been a subject of medical concern.[5] Medieval medical writers regularly devote a chapter to love in sections dealing with such mental diseases as madness, melancholy, hydrophobia, frenzy. In classical works I have found no mention of melancholy in connection with the lover's malady. Medieval writers, however, usually characterize it as a melancholic ailment.

John L. Lowes, in explaining the term *hereos*, which occurs in Chaucer's description of Arcite's lovesickness ("Knight's Tale," l. 1374), has revealed

---

1 Jacques Ferrand, *Erotomania or a Treatise . . . of Love, or Erotique Melancholy*, tr. Edmund Chilmead (Oxford, 1640), p. 28. The French original of this work appeared first in 1612.

2 *Anatomy*, III, 63.

3 *Synopsis*, VIII, ix.

4 See the index to the Kühn edition *(amor)*.

5 *Galeni Opera*, XIV, 630–31; XVIII B, 18.

a great deal about the history of the love malady in medical tradition and about the symptoms of the disease as they are listed in medieval medical literature.[6] His etymological findings also are interesting. *Hereos,* he shows, is derived through devious ways from the name of the Greek god of love. The Middle Ages and the Renaissance, unconscious of this derivation, associated the term with the Latin words *herus* and *heros.* Through this association arose the idea that the lover's malady was an affliction peculiar to the aristocratic or the great of heart.[7] Lowes explains thus both the derivation of the expression *heroical love* and its unetymological connotations.

II

Erotic love, since it is a species of desire, is a warm and moist (or sanguine) passion. The person who by nature or by accident has a high proportion of blood in his system is predisposed to love just as he is predisposed in general to warm and moist passions, to other kinds of desire and to joy and hope. A surplus of blood, moreover, inclines men particularly to love for the physiological reason that blood is "the Material cause of seed."[8] The sperm is "nothing else but Blood, made White by the Naturall Heat, and an Excrement of the third Digestion."[9]

... after the third and last concoction: which is doone in euerie part of the bodie that is nourished, there is left some part of profitable bloud, not needefull to the partes, ordeyned by nature for procreation, which ... is woonderfullie conueighed and carried to the genitories, where by their proper nature that which before was plaine bloud, is now transformed and changed into seede.[10]

When blood abounds in a body, seed also abounds. Abundance of seed causes amorous disposition.

Moderate indulgence in venery is healthful, for the seed should occasionally be evacuated;[11] but incontinence is highly injurious. A great deal of

---

6 "The Loveres Maladye of Hereos," *Modern Philology,* XI (1914), 491–546. The symptoms which Lowes has noted belong altogether to the later, or melancholic, stage of the disease.

7 See Ferrand *Erotomania,* p. 17; Burton, *Anatomy,* III, 43, 62. An occasional variant upon *heroical melancholy* is *knight's melancholy;* see Du Laurens, *Discourse,* p. 89, and Burton, *Anatomy,* I, 200.

8 Ferrand, *Erotomania,* p. 64.

9 *Ibid.,* p. 261. Concerning the three digestions, see Chap. I, note 13.

10 Cogan, *Haven of Health,* p. 240.

11 *Ibid.,* p. 241; Vaughan, *Directions,* p. 69; Venner, *Via Recta,* p. 221. Young persons and persons of sanguine complexion, since they have blood to spare, can safely indulge more often than others; intemperance is especially dangerous to persons of choleric or melancholy complexion (Cogan, *Haven of Health,* pp. 239–40, 244; Venner, *Via Recta,* p. 221).

blood goes into the generation of a very small quantity of seed. The loss of seed "harmeth a man more, then if hee should bleed forty times as much."[12] "And this is the cause why such as vse immoderate *Venus*, be short liued, and as the Sparowes, through incontinencie consume themselues."[13] Loss of blood seems a very serious matter to the Renaissance physiologist, for the primary qualities of a living body, he believes, are heat and moisture. Immoderate expenditure of blood hastens age and death.

A large quantity of blood in the body, then, produces amorous inclinations. "Abundance of Blood of a good temperature, and full of spirits" is a "Cause of Love."[14] Of all complexions, therefore, the sanguine is "most enclined to *Venus*, by reason of abundance of bloud, hoat and moyst."[15] Although sanguine men are blessed with many virtues, they are "tainted with" one fault, "and that is, (by reason of that lively abounding humor) they are somewhat too prone to Venery."[16] Because the liver is the organ which produces blood, it is very often associated with love. Those of sanguine complexion "are most capable of loue," for "the bounty of the liuer whereas the blood is framed, induceth to loue."[17] Since youth is the sanguine age, young people "are soon caught ... most apt to love."[18] Youths "are hot and fiery by reason of the blood which boyles in their veines; and what they once desire they affect with vehemency. Yet they shew this heate more particularly in the motions of Loue, whereunto their age which is in the flower, giues them a violent inclination."[19]

Even though one is not sanguine by nature, he may develop a sanguine, and therefore an amorous, disposition. Anything which engenders blood may be an antecedent cause of love. Other warm and moist passions may prepare the way for love. Ferrand mentions joy in particular.[20] Diet is perhaps the most frequent cause. "*Venus* delights in Fulnesse and variety of dainties."[21] Highly nutritive foods—that is, warm and moist foods—are readily converted into good blood enlivened by abundant spirit. The list of

---

[12] Vaughan, *Directions*, p. 70.

[13] Cogan, *Haven of Health*, p. 242. "Facit . . . ad vitae longitudinem atque robur, Veneris paruus usus; namque plurimum in ea effunditur ex arteriali illo sanguine atque purissimo spiritu, quod his indigeat generatio, propter quam Venus ipsa constituta est."— Jerome Cardan, *De Subtilitate Libri XXI* (Basel, 1554), p. 363. See also Aristotle, *Parva Naturalia*, 466b.

[14] Ferrand, *Erotomania*, p. 64.

[15] Cogan, *Haven of Health*, p. 244.

[16] Walkington, *Optick Glasse*, p. 117.

[17] Coeffeteau, *Passions*, p. 551. Cf. pp. 22, 26.

[18] Burton, *Anatomy*, III, 66.

[19] Coeffeteau, *Passions*, pp. 655–66.

[20] *Erotomania*, p. 61. Fear and grief, he says, make one averse to love by cooling and drying the body.

[21] *Ibid.*, p. 241.

provocative dishes includes especially white bread, veal, pork, capon, partridge, eggs, potatoes.[22] Wine is

> a great encreaser of the vitall spirites, and a restorer of all powers and actions of the bodie . . . *the vine* may seeme as it were *life: because it greatelie preserueth life.* And no maruaile, considering that *life,* as *Aristotle* affirmeth, standeth chiefly *in heate and moysture.* Which two qualities are the very nature of wine.[23]

Wine "maketh fresh and healthie bloud . . . it prouoketh venery, and maketh women fruitfull."[24] The sweet wines malmsey and muscatel are "very hot," are very nourishing, and "mightily [cherish] the naturall heat."[25] These "are only for married folkes."[26]

Idleness and ease result in a redundancy of blood which in an active person would be consumed in exercise. Love "tyrannizeth in an idle person." Continence is "almost impossible" for those who are "young, fortunate, rich, high-fed, and idle withal."[27] Those persons are especially prone to love who "live at ease, and feed high: except by frequent and violent Exercise, or Labour, they consume the superfluity of Blood, which otherwise would be converted into Seed."[28] Court life fosters love, for it is an easy and idle life, its diet is rich and choice, and it keeps the sexes continually together. Love flourishes "in great houses, Princes' Courts, where they are idle *in summo gradu,* fare well, live at ease, and cannot tell otherwise how to spend their time."[29]

Hot and dry humors as well as blood may incline one to love. According to some authors, choleric persons are amorous.[30] Adust melancholy humors which are hot and flatulent also are said to cause erotic impulses.[31] One

---

[22] The curious reader may pursue this subject in any of the many dietaries of the period. See Chap. I, note 19. The sanguine foods are ordinarily those which authorities recommend most highly.

[23] Cogan, *Haven of Health,* pp. 208-9. Cf. Elyot, *Castel of Helth,* fol. 33ʳ; Vaughan, *Directions,* p. 19; Venner, *Via Recta,* p. 20. See also M. P. Tilley, "Good Drink Makes Good Blood," *Modern Language Notes,* XXXIX (1924), 153-55.

[24] Wirtzung, *Praxis,* p. 783.

[25] Venner, *Via Recta,* pp. 23-24.

[26] Vaughan, *Directions,* p. 20.

[27] Burton, *Anatomy,* III, 69. Cf. pp. 62, 67, 70, 117. "Paratiores ad id malum esse putantur, qui ingentes iecoris fibras habent, & qui semine abundant, ociosam vitam agunt, & delicate uiuunt. Nam & seminis abundantia & otium sunt caussa amoris insani."—Foreest, *Observationum,* p. 352.

[28] Ferrand, *Erotomania,* p. 59. Labor, says Bright, cools and dries the body (*Treatise,* p. 248).

[29] Burton, *Anatomy,* III, 119.

[30] *Batman uppon Bartholome,* fol. 32ᵛ; Ferrand, *Erotomania,* pp. 213, 241.

[31] Lemnius, *Touchstone,* fol. 149ᵛ; Bright, *Treatise,* p. 176; Burton, *Anatomy,* I, 475; III, 66; Ferrand, *Erotomania,* pp. 64-66. See also Aristotle, *Problemata,* XXX, i (953ᵇ).

authority includes "hot, provocative, Flatulent and Melancholy Meats" among the causes of love.[32] Love is much more often associated with blood, however, than with any other humor.

Thus far I have dealt only with the antecedent causes of love. The immediate cause, of course, is the beloved. Love at first sight is a natural thing if one is physically predisposed. Falling in love, moreover, is a rude and painful shock which throws into confusion all the normal processes of body and mind. The infection enters through the eyes[33] and produces a swift and violent reaction. It passes

through the veines vnto the liuer, doth suddenly imprint a burning desire ... setteth concupiscence on fire ... posteth in haste to the heart ... afterward assaileth and setteth vpon reason, and all the other principall powers of the minde ... and maketh them her vassals and slaues ... the man is quite vndone and cast away, the sences are wandring ... reason is confounded, the imagination corrupted, the talke fond and sencelesse. ...[34]

The damage may be done before one has time to do anything about it, and once love has entered, "all's utterly lost; *Actum est de Homine*."[35]

Since love is a warm passion, it causes the heart to open and to emit blood and heat-bearing spirit. Also it encourages the generation of blood. Lovers become uncomfortably hot. According to one writer, they "are like to them that are rosted by a soft fire."[36] Others speak of fires that are anything but soft. The flames of love, which are comparable to the flames of Aetna, scorch "the very inwards and marrowes, of those that entertaine it into their bosome."[37] The heat may be so fierce as to be mortal: "I haue seene a Natomie made of some of those that haue dyed of this malady, that had their bowels shrunke, their poore heart all burned, their Liuer and Lightes all vaded and consumed, their Braines endomaged. ..."[38] Let no man call love "the sweete passion or affection, seeing of all other miseries, this is the greatest miserie."[39] The "griping griefes" of lovers are "of all other most paine-

---

[32] Ferrand, *Erotomania*, p. 48. Aphrodisiacs are ordinarily hot and dry foods. See Wirtzung, *Praxis*, p. 294.

[33] Some authors believe that spirits engendered in the heart of the beloved emanate from her eyes, enter the eyes of the lover, penetrate to his heart, and spread through his body. These spirits, desiring always to return to the place of their origin, cause an intense yearning in the lover. See Pierre Boaistuau, *Theatrum Mundi*, tr. John Alday (London, 1581), pp. 193–94; Valleriole, *Libri Sex*, pp. 98–102; Plato, *Phaedrus*, 251, 255.

[34] Du Laurens, *Discourse*, p. 118.

[35] Ferrand, *Erotomania*, p. 68.

[36] La Primaudaye, *Academie*, p. 491.

[37] Robert Henderson, *The Arraignement of the Whole Creature* (London, 1631), p. 264. Cf. Burton, *Anatomy*, III, 171.

[38] Boaistuau, *Theatrum Mundi*, p. 192. Cf. Burton, *Anatomy*, III, 173.

[39] Du Laurens, *Discourse*, p. 119.

full: seeing that so many of them do willingly runne into the euerlasting paines of hell fire, by cruelly murthering them selues, that they may thereby escape and rid them from the broyling brandes of *Cupide*."[40]

The erotic impulse is overwhelmingly powerful. It impels men headlong into folly and evil. If love is directed by reason and if it has social and religious sanctions, it is conducive to man's physical and spiritual welfare. But of all the passions (except perhaps anger) it is the strongest and most violent and therefore the one most like to vanquish right reason. Moralists grow splendidly indignant when they contemplate the folly and sin of men under love's dominion:

when like a wild and vntamed beast it exceedes the bounds of reason, there is no misery which it brings not into the world, nor any disorder which it causeth not in our liues. It is as it were a fatall source, from whence flow all kinds of horror, vncleanenes, adulteries, incests, sacrileges, quarrells, warres, treasons, murders, parricides, cruelties, and violences; besides the particular torments it giues vnto the soules of such as giue themselues to be surprized, filling them with enuies, iealousies, cares, melancholies, terrors, yea and madnesse; drawing them many times to despaire, and to do things whereat heauen and earth blush and are ashamed.[41]

"Human, divine laws, precepts, exhortations, fear of God and man, fair, foul means, fame, fortunes, shame, disgrace, honour, cannot oppose, stave off, or withstand the fury of it, *omnia vincit amor, &c.*"[42]

Because of the physical tortures which love inflicts, the mental aberrations which it causes, and the spiritual calamities which rise from it, the physicians and moralists of the Renaissance find it a matter for grave concern.

III

Lovesickness as I have thus far described it is clearly not a melancholy disease. If the patient is not relieved, however, either by consummation or by medical intervention, his physical and mental distresses will engender melan-

---

[40] John Bishop, *Beautifull Blossomes* (London, 1577), fol. 52ᵛ.

[41] Coeffeteau, *Passions*, pp. 154–55.

[42] Burton, *Anatomy*, III, 61. Examples of this kind of invective on the subject of love are common. See, for instance, Rogers, *Anatomie*, fols. 18ᵛ ff.; Bishop, *Blossomes*, fol. 50ᵛ; Wright, *Passions*, p. 203; Charron, *Of Wisdome*, p. 83; Henderson, *Arraignement*, pp. 258–65; Burton, *Anatomy*, III, 54, 177, 213–14.

choly humors.[43] There are two stages of the love malady: a sanguine stage, in which the lover is hot and moist and abounds with blood; and a melancholy stage, in which he is cold and dry, weak and woebegone, and subject to all the physical debilities, the despondencies, and the mental vagaries which medical writers attribute to superabundance of the melancholy humor. These stages are almost never clearly distinguished in the medical writings, yet the distinction is logically necessary. The later stage is love melancholy. Broadly speaking, its cause is unsatisfied love.

Love, if it is thwarted, cools and dries the body in various ways. It does so, in the first place, through the continual mental activity which it provokes. The lover's mind is constantly and anxiously intent upon his mistress' charms and upon his hopes, fears, and despairs. In thus busying the mind, love "so drieth the humours, as that the whole frame of temperature, especially that of the braine, is ouerthrowne and marred."[44] For mental activity consumes heat and moisture. The lover's melancholy is in some degree due to the same causes as the scholar's (see above, pp. 24–26).

The lover's diverse and turbulent emotions, moreover, breed melancholy. Love "is fire, ice, hot, cold, itch, fever, frenzy, pleurisy, what not?"[45] The hot passions which assail the lover—desire, hope, joy, and anger—may produce melancholy adust by burning the humors. This eventually becomes black, heavy, cold, and dry. Thus the lover's passions render his "bloud . . . adust, earthy, and Melancholy."[46] The lover's fears and sorrows, cold and dry passions, engender natural melancholy. Although he is sometimes merry and joyful, "yet most part, Love is a plague, a torture, an hell, a bitter-sweet passion at last."[47] The lover has many fears. He trembles with agitation when he is in his mistress' presence and is continually tortured by anxiety concerning the success of his wooing. Of all the passions, however, "Sorrow hath the greatest share."[48] For love melancholy comes of unsatisfied love.

There are other reasons for the lover's melancholic constitution. One is insomnia, caused by "diverse Imaginations and Fancies that steale into" his brain. Lack of sleep renders "the Braine . . . Dry and Cold."[49] Another

---

[43] According to Constantinus, "si non amantibus succuratur, ut cogitatio eorum auferatur, & anima leuietur, in passionem melancholicam necesse est incidant, & sicut ex nimio labore corporis in passionem laboriosam incidunt, itidem ex labore animae in melancholiam."—*Opera*, p. 18.

[44] Du Laurens, *Discourse*, p. 120.

[45] Burton, *Anatomy*, III, 157. "Haec mentis conturbatio, composita quaedam ex omnibus reliquis animi passionibus est affectio, cum nunc gaudij, nunc tristitiae, nunc irae in ea effectus eluceant, nihilque sit amantibus inconstantius."—Plater, *Praxeos*, p. 97.

[46] Ferrand, *Erotomania*, p. 10.

[47] Burton, *Anatomy*, III, 162.

[48] *Ibid.*, p. 164.

[49] Ferrand, *Erotomania*, p. 131.

reason is that "Digestion is very bad," because "the spirits and Naturall Heat are withdrawne from the stomacke, to the Braine."[50] Indigestion creates crudities and melancholy. Another reason is unevacuated seed, which suffers melancholic corruption and "by sending up divers noysome vapours to the Braine . . . [disturbs] the operation of its cheifest Faculties."[51]

Love melancholy is easily recognized. One finds the lover "souning . . . weeping, sobbing, sighing, and redoubling his sighes."[52] Lovers characteristically stand "as if they were either in some deepe contemplation, or else were earnestly fixt in beholding something or other that much delighted them."[53] They cannot converse coherently; their "words are short & scarce intelligible," for their thoughts are entirely of the beloved.[54] Their moods are extremely variable because of "the Diversity of those objects they fancy to themselves"; there is "no order or equality at all in their Gesture, Motions, or Actions"; they are "now very jocund and laughing; and presently within a moment [they fall] a weeping."[55] Because the lover is assailed successively by diverse passions, "sometime he is as hot as fire, and vpon the sudden he findeth himselfe as colde as ice."[56] He is heedless of personal appearance and of all practical concerns: " 'tis the humour of them all, to be careless of their persons, and their estates . . . their beards flag . . . they care not, as they say, which end goes forward."[57] Lovers avoid "company, louing solitarines, the better to feed and follow [their] foolish imaginations."[58] In their solitude they sometimes break forth into passionate soliloquy; "sodainly you shall see them drowned in teares, making the ayre to sounde with their cryes, sighs, plaints, murmurings and imprecations: another time you shall see them cold, frozen and in a traunce."[59]

Certainly physiological symptoms deserve emphasis. Lovers have no appetite and sleep badly.[60] They become extremely lean because of their lack of heat and moisture.[61] Their eyes are "hollow, and sunke into their head, dry, and without teares; yet alwaies twinkling with a kind of smiling

[50] *Ibid.*, p. 125.

[51] *Ibid.*, p. 261. Cf. Vaughan, *Directions*, pp. 96–97.

[52] Du Laurens, *Discourse*, p. 118. The lover finds some relief from his anguish in tears (Burton, *Anatomy*, III, 172).

[53] Ferrand, *Erotomania*, p. 107.

[54] Coeffeteau, *Passions*, p. 173.

[55] Ferrand, *Erotomania*, pp. 109, 112, 107.

[56] Du Laurens, *Discourse*, p. 118.

[57] Burton, *Anatomy*, III, 174.

[58] Du Laurens, *Discourse*, p. 118.

[59] Boaistuau, *Theatrum Mundi*, p. 194.

[60] Ferrand, *Erotomania*, pp. 68, 131; Burton, *Anatomy*, III, 155.

[61] Du Laurens, *Discourse*, p. 118; Ferrand, *Erotomania*, p. 68; Burton, *Anatomy*, III, 153.

looke."[62] Their skin is pale and curiously discolored. A lover's pallor, which is due to corrupted humors, is not "simple Decoloration ... But rather a mixt Colour of White, & Yellow; or of White, Yellow, & Green."[63] The lover's "heart doth alwaies quake, and his pulse keepeth no true course, it is little, vnequall, and beating thicke, changing it selfe vpon the sudden, not onely at the sight, but euen at the very name of the obiect which he affecteth."[64]

Lovers necessarily suffer some degree of mental derangement; "they are very slaves, drudges for the time, mad-men, fools, dizzards, *atrabilarii*, beside themselves, and as blind as Beetles."[65] Those "that are in Love have their imagination depraved, and their judgement corrupted," for "a Lover cannot give a right judgement of the thing he loves."[66] Like many other melancholy men, the lover has his obsession—his mistress—and his delusion—her perfection: "Every Lover admires his Mistress, though she be very deformed of her self, ill-favoured, wrinkled, pimpled."[67] The lover's inability to see his mistress' shortcomings might not appear to be downright insanity. Yet some lovers do indeed go stark mad. One medical writer observes that a lover with a corrupted imagination is likely to see the image of his mistress and to run after it, "kissing this his idoll in the ayre, daintily intertaining and welcomming it." He goes on to tell the story of a lover who paid continual court to his own shadow.[68] Another physician reports a more violent case: A certain handsome youth, pining for a beautiful girl whom he could not have, began to rave. His parents were forced to bind him in chains. He lived miserably for some time continually imprisoned and finally died still mad.[69] Mad lovers do prodigious things. There is the mad lover, for instance, who attempted to assassinate the Duke of Venice.[70] One writer says that lovers become wolf-mad.[71] Another declares that, if lovers are jealous, "they be-

---

[62] Ferrand, *Erotomania*, p. 125. Cf. Burton, *Anatomy*, III, 153.

[63] Ferrand, *Erotomania*, p. 121. See also pp. 122–23. This is the explanation of the "green and yellow melancholy" of Viola's father's daughter in *Twelfth Night* (II, iv, 115). Cf. *Love's Labor's Lost*, I, ii, 91; Ford, *The Fancies Chaste and Noble*, in *Works*, II, 269. Black bile normally causes discoloration of the skin. The *Regimen Sanitatis Salerni* mentions "earthye browne" and "grene" as melancholic hues (fol. cxliiiᵛ). Lemnius describes the melancholic's face as "pale, yelowyshe & swarty" (*Touchstone*, fol. 146ʳ). Cf. Burton, *Anatomy*, I, 475.

[64] Du Laurens, *Discourse*, p. 118.

[65] Burton, *Anatomy*, III, 176.

[66] Ferrand, *Erotomania*, p. 31. Cf. Burton, *Anatomy*, III, 64.

[67] Burton, *Anatomy*, III, 178.

[68] Du Laurens, *Discourse*, pp. 120–21.

[69] Foreest, *Observationum*, p. 351.

[70] Vaughan, *Directions*, pp. 95–96.

[71] Ferrand, *Erotomania*, pp. 10, 206, 340–41. At some time in its history *amor* seems to have borrowed some features from lycanthropia. This was due, I suspect, to a confusion of terms in Rhazes' *Continens* (fols. 18ᵛ, 20ʳ).

come madde, and playe the *Lycantropes*, and goe all the night like raging wolues."[72]

Many lovers commit suicide. Others have a gentler but no less tragic end; they waste away and die. "It is so well known in every village, how many have either died for love, or voluntarily made away themselves, that I need not much labour to prove it. . . . Death is the common *Catastrophe* to such persons."[73]

IV

The physician who attends a lovesick patient must be an ingenious psychological strategist. The primary difficulty is that the patient will not cooperate. He does not want to be cured (except by consummation). He is, moreover, very secretive regarding the cause of his ailment. But love "will hardly be hid, though they do all they can to hide it, it must out . . . words, looks, gestures, all will betray them: but two of the most notable signs are observed by the Pulse and Countenance."[74]

In spite of the patient's reticence, the wise physician has no trouble in diagnosis. In order to administer intelligent treatment, however, he should know whom the patient loves. To find out, he must watch the patient closely. He must note who is present when he blushes. He may be fortunate enough to have his finger on the patient's pulse when the beloved enters, and then the whole matter is clear.[75] A useful device is to name over a list of persons with the fingers on the patient's pulse; if the beloved is named, the pulse will become quick and irregular.[76]

Medical writers of the Renaissance tell many stories of clever physicians who discover the tender secrets of lovesick patients. The most popular of these, and perhaps the most representative, is the tale of Antiochus, drawn from classical sources.[77] Antiochus, the son of Seleucus, King of Syria, fell deeply in love with his young stepmother, Stratonice. As Plutarch tells the story (*Demetrius*, XXXVIII), the young man struggled very hard to over-

---

[72] Boaistuau, *Theatrum Mundi*, p. 195.

[73] Burton, *Anatomy*, III, 215.

[74] *Ibid.*, 155–56.

[75] Ferrand once had this good fortune (*Erotomania*, pp. 117–19).

[76] See Burton, *Anatomy*, III, 156–57; Avicenna, *Canon*, p. 380.

[77] Concerning the literary history of this tale, see Hjalmar Crohns, "Zur Geschichte der Liebe als 'Krankheit,'" *Archiv für Kultur-Geschichte*, III (1905), 66–86; Ruth Lee Kennedy, "The Theme of 'Stratonice' in the Drama of the Spanish Peninsula," *Publications of the Modern Language Association*, LV (1940), 1010–32. The story appears in Painter's *Palace of Pleasure* (novel 27). Renaissance writers often refer also to a passage in Galen's works (*Opera*, XIV, 630–33) in which Galen matches the Erasistratus story with a case from his own practice.

come his unlawful passion. Failing, he attempted self-starvation. Naturally he confided his secret to no one. Erasistratus, his physician, saw readily that the Prince was in love, but to discover the object of his passion was a matter of greater difficulty. The doctor kept watch in the Prince's chamber, observing him closely whenever any of the beauties of the court appeared. When Stratonice entered, the Prince showed all the external signs of passionate love. Erasistratus delicately imparted his discovery to the anxious father, who, to save his son's life, gave his wife to him and, in sheer benevolence, added his crown.

When the doctor has the facts, his course of action will be determined by circumstances. If marriage—or perhaps even extramarital consummation—is possible, he will do what he can to bring it about. The best cure is *"to let them have their desire."*[78] Upon possession of the beloved, the lover's sorrow vanishes and with it his melancholy. "But this course of cure being such, as neither ought nor can alwaies be put in practise, as being contrary vnto the lawes of God and men,"[79] the doctor must often adopt other methods. Medical works show that the physician is well provided with therapeutic measures, both physical and mental.

The doctor's choice among physical remedies will depend upon the stage of the disease. If it is still in the early, sanguine stage, he will take measures to reduce the excess of blood in the patient's veins. (Devices for accomplishing this are recommended both as preventives and cures.) Bloodletting is an obviously logical method of treatment. Since abundant blood renders the body spermatic, it is highly advisable "to take away the superfluity of Blood, by opening the Liver Veine in the right arme."[80] Coition serves the same purpose. The patient must revise his diet and habits: "As an idle sedentary life, liberal feeding, are great causes of [love], so the opposite, labour, slender and sparing diet, with continual business, are the best and most ordinary means to prevent it."[81] The lover may subdue the flesh "by earnest studie and meditation, by often fasting, by much labour, by hard fare, by hard lodging, and such like."[82] His "meats must be but very litle nutritive; but rather Refrigerative and of a cooling quality. And therefore ye must give him in his broths, and salads, Purslane, Sorrell, Endive, Succory, and Lettuce."[83] The lover must "drinke water, and no wine upon any

---

78 Burton, *Anatomy*, III, 263.

79 Du Laurens, *Discourse*, p. 122.

80 Ferrand, *Erotomania*, p. 261.

81 Burton, *Anatomy*, III, 218. Cf. *ibid.*, pp. 220–21; Du Laurens, *Discourse*, p. 123; Vaughan, *Directions*, p. 91.

82 Cogan, *Haven of Health*, p. 245.

83 Ferrand, *Erotomania*, pp. 241–42. Ferrand advises against both hot and moist and hot and dry foods.

tearmes: because that wine inflames the blood, and makes men the more prone to lust; as *Aristotle* saies."[84]

If the malady has reached its cold and dry stage, lovers are treated in the "maner . . . appoynted for the melancholike."[85] The noxious humors are evacuated by purging or phlebotomy. The patient should be warmed and moistened with wine and with foods which produce good blood.[86] Warm baths are helpful. If the patient cannot sleep, the physician should administer soporifics, for sleep warms and moistens. His surroundings should be pleasant, and he should be made as merry as possible. Gaiety warms and moistens, just as sorrow cools and dries. Music, which is good for any melancholy man because it enlivens his sluggish spirit, is sometimes recommended specifically for lovers.[87]

The psychological remedies cannot be readily classified according to the stage of the disease to which they are applicable.[88] They include recreations of various sorts. The patient should be continually occupied at something to prevent thoughts of love. He should never be left alone and should not be allowed to read love poetry, hear amorous songs, or see pictures suggesting love. Travel is good for a lover. It not only diverts his thoughts from the mistress with new and varied experiences but it takes him where he cannot see her. By all means, he should not see her, for when he does the old fire is rekindled. He may be introduced, however, to other beauties, for "one fire drives out another."[89]

The physician or the lover's friends should reason with him, pointing out to him the dangerous folly of his ways. The frailties and imperfections of women in general and the shortcomings of his sweetheart in particular should be forcibly called to his attention. Slander is justifiable. Religion also offers help. Burton says that one should represent to the lover "the miserable events and dangers which will surely happen, the pains of Hell, joys of Paradise, and the like."[90] Ferrand advises "that some learned Divine should inculcate into him the feare of Death and Hell; and so by this meanes stirre him up to devotion and frequency of prayer. . . . And I would have him frequent the company of Religious people." He approves of solitude

---

[84] *Ibid.*, p. 238. See Aristotle, *Problemata*, 953[b].

[85] Du Laurens, *Discourse*, p. 124. The author advises such treatment only after other measures have failed.

[86] Ferrand prescribes fasting for love in the early (warm and moist) stage, nourishing foods in the late (cold and dry) stage (*Erotomania*, pp. 331–33).

[87] See Burton, *Anatomy*, III, 222–23.

[88] The following is based principally upon Du Laurens, *Discourse*, pp. 122–23; Ferrand, *Erotomania*, pp. 217 ff.; Burton, *Anatomy*, III, 224 ff.

[89] Burton, *Anatomy*, III, 234. Yet Benvolio uses this method in Romeo's case with disastrous results.

[90] *Ibid.*, p. 236.

as a preventive "provided alwaies, that we join with it Fasting, Watching and Prayer."[91] The lover should confide in his friends and give them opportunity to help him with counsel and persuasion. He should strive with all his power, moreover, to rule his passion with reason, to employ "that Soveraigne Remedy ... *The Perfection of Wisdome*."[92]

If a lover has become irrational and has developed a hallucination, the physician must remember the principles applicable in all cases of melancholy involving delusion. One must never contradict the patient but must humor him even to the point of agreeing with the most preposterous assertions. One must contrive a means of uprooting the patient's fanciful notions without betraying any skepticism concerning them. The shrewd physician often resorts to ingenious deceptions.

A great many of the curative methods recommended in scientific treatises may be found also in literary works (though not, of course, the strictly surgical and pharmaceutical remedies). John Lyly's "A cooling Carde for Philautus and all fond louers," one of the essays appended to *Euphues*, advises virtually the same means of subduing love that one finds in the medical works. One finds them again in Beaumont's *The Remedy of Love* and in Overbury's poem of the same title. The remedies of love, in fact, constitute a curious little literary genre, all of them apparently inspired more or less directly by Ovid's *De Remedio Amoris*.

V

Burton devotes a section of the *Anatomy* to jealousy, which he defines as "a bastard-branch, or kind of Love-Melancholy, which, as *Heroical* Love goeth commonly before marriage, doth usually follow."[93] Burton's treatment of jealousy is notable for the fact that it contains little citation of medical authority,[94] whereas in other parts of the *Anatomy* the names of

---

91 *Erotomania*, pp. 255, 328. For the sanguine lover, fasting and watching have the physiological effect of ridding the body of heat, blood, and spirit and thus of fleshly appetites.

92 *Ibid.*, p. 363.

93 *Anatomy*, III, 295. Like Burton, I confine myself in this section to marital jealousy.

94 Burton cites "*Valescus de Taranta cap. de Melancholia, Aelian Montaltus, Felix Platerus, Guianerius*" (*ibid.*, p. 295). I have been able to consult Valesco and Plater. Valesco mentions jealousy among the causes of melancholy (*Philonium Pharmaceuticum, et Cheirurgicum, de Medendis Omnibus ... Affectibus* [Frankfurt, 1599], p. 56). Plater describes eight rather lurid cases of psychopathic jealousy; two of the patients were melancholy men (*Observationum ... Libri Tres*, pp. 52–54). He later describes a case of melancholic insanity "*ob zelotypiam, & terrorem*" (pp. 77–79). Both authors seem to think of jealousy as an occasional cause of melancholy. Neither distinguishes a melancholy due to jealousy or a jealousy due to melancholy as a psychopathological type.

medical writers follow one another in rapid succession. The concept of melancholy jealousy is popular rather than scientific. Yet since it appears rather often in Elizabethan literature, especially in the drama, it seems worthwhile to outline its rather slender scientific basis.

Jealousy "is a certaine Feare or Doubt, least any one whom we would not, should enioy a Beautie that wee make account of."[95] It is a compound, hot-and-cold passion, a mixture of love and fear.[96] Jealousy is one of the passions to which melancholy persons are especially prone.[97] Suspicion, the species of fear which appears in jealousy, also is often specifically named among the melancholy passions.[98] Men are especially subject to jealousy in old age, the melancholic period of life. Old men "are cold and dry by nature. . . . Old age is a disease of itself, loathsome, full of suspicion and fear."[99] It is clear, then, that melancholy inclines men to jealousy. On the other hand, jealousy may cause melancholy. Any immoderate passion may engender black bile, and jealousy is one of the most uncontrollable of the passions. Being hot and cold, it may produce both the adust and natural humors. Jealousy, then, is "symptom and cause of Melancholy, as *Plater* and *Valescus* teach us: melancholy men are apt to be jealous, and jealous apt to be melancholy."[100]

Jealousy and melancholy aggravate each other in a vicious cycle until they affect both health and sanity. The jealous man becomes "meagre"[101] and has "a pale, leane, and amazed kind of visage."[102] Reason no longer controls his behavior. He makes

strange gestures of staring, frowning, grinning, rolling of eyes, manacing, ghastly looks, broken pace, interrupt, precipitate, half-turns. He will sometimes sigh, weep, sob for anger . . . rave, roar, and lay about him like a mad man, thump her sides, drag her about perchance, drive her out of doors . . . she is a whore, &c., by and by with all submiss compliment intreat her fair.[103]

He is excessively, absurdly, and morbidly suspicious. He watches his wife

---

[95] Benedetto Varchi, *The Blazon of Jealousie*, tr. Robert Tofte (London, 1615), p. 12.

[96] *Ibid.*, pp. 36–39. Bright says that jealousy is compounded of love and grief (*Treatise*, p. 83). In characterizing jealousy, the authors are inclined to emphasize its heat rather than its cold. Varchi associates it with the choleric complexion (p. 29).

[97] See Bright, *Treatise*, pp. 130, 133; Burton, *Anatomy*, I, 449–50. In these passages the authors are using the word jealousy in the broader sense.

[98] Bright, *Treatise*, p. 124; Du Laurens, *Discourse*, p. 89; Burton, *Anatomy*, I, 449–50.

[99] Burton, *Anatomy*, III, 306. The old man's jealousy is due not only to his melancholy nature but to his impotency.

[100] *Ibid.*, p. 305.

[101] Du Bosc, *The Compleat Woman*, p. 68.

[102] Ferrand, *Erotomania*, p. 189.

[103] Burton, *Anatomy*, III, 322.

as a Cat doth a Mouse . . . accurately observing on whom she looks, who looks at her . . . why did she smile, why did she pity him, commend him . . . why did she offer to kiss, to dance? &c., a whore, a whore, an arrant whore! . . . I'st not a man in woman's apparel? is not somebody in that great chest, or behind the door, or hangings, or in some of those barrels? . . . If a dear friend or near kinsman come as guest to his house, to visit him, he will never let him be out of his own sight and company, lest peradventure, &c. If the necessity of his business be such that he must go from home, he doth either lock her up, or commit her with a deal of injunctions and protestations to some trusty friends, him and her he sets and bribes to oversee: one servant is set in his absence to watch another, and all to observe his wife, and yet all this will not serve.[104]

Jealous men sometimes go stark mad and many commit murder or suicide.[105] Writers on the subject have little to suggest for remedy beyond "Wisdome, Discretion, and Patience."[106]

Jealousy is most ignoble—"a weake maladie of the soule, absurd, vaine"— and most excruciating—"the Gaule that corrupteth all the Hony of our Life."[107] Jealous persons live "in a continuall Hell, take no rest in the day; neither can they sleepe at all in the nights."[108] It brings tragic disasters: "most cruell reuengements, and most horrible and sauage murthers." Jealous men act "many times against their owne reputations and Honours, and against their owne proper selfes, and lifes."[109]

---

104 *Ibid.*, pp. 322–23.
105 *Ibid.*, pp. 329–31.
106 Varchi, *Blazon of Jealousie*, p. 59.
107 Charron, *Of Wisdome*, pp. 91–92.
108 Varchi, *Blazon of Jealousie*, pp. 44–45.
109 *Ibid.*, p. 60.

Chapter VII. THE LOVER'S MALADY IN ELIZA-BETHAN LITERATURE

I

To the Elizabethans, if their literature is an accurate index of their thinking, the expression "lovesick" meant literally what it said. Their novels and their plays reveal a belief that lovesickness may be a very critical malady. Literary characters affected by it are physically disordered and mentally unbalanced. Some of them go mad. Some of them die. In large part the Elizabethans owed their ideas concerning the love malady to psychological and medical theory.

In literary works, just as in scientific works, one finds the sanguine and melancholy stages of the lover's malady. Sometimes love is a hot and excited condition of body and mind which spurs to action; sometimes it is a cold, weak, and passive debility. In the first stage, desire is the dominant passion; in the second, grief is the dominant passion. The two phases, however, are by no means clearly distinguished in Elizabethan literary works. Fernando of Ford's *Love's Sacrifice*, as an example, complains both of plethora of blood and of extreme emaciation.[1]

Sanguine lovesickness is not a melancholic disease and thus in a sense lies outside the field of this study. The process of falling in love, also, is hardly a melancholic subject. Yet a discussion of love melancholy with no reference to the earlier phases of the malady would be oddly incomplete. It would dissociate matters which in the Elizabethan mind were very closely associated. This chapter, then, will deal with the lover's malady in its entirety, not merely with love melancholy.

II

Love at first sight is a very common occurrence in Elizabethan literature. Falling in love,[2] as Elizabethan writers represent it, is just such a rude and

---

[1] *Works*, II, 21, 34, 48.

[2] Elizabethan writers are well acquainted with the theory that the infecting agent is a spirit emanating from the eyes of the beloved (Chap. VI, note 33). See, for instance, Sidney, *Arcadia*, in *Works*, I, 351; Lodge, *A Margarite of America* (in *Works*, vol. III), pp. 53, 75; *Love's Labor's Lost*, IV, iii, 29; *Lust's Dominion*, p. 127; *A Wife for a Month*, Beaumont and Fletcher, V, 3; Thomas Middleton, *The Changeling*, in *Works*, ed. A. H. Bullen (London, 1885–86), VI, 66. Cf. Dante, *The New Life*, XIX.

sudden shock as the medical writers indicate. The swift onset of love, like that of any strong and sudden passion, agitates the heart violently. Euphrasia, in *Philaster*, describes the experience:

> My bloud flew out, and back again as fast
> As I had puft it forth, and suck't it in
> Like breath.[3]

Elizabethan authors seem to believe that for a time the heart fails in its function, the vital spirit ceases to flow, and the animation of the body is suspended. The lover therefore stands tongue-tied, gazing at the lady in wide-eyed and statuesque stupor.

When Arsadachus of Lodge's *A Margarite of America* first sees the lovely Diana, he is "so sodainely altered, that as such as beheld the head of *Medus* were altred from their shapes, so he . . . [is] rauished from his sences."[4] In *Love's Labor's Lost* the King of Navarre meets the Princess of France for the first time: "all his senses [are] lock'd in his eye"; his face is covered with "amazes . . . his eyes enchanted with gazes" (II, i, 240–45). In *As You Like It* Orlando, overcome by the charms of Rosalind, stands in her presence like "a quintain, a mere lifeless block" (I, ii, 268). Sir Francis Acton, in *A Woman Killed with Kindness*, sees a certain lady for the first time: "stay; my heart . . . I am inchanted, all my spirits are fled." His companion exclaims: "Sir Francis, why Sir Francis, zounds, in a trance?"[5]

The lover very soon realizes that something has gone wrong. A young man in *Love's Pilgrimage* who has just fallen in love cries out: "bless me from a feaver / I am not well o'th suddain."[6] The infection of love spreads swiftly:

> What strange new motions do I feel? my veins
> Burn with an unknown fire: in every part
> I suffer alteration: I am poyson'd,
> Yet languish with desire again to tast it.[7]

---

[3] *Beaumont and Fletcher*, I, 146.

[4] *Works*, vol. III; p. 64. Cf. Lodge, *Rosalynde* (in *Works*, vol. I), p. 23; Sidney, *Arcadia*, in *Works*, I, 90; Greene, *Menaphon*, in *Works*, VI, 50, 115. Lovers of the novels continue to become spellbound in the mistress' presence long after they have fallen in love.

[5] Heywood, *Works*, II, 116. Sir Francis' speech is apparently a conventional aside representing the speaker's thoughts. Under the circumstances Sir Francis could not actually speak.

[6] *Beaumont and Fletcher*, VI, 282. Cf. *Wit Without Money*, *ibid.*, II, 175; *Four Plays in One*, *ibid.*, X, 298; Brome, *The Queen's Exchange*, in *Works*, III, 476–77.

[7] *Love's Cure*, Beaumont and Fletcher, VII, 220. All this results from a kiss. Cf. Jonson, VII, 23, 32.

III

When Elizabethan authors write on the subject of love, they frequently use phraseology which shows that their conception of love has been greatly influenced by the physiological psychology. To them, as to the physicians and psychologists, love is a fervid and compulsive passion due to a specific physiological condition, a passion of such devastating effect that it may be considered a disease. The phraseological evidence of this view is very abundant in the drama, although less plentiful in other genres.[8] The documentation in this section has been taken altogether from the drama. It would be possible to gather much more from that source.

Some lovers of the drama suffer alternately from heat (due to desire) and cold (due to sorrow).[9] Much more frequently, however, love is characterized simply as a hot passion.[10] It is evident that, to the dramatists, the heat of love is not figurative; it is literal and painful. One dramatic character declares that his heart "is scorcht with loue."[11] Another is tormented by "marrow burning loue."[12] Another, upon falling in love, feels a fire "Burning mine entrails."[13] "Lust is like *Aetna*."[14] Both illicit passion and legitimate love are fervid. Fletcher draws a hazy distinction of degree between "looser thoughts, ill tempered fires" and "True Love . . . Whose moderate heat can ne'r consume."[15] In the Elizabethan drama, however, there is no real physiological differentiation, on this basis or any other, between "lust" and "love."

The dramatists commonly attribute love to redundancy of blood. Love is "the naturall sinne of [the] sanguine complection."[16] It is a "*Disease of*

---

[8] The tormenting heat of love, however, is very frequently mentioned in Elizabethan novels and amatory verse.

[9] *Jonson*, VI, 481; VII, 32.

[10] The association between love and heat is a very old and familiar one. See Sappho, fragment II, ll. 9-10; Euripides, *Hippolytus*, ll. 533, 1300; Theocritus, Idyll II, ll. 40, 133-34; Ovid, *Remedia Amoris*, ll. 105, 117-20, 491; Ovid, *Amores*, I, i, 26; III, i, 20, etc. This association may not have originated in scientific theory, yet scientific theory undoubtedly strengthened it.

[11] Lyly, *Works*, III, 255.

[12] Kyd, *Works*, p. 217.

[13] Chapman, *Plays*, p. 4, Cf. p. 61.

[14] Marston, *Plays*, III, 59.

[15] *Beaumont and Fletcher*, II, 438.

[16] Marston, *Plays*, II, 176.

bloud, and idle hours."[17] An amorous gallant is said to be "bloud-full."[18] A certain lecher's "veines are sweld with lust."[19] Lust is a "plurisy."[20] It is sometimes compared to a flood or tide.[21] A lover's blood, of course, is hot:

> My veins are all on fire, and burn like *Aetna*,
> Youth and desire beat larums to my blood.[22]

Because it produces blood, the liver is often held responsible for love. In *As You Like It*, Rosalind, describing a cure for love to Orlando, undertakes to wash his "liver as clean as a sound sheep's heart" (III, ii, 449-50). Falstaff, says Pistol in *The Merry Wives of Windsor*, loves Mistress Ford "With liver burning hot" (II, i, 119). One frequently finds such phrases as "my venerean gentleman's hot liver."[23] The vital spirits also, because they are the vehicle of the warmth and moisture of the blood, are associated with sexual activity. The central character of *The Woman Hater* is asked in mockery whether he has "blood and Spirit" in his veins. Surely he has "no liver," for if he did, it would "send a lively and desiring heat" throughout his body.[24] An elderly bridegroom in Tomkis' *Albumazar* is confident of his abilities because he feels that his arteries are "Blown full with youthful spirits."[25]

Sexual indulgence consumes blood and spirit and consequently robs one of the precious heat and moisture which are essential to life. Eleazar the Moor, in *Lust's Dominion*, says that venery has wasted his spirits, "Ravish'd [his] youth," dried his body "to anatomy."[26] Lust brings only "foul disease, with present age and pain, / And then a Grave."[27] In old age sexual activity is not only unbecoming but also, because heat and moisture are waning, unsafe. An old man given to sexual incontinence is characterized as a person of "spend-thrift veynes," "A parcht and iuicelesse luxur."[28]

The Elizabethan dramatists know that idleness, rich food, and wine cause

---

17 *Beaumont and Fletcher*, V, 112.
18 Marston, *Plays*, I, 179. Cf. Massinger, *Plays*, II, 38; Ford, *Works*, I, 160.
19 Tourneur, *Works*, p. 107. Cf. Massinger, *Plays*, II, 299, 465.
20 Ford, *Works*, I, 177, 293. Ford uses the word in the sense of "plethora" (see *pleurisy* in *A New English Dictionary*). Cf. Tourneur, *Works*, p. 216, and Burton, *Anatomy*, III, 263.
21 Marston, *Plays*, III, 48; Middleton, *Works*, VI, 128; Ford, *Works*, II, 21, 48, 239.
22 *Beaumont and Fletcher*, V, 33.
23 Chapman, *Plays*, p. 332.
24 *Beaumont and Fletcher*, X, 97.
25 *Old Plays*, ed. Dodsley and Hazlitt, XI, 308.
26 P. 9.
27 *Beaumont and Fletcher*, II, 443.
28 Tourneur, *Works*, p. 79. Cf. Marlowe, *Works*, p. 430; *Beaumont and Fletcher*, II, 45.

amorous inclinations.[29] Chastity is hardly possible among "women of young spirit and full age,"

> such as feede well and taste choice cates,
> That straight dissolve to puritie of blood,
> That keepe the veines full, and enflame the appetite,
> Making the spirit able, strong, and prone.[30]

In *The Faithful Shepherdess* the Priest of Pan sprinkles the young rustics with water:

> Shepherds, thus I purge away,
> Whatsoever this great day,
> Or the past hours gave not good,
> To corrupt your Maiden blood:
> From the high rebellious heat
> Of the Grapes, and strength of meat;
> From the wanton quick desires,
> They do kindle by their fires,
> I do wash you with this water,
> Be you pure and fair hereafter.
> From your Liver and your Veins,
> Thus I take away the stains.
> All your thoughts be smooth and fair,
> Be ye fresh and free as Air.
> Never more let lustful heat
> Through your purged conduits beat.[31]

The idle and luxurious life of courts is an erotic life. Marston's Malevole would rather leave a lady in a bordello than "in an *Italian* lascivious Pallace," for in the latter place she is

> incensed with wanton sweetes,
> Her veines fild hie with heating delicates,

---

[29] Certain foods are considered specifically aphrodisiac. These include especially eggs, potatoes, and eryngo. Eryngo, defined by *A New English Dictionary* as "The candied root of the Sea Holly . . . ," is the aphrodisiac most frequently mentioned in the drama. Eryngo, it happens, is not a sanguine but a choleric food, "hot and dry in the second degree."—Venner, *Via Recta*, p. 136. It warms "the parts of generation."—Wirtzung, *Praxis*, p. 717. The aphrodisiac qualities of wine are often referred to. A favorite mixture is eggs and muscadine (muscatel). One finds indications in the drama that the blades of London made dietary preparations for their pleasures.

[30] Heywood, *Works*, V, 207–8.

[31] *Beaumont and Fletcher*, II, 375–76.

Soft rest, sweete Musick, amorous Masquerers, / lascivious banquets, sinne it selfe gilt ore."[32]

Similar opinions appear in *The Tragedy of Nero:*

> Chastitie! foole! a word not knowne in Courts.
> Well may it lodge in meane and countrey homes
> Where povertie and labour keepes them downe,
> Short sleepes and hands made·hard with *Thuscan* Woll,
> But never comes to great mens Pallaces
> Where ease and riches stirring thoughts beget,
> Provoking meates and surfet wines inflame.[33]

The playwrights evidently know a great deal about the prevention and cure of erotic desire. They understand that the most effective way to subdue it is to reduce the amount of blood in the body. Labor (which consumes blood), lean diet, and water (instead of wine) are antedotes for love. Clorin outlines a way of life for the erring young men and women of *The Faithful Shepherdess:*

> correct the bloud
> With thrifty bits and labour, let the floud,
> Or the next neighbouring spring give remedy
> To greedy thirst, and travel[,] not the tree
> That hangs with wanton clusters.[34]

In *Measure for Measure,* Lucio is "fain to dine and sup with water and bran" when he sees that Claudio must die for adultery (IV, iii, 163–64). Othello, finding Desdemona's hand "Hot, hot, and moist," recommends religious devotion and spare living to her:

> this hand of yours requires
> A sequester from liberty, fasting and prayer,
> Much castigation, exercise devout;
> For here's a young and sweating devil here,
> That commonly rebels. (III, iv, 40–44)

Dramatists sometimes refer facetiously or sardonically to bloodletting as a remedy of love. In *Love's Labor's Lost* Dumaine says that he would like to forget his mistress but cannot because she reigns in his blood as a fever. In

---

32 Marston, *Plays,* I, 179.
33 *Old Plays,* ed. Bullen, I, 15. Cf. Massinger, *Plays,* II, 244.
34 *Beaumont and Fletcher,* II, 442. Cf. *ibid.,* p. 195.

that case, Berowne remarks, "incision / Would let her out in saucers" (IV, iii, 97–98). Eleazar the Moor, knowing that the king is trying to cuckold him, boasts that with his "falchions point" he will "lance those swelling veins in which hot lust / Does keep his Revels."[35] Purgation is another cure for love. In Chapman's *May-Day* a mocking gallant counsels a lovesick friend to "purge for her, for love is but a humour."[36] Many persons in Chapman's Elizabethan audience would have considered this intelligent advice.

The torments of love are excruciating. Consider, for instance, the condition of Tellus in Lyly's *Endimion*. When she fell in love, she says, she felt "a continuall burning in all my bowels, and a bursting almost in euerie vaine."[37] Then there is the case of a young lady in Jonson's *The New Inn*:

> My fires, and feares, are met: I burne, and freeze,
> My liuer's one great coale, my heart shrunke vp
> With all the [fibres], and the masse of blood
> Within me, is a standing lake of fire,
> Curl'd with the cold wind of my gelid sighs,
>
> . . . .
>
> Vntil I see him, I am drunke with thirst,
> And surfeted with hunger of his presence.[38]

A person in this condition could hardly be expected to act rationally.

Love seizes upon a great many unwilling victims in Elizabethan drama and fiction. One gets the impression that no one is safe (the psychologists might not agree to this). If any man were immune, it would be Angelo, of *Measure for Measure*,

> a man whose blood
> Is very snow-broth; one who never feels
> The wanton stings and motions of the sense,
> But doth rebate and blunt his natural edge
> With profits of the mind, study and fast. (I, iv, 57–61)

Yet Angelo falls furiously in love at first sight.

---

[35] *Lust's Dominion*, p. 52.

[36] *Plays*, p. 278. Still another cure, an obviously logical one, is employed in Massinger's *The Parliament of Love*. A physician protects his wife from a salacious gallant by giving him a "cooler" (*Plays*, II, 294), that is, a medicine to cool the blood. This episode constitutes one of the principal interests of the play. See especially pp. 299–302.

[37] *Works*, III, 74.

[38] *Jonson*, VI, 481.

IV

As I have noted before, psychological conflict—that is, conflict between reason and passion—is a frequent theme in the Elizabethan drama. For dramatic purposes, love is a particularly suitable opponent for reason both because of the tyrannical violence and power attributed to it and because of playgoers' perennial interest in it. To the Elizabethan, a conflict between reason and love would necessarily be a conflict between virtue and vice. Romanticism has greatly changed our thinking on this subject.

In Elizabethan plays, then, love frequently clashes with right reason.[39] In representing this subjective struggle, the playwright sometimes gives his audience a study in the contemporary psychology and ethics. An honorable and scrupulous person falls in love with a lady betrothed to his friend, with someone too closely related to him by blood, with someone already married. To save himself from moral disaster, he must oppose the desires of the flesh with all the power of intellect and will. A character in Fletcher's *The Faithful Shepherdess* phrases his virtuous determination to resist erotic passion in physiological language:

> I charge you all my veins
> Through which the blood and spirit take their way,
> Lock up your disobedient heats, and stay
> Those mutinous desires.[40]

Many characters, however, find love stronger than reason and are driven into evil courses which lead to tragedy or near tragedy.

The struggle between these two psychological opponents is very fierce. Tamyra, in love with Bussy D'Ambois, is torn by conflicting impulses:

> My licentious fancy
> Riots within me; not my name and house
> Nor my religion, to this hour observed,

---

[39] The conflict between love and right reason is a major interest in many Elizabethan plays in addition to those mentioned below, among them: Whetstone's *Promos and Cassandra*, *The Two Gentlemen of Verona*, *Measure for Measure*, *A Warning for Fair Women*, *A King and No King*, *Monsieur Thomas*, Marston's *The Dutch Courtezan*, Massinger's *The Unnatural Combat*, Brome's *The Queen's Exchange*, Glapthorne's (?) *Revenge for Honour*. See also Kyd, *Soliman and Perseda*, in *Works*, pp. 209, 217; *The Second Maiden's Tragedy* (Malone reprints), p. 27; *Bonduca*, in *Beaumont and Fletcher*, VI, 99; Heywood, *A Woman Killed with Kindness*, in *Works*, II, 108; Middleton, *Women Beware Women*, in *Works*, VI, 251.

[40] *Beaumont and Fletcher*, II, 396.

> Can stand above it; I must utter that
> That will in parting break more strings in me
> Than death when life parts; and that holy man
> That, from my cradle, counsell'd for my soul,
> I now must make an agent for my blood.[41]

The friar who acts as the lover's mediator justifies the amour on the ground that "our affections' storm, / Raised in our blood, no reason can reform."[42] The events of the tragedy make it appear that the friar is right.

A similar psychological battle occurs in "The Triumph of Honor," one of the dramatic sketches included in *Four Plays in One*. Martius falls precipitantly in love with the wife of a man whom he greatly admires. He is deeply ashamed and struggles manfully with his passion, reminding himself that "He conquers best, conquers his lewd desires." But when he sees the lady,

> the wild rage of my blood
> Doth Ocean-like oreflow the shallow shore
> Of my weak virtue.

He must have her "or perish."[43] Martius, however, masters his passion, and the playlet has a happy ending much like that of Chaucer's "Franklin's Tale."

Lessingham, of Webster's *A Cure for a Cuckold*, is commanded by the unresponsive lady whom he loves to kill his best friend as proof of his affection for her. Lessingham regards the deed with loathing, yet feels an irresistible compulsion: "this woman has a power of me / Beyond all vertue—vertue! almost grace."[44] He actually attempts to carry out the lady's injunction. At the close of the play, he asks his friend's forgiveness on the ground that "some wilde distractions" had overcome "the goodness you once knew in me."[45] This explanation satisfies the friend.

Ford's *Love's Sacrifice* presents another violent struggle between love and right reason. Fernando is in love with the wife of his friend and benefactor. He soliloquizes passionately, "striking his breast! ... tearing his hair!"[46] He

---

[41] Chapman, *Plays*, p. 150. Cf. Marston, *The Insatiate Countess*, *Plays*, III, 31–32.

[42] P. 152.

[43] *Beaumont and Fletcher*, X, 303–4. Martius withdraws into "retir'd melancholy" (p. 303).

[44] *Works*, III, 37.

[45] Pp. 94–95. Clare, Lessingham's beloved, is also mentally and morally unbalanced by love. Both characters are represented as touched by melancholy (pp. 33, 76, 79).

[46] *Works*, II, 36–37. Fernando says that love has changed him "to a lean anatomy" (p. 34).

cannot hide his secret. A villainous intriguer provokes him to betray it by showing him a picture of his beloved,[47] a device which reminds one of the stratagems employed by Erasistratus and Galen for similar purposes. Fernando's love is physical and mental agony:

> unbounded anguish as the rage
> Of flames beyond all utterance of words
> Devour me, lighten'd by your sacred eyes.[48]

> Traitor to friendship, whither shall I run,
> That, lost to reason, cannot sway the float
> Of the unruly faction in my blood?[49]

He is, he thinks, "be-leper'd" in his soul, yet he finds that he "must speak or burst."[50] His speaking leads to tragedy for all three members of the triangle.

In 'Tis Pity She's a Whore Ford presents what is perhaps the most detailed study of the love-reason conflict in the drama. Giovanni is in love with his own sister, Annabella. He has fought his passion with all his moral strength and is profoundly wearied by the struggle:

> I have too long suppress'd the hidden flames
> That almost have consum'd me: I have spent
> Many a silent night in sighs and groans;
> Ran over all my thoughts, despis'd my fate,
> Reason'd against the reasons of my love,
> Done all that smooth-cheek'd virtue could advise;
> But found all bootless.[51]

He has tried all that "judgment or endeavours" could do. He has wept and prayed,

> even starv'd
> My veins with daily fasts: what wit or art
> Could counsel, I have practis'd.

---

[47] Pp. 38–39.
[48] P. 47.
[49] P. 21.
[50] Pp. 34, 36.
[51] Works, I, 125. Giovanni has developed melancholic symptoms. He "Walks careless of himself . . . some woful thing . . . some shadow of a man . . . he beats his breast and wipes his eyes, / Drown'd all in tears" (Works, I, 122). He mopes in solitude (p. 153).

But "The more I strive, I love."[52] He seeks the counsel of Friar Bonaventura, his tutor and spiritual father, who, deeply shocked, represents to him the enormity and sacrilege of his desires and earnestly begs him to avail himself of the aids of religion. Reason is losing the battle with passion, however, for reason has begun to take passion's part. Giovanni plausibly argues with the friar that blood relationship is a reason for, not a reason against, sex relationship.[53] Finding at last that he "must speak, or burst,"[54] he declares himself to Annabella. He discovers that she loves him, and their love is consummated. His reason, now completely depraved, no longer struggles against his passion but triumphantly justifies it. He cleverly demonstrates to the horrified Bonaventura that it is altogether right and proper for him to love his sister, basing his reasoning on the very Platonic principles which the friar has taught him.[55] The play ends with the death of all the principal persons.

The characters just discussed are not mean or evil persons. Their creators clearly mean to win for them the respect and sympathy of the audience. Giovanni, the worst sinner of all, is a "miracle of wit" and has been esteemed "A wonder of [his] age":

> How did the University applaud
> Thy government, behaviour, learning, speech,
> Sweetness, and all that could make up a man![56]

In the Elizabethan drama, however, the most admirable people, if they fall in love, may plan or commit the most odious crimes. Such erotic sinners are motivated by a passion which they have not invited, which they loathe and combat with all their power, which they obey only because of its irresistible compulsion. They simply cannot help themselves. They are diseased, insane. Immoral acts or intentions due to love therefore are forgiven with remarkable readiness in the old drama. At the close of *The Two Gentlemen of Verona* no one seems to think the worse of Proteus for his contemplated sins. Angelo is not treated as a criminal in *Measure for Measure*. A soldier in Marston's *The Insatiate Countess* commits murder for love. His victim has given him a good character:

---

[52] P. 122.

[53] See p. 114. Cf. p. 126. Other dramatic characters who have been overpowered by incestuous desire similarly attempt to justify the passion. See Massinger, *The Unnatural Combat*, in *Plays*, I, 216–17; Brome, *The Love-sick Court*, in *Works*, II, 132. Such argument is supposed to indicate the corruption of reason by passion.

[54] P. 123.

[55] P. 146.

[56] P. 115.

> I know thee valiant Spaniard, and to thee
> Murders more hatefull, then is sacrilege.
> Thy actions ever have bene honourable.[57]

The governor, pitying his "bewich't fortunes," not only pardons him but offers him a colonel's commission.[58] Men in love are not responsible.

Elizabethan Englishmen think of passion as a physical state, or as a physical process. When love overpowers reason, flesh overpowers spirit, the subhuman element in human nature vanquishes the human. With this idea in mind, Tamyra in *Bussy D'Ambois*, attempts to justify her unlawful love:

> Our bodies are but thick clouds to our souls,
> Through which they cannot shine when they desire:
> . . . .
> O, how can we . . . .
> Disperse our passions' fumes, with our weak labours,
> That are more thick and black than all earth's vapours?[59]

The adulterous heroine of Webster's *The White Devil*, as she lies bleeding to death, lays the blame for her transgressions upon her physical nature: "my greatest sinne lay in my blood. / Now my blood paies for't."[60] To an Elizabethan these might seem valid self-vindications. The drama of the period demonstrates over and over the inability of the human intellect to control the impulses of the flesh. Passion may drive the most reasonable and virtuous persons into sin and calamity.

V

Love is commonly regarded, then, as an ignoble impulse arising from a physical condition, as a disease of body and mind, as a dangerous threat to virtue and happiness. Unless it is strictly controlled and directed by reason, it is a great evil. This is the view of the psychologist and moralist. In Elizabethan literature one finds another view of love, however, according to which love is a great good, a sweet and ennobling longing of the soul. This view, inherited from the Middle Ages, is in the courtly love tradition.

In some literary works, the courtly love tradition is clearly the dominant

---

57 *Plays*, III, 66.
58 P. 69.
59 Chapman, *Plays*, p. 154.
60 *Works*, I, 190. Cf. the dying words of Beaumelle in Massinger's *The Fatal Dowry*, in *Plays*, III, 444.

influence. The pensive lovers in Lodge's *Rosalynde*, for instance, act as courtly lovers are supposed to act, and their conduct bears the stamp of the author's approval. In other works, notably in plays dealing with the love-reason conflict, the scientific and ethical tradition is dominant. The behavior of hot and headlong sinners like Angelo and Giovanni illustrates the dangerous and evil power which the psychologists and moralists see in erotic passion. The authors may approve of the persons, but they do not approve of the passion or of the behavior which it motivates. (In many works, of course, the author takes no serious attitude at all.)

It is not always easy to define an author's attitude, for these two antithetical views are strangely interwoven in the thought and literature of Elizabethan and early Stuart England. One finds both, for example, in Sidney's *Arcadia*. Musidorus admonishes his lovesick friend Pyrocles earnestly, even harshly, although there is nothing obviously reprehensible about Pyrocles' love except the mere fact that it is love. Musidorus reminds Pyrocles that, "if we wil be men," reason must rule the sensitive faculties. Yet Pyrocles has allowed himself to be overcome forsooth by "love, a passion, and the basest and fruitlessest of all passions . . . it utterly subverts the course of nature, in making reason give place to sense, & man to woman." He beseeches his friend to purge himself "of this vile infection."[61] Pyrocles replies that Musidorus is like a physician who, instead of treating his patient, scolds him for his illness and bids "him be sick no more. . . . I am sicke, & sicke to the death." He declares that he has resisted his passion to the extent of his power, calling to his aid such philosophy as he knew. In spite of his utmost effort, however, love has conquered reason: "me thought even reason did assure me, that all eies did degenerate from their creation, which did not honour such a beautie."[62] It is admitted by both parties, then, that Pyrocles is in the grip of a dangerous evil. Yet no reader of the *Arcadia* ever got the impression that its characters or its author really considered love ignoble or degrading. Love is Sidney's theme and he treats it with affectionate respect. The whole novel, in spite of these touches of classical ethics, is permeated with the ideas and attitudes associated with courtly love.

Iago has heard that "base men being in love have then a nobility in their natures more than is native to them" (*Othello*, II, i, 218–20). Yet himself seems convinced that love "is merely a lust of the blood and a permission of the will" (I, iii, 339–40). Although Iago is a villain, the discourse on love which he delivers to Roderigo is good Elizabethan ethics (I, iii, 323–37). Writing in his own person, Shakespeare characterizes "lust in action" as an "expense of spirit in a waste of shame" (Sonnet cxxix). In the essay "Of

---

[61] *Works*, I, 77–78, 82. Musidorus later recants (pp. 113–14).
[62] Pp. 82, 85.

Love," Bacon declares that "great spirits and great business do keep out this weak passion." Man, who is "made for the contemplation of heaven and all noble objects," degrades himself grossly when he does "nothing but kneel before a little idol." Sir William Cornwallyes has great contempt for the lover's "Rimes, and Songs full of passion" and for "crossed armes, and the Hat pulled down."[63] A very large number of Elizabethan and early Stuart Englishmen held such opinions.

VI

Many characters of Elizabethan literature become weak, ill and despondent as a result of love. These are victims of love melancholy proper, the grief-stricken phase of the lover's malady.

The Elizabethan idea of love melancholy may have been as much a product of literary as of scientific influences. It had abundant literary precedent. Love is represented as a wasting disease in various works of ancient times.[64] The pining lover is a conventional figure also in romances, allegories, and amatory lyrics of the Middle Ages and the early Renaissance. His appearance in these is clearly due to the influence of the courtly love system, according to which despondent sickliness is a necessary concomitant of love.[65] Although Elizabethan and early Stuart England was not greatly inclined toward romantic idealization of love, the melancholy lovers in its literature have much in common—sometimes fundamentally, sometimes superficially—with the lover of the courtly love tradition.

There are many melancholy lovers in Elizabethan literature whose despondencies and debilities are sufficiently explained by literary precedents. Even if one is content to account for them thus, however, he does not exclude an indirect scientific influence. Lowes observes that, in their descriptions of the lover's malady, medieval poets and medieval physicians doubtless exercised mutual influence.[66] Such a mutual influence probably operated

---

63 *Essayes* (London, 1632), no. 5 ("Of Loue").

64 See Ovid, *Ars Amatoria*, I, 723–38; Ovid, *Heroides*, XI, 25–36; Theocritus, Idyll I, ll. 131, 138–41; Idyll II, ll. 82–89; Idyll XIV, ll. 3–6; Euripides, *Hippolytus*, ll. 131–52; Sappho, Fragment II; II Samuel, 13:1–14. I have been able to trace lovesickness farther back in literature than in medical treatises.

65 See especially Lewis Freeman Mott, *The System of Courtly Love* (New York, 1896), pp. 10–12, 33–34, 59, 130, *et passim*; William Allan Neilson, *The Origins and Sources of* The Court of Love (Boston, 1899), pp. 172, 179, *et passim*; William George Dodd, *Courtly Love in Chaucer and Gower* (Boston, 1913), pp. 13–15, *et passim*; Andreas Capellanus, *The Art of Courtly Love*, tr. John Jay Parry (New York, 1941), pp. 5, 6, 9, 185.

66 "The Loveres Maladye," p. 543.

throughout the long and parallel histories of the literary and scientific concepts of lovesickness.

In any case literary influences do not wholly account for the manner in which lovesickness is represented in Elizabethan works. Several writers of the period, most of them dramatists, show a knowledge of the medical and psychiatric aspects of the malady which they could hardly have gained from reading the amatory literature of earlier times. Representations of despondent love, moreover, contain many indications of the current interest in melancholy and of the ideas popularly associated with it. In Elizabethan literature *melancholy* is used in connection with love much more often than before.[67] Englishmen have begun to think of the melancholy lover as a type related to the malcontent. Writers often speak of the lover's "discontent" and describe him as "discontented," although these words do not seem particularly applicable. Pining lovers are sometimes called malcontents.[68] The melancholy lover has borrowed the characteristic pose of the malcontent with clothing disordered, hat pulled over the eyes, and arms folded. Folded arms are mentioned very often; the "cross arms" are, in fact, "the lover's sign."[69]

Love melancholy is logically due to the sorrow of unsatisfied love. The fact that the lover in Elizabethan literature often assumes the melancholy attitude immediately upon falling in love, even before he knows the lady's feeling toward him, is largely due, I think, to the influence of the courtly love tradition. The courtly lover necessarily languishes because he of course assumes that he will be frustrated. It would be highly presumptuous of him to think that his divinity would treat him with anything but lofty contempt.

Elizabethan sonneteers, inspired by the love poets of Italy, complain pathetically of their weakness of body and excruciating despondency of mind. They suffer exquisite pain from the fires and chills of love; they cannot sleep; they are fond of pensive solitude; they sigh, weep, and long for death; they grow pale and feeble. Anyone who is even superficially acquainted with the sonnet sequences will recognize the following, from Thomas Watson's *The Tears of Fancie*, as typical:

> The priuate place which I did choose to waile,
> And deere lament my loues pride was a groue;

---

[67] In the Tudor drama written before 1580, I have found no instance in which *melancholy* is used in connection with love (see Chap. IV, note 1). Love is not a frequent theme in the older drama, to be sure, but it appears at least occasionally. Chaucer is very definitely conscious of the connection between love and melancholy ("Knight's Tale," l. 1375).

[68] See *Love's Labor's Lost*, III, i, 193; Dekker, *A Knight's Conjuring*, ed. Edward F. Rimbault (London, 1842), p. 73.

[69] Middleton, *Works*, VI, 186.

Plac'd twixt two hills within a lowlie dale,
Which now by fame was cald the vale of loue.
The vale of loue for there I spent my plainings,
Plaints that bewraid my sicke harts bitter wounding:
Loue sicke harts deepe wounds with dispaire me paining,
The bordering hills my sorrowing plaints resounding.
Each tree did beare the figure of her name,
Which my faint hand vppon their backs ingraued:
And euery tree did seeme her sore to blame,
Calling her proud that mee of ioyes depraued.
But vaine for shee had vowed to forsake mee,
And I to endles anguish must betake mee.[70]

This wretched amorous languor is, of course, regarded as a kind of melancholy. In his preface to Sidney's *Astrophel and Stella*, Nashe invites "idle eares to the admiration of [Sidney's] melancholy."[71] Lodge uses "melancholie" in the sense of love lyric.[72]

There is much melancholic misery also in Elizabethan amatory poems written in forms other than the sonnet—in Lodge's *Glaucus and Silla*, J. C.'s *Alcilia: Philoparthen's Loving Folly*, Robert Tofte's *Alba: The Month's Minde of a Melancholy Lover*, Nicholas Breton's *The Passionate Shepheard*, and many others. The poems mentioned, each of which consists mainly or wholly of a lover's lament, are closely akin to the sonnets in content and style. Even in Spenser's *The Faerie Queene*, in which love is merely an incidental theme, one finds the lover's malady: Rebuked by Belphebe, Timias, Prince Arthur's squire, retires to a "gloomy glade" where mossy trees cover "all with shade / And sad melancholy" (IV, vii, 38). There he builds a cabin and dwells in wretched despondency. Through long fasting and self-neglect, he becomes "pale and wan, / All overgrowen with rude and rugged haire" (IV, vii, 43). He loses the power of speech. When Belphebe sees him once more, she fails to recognize him. He is like a "ghost late risen from his grave" (IV, viii, 12). Restoration to the lady's gracious favor cures him.

The conventional traits appear again in the very numerous melancholy lovers who wander disconsolately through Elizabethan prose fiction—through Lyly's two novels, Sidney's *Arcadia*, Green's *Menaphon* and *The*

---

70 *Elizabethan Sonnets*, ed. Sydney Lee (Westminster, 1904), I, 147. Lisle Cecil John, in *The Elizabethan Sonnet Sequences: Studies in Conventional Conceits* (New York, 1938), pp. 79-109, 196-97, reviews the melancholic symptoms of love which appear in the sonnets. The volume also deals with the literary antecedents of the English sonnet.

71 Nashe, *Works*, III, 330. In *Astrophel and Stella*, sonnets xxiii, xxvii, xciv, and cviii furnish good illustrations of Sidney's melancholy. Sidney occasionally displays some rather specific physiological knowledge.

72 *A Margarite of America* (*Works*, vol. III), p. 24. Cf. "*Italian* melancholie," p. 78.

Carde of Fancie, Lodge's *Rosalynde* and *A Margarite of America*, and many more. There is no great individuality among these characters. They tend to be lean, pale, and hollow eyed; they sigh and lament; they continually seek solitude and, having found it, deliver pathetic soliloquies, which the writers call "passions"; they often stand or sit, with arms crossed, in a "dump" or a "muse," from which it is hard to arouse them; they have no appetite and sleep very badly; in the presence of the beloved they tremble and become petrified and speechless. Some of the cases in the novels are severe. Castania, in Greene's *The Carde of Fancie*, is "constrained to keep her bed," and her brother Tharsalio, on shipboard, is "constrayned to keepe his Cabbine";[73] Phoebe, in Lodge's *Rosalynde*, becomes dangerously lovesick;[74] Zelmane, in Sidney's *Arcadia*, dies of love.[75] As a rule these lovers are very secretive regarding the cause of their illness. Sometimes the novelist elaborates on the mystification of anxious parents and friends; sometimes inept physicians fail in diagnosis; occasionally a clever character displays his acumen in recognizing love by its symptoms.[76]

I shall describe two of the many cases of melancholic lovesickness which occur in the novels—those of Fidus, in *Euphues and His England*, and Amphialus, in the *Arcadia*. Fidus tells his own story.[77] Having fallen in love with Iffida and having received no encouragement, he moped in solitude. "At the last with continual abstinence from meat, from company, from sleepe, my body began to consume, & my head to waxe idle." His anxious and mystified father summoned divers physicians, among them a shrewd Italian. This man, after "feeling my pulses, casting my water, & marking my lookes," diagnosed the case as love. "Your humour," he said to Fidus, "is to be purged not by the Apothecaries confections, but by the following of good counsaile." If Fidus would confide in him, he could offer relief; otherwise "you shall but shorten your lyfe." Fidus was thus persuaded to tell the physician the name of his beloved, and the doctor brought Iffida to his bedside. She found him greatly "altered in a moneth, wasted to the harde bones, more lyke a ghoast then a lyuing creature." She was overcome with pity but could not return Fidus' love because she was plighted to another. She remained with him, however, and nursed him back to health. Since her

---

[73] *Works*, IV, 94, 151.

[74] P. 115 (*Works*, vol. I).

[75] *Works*, I, 295–99.

[76] See Greene, *The Carde of Fancie*, in *Works*, IV, 94–95, and *Planetomachia*, in *Works*, V, 131–32.

[77] Lyly, *Works*, II, 72–74. At the close of the novel, Euphues himself retires to live in melancholy solitude on "the Mount of *Silixsedra*," "both tormented in body and grieued in minde" (p. 228). Apparently the cause is hopeless love of Camilla.

death he has lived as a hermit. Fidus' lovesickness is a highly conventional case which is developed in somewhat greater detail than most.

In the *Arcadia* Amphialus is in love with Philoclea, who is herself in love with Pyrocles. In her presence Amphialus loses the power of coherent speech and stands rapt "as if with the sight of *Gorgons* head."[78] His "un-luckie love" fills his mind "with melancholie."[79] Amphialus unwittingly kills a young woman, and shame and remorse for this deed complicate his love melancholy. Thereupon Amphialus gets "him to his bed, not so much to rest his restles minde, as to avoyd all companie. . . . And then melancholie (onely riche in unfortunate remembrances)" brings before him all the shames and sorrows of his past life, over which he broods miserably. He lies awake all night and when day comes shuts out the light. The greatest of his sorrows, so great that the rest seem inconsequential, is "his fatall love to *Philoclea*."[80] There comes a challenge to combat, however, which rouses Amphialus from his bed. In the battle, he is severely wounded. Lying abed once more, he seems likely to die, for although the surgeons make progress toward curing his physical hurt, "Sorrowe and shame (like two corrupted servaunts)" lay siege to his life, encouraging the wish to die. His "melancholy" detests "all company, so as not the very surgeons nor servants durst speak unto him in doing him service."[81] Later, attempting suicide, he wounds himself. As the story breaks off unfinished, it seems likely that he will die. The love melancholy of Amphialus is the least conventional case that I have found in prose fiction, both because it has medical complications and because Amphialus' lethargic brooding and black despair have more in common with the grief-stricken melancholy described in medical texts than with the usual sentimental love languor.

The conventional figure of the woebegone and debilitated lover appears very frequently also in the drama. Among the earlier examples are various characters in the plays of John Lyly. Endimion, for instance, is cruelly tormented by his hopeless love for Cynthia. He lives in "deepe melancholy,"[82] seeks solitude, and soliloquizes passionately. Tears, sighs, "hollowe eyes," and "broken sleepes"[83] indicate the depth of his misery. Apelles suffers extremities for love of Campaspe and is cleverly tricked into betraying his

---

[78] Sidney, *Works*, I, 375.

[79] P. 441.

[80] Pp. 450–51. Among the past deeds over which Amphialus broods is the involuntary killing of his friend Philoxenus. Immediately after this deed, Amphialus suffered a grief-stricken fit of melancholy (pp. 71–74, 98–99). Amphialus is very susceptible to melancholy, as his mother realizes (p. 419).

[81] Pp. 464–65.

[82] Lyly, *Endimion*, in *Works*, III, 38.

[83] P. 31. Tellus is lovesick for Endimion (pp. 53, 74).

secret by his rival, Alexander the Great.[84] Peele's *The Arraignment of Paris* presents a tragic case. The shepherd Colin, whose companions pity him deeply for his "uncouth fit," his "malady,"[85] pines away and dies for love of the flint-hearted Thestylis. In Dekker's *Old Fortunatus*, Orleans, in love, enters *"melancholike"* and complains that he is "sicke." He looks "leane, and [like] a louer" and is "long tormented" in "sorrowes Jayle."[86] Eurione, of Chapman's *Monsieur D'Olive*, suffers from "a maiden melancholy," the result of her love for the Count St. Anne.[87] Aspatia, in *The Maid's Tragedy*, loves Amintor hopelessly. She

> Walks discontented, with her watry eyes
> Bent on the earth: the unfrequented woods
> Are her delight.

She sings mournful love songs, tells tales of tragic love, and "carries with her an infectious grief."[88] Her death is virtual suicide. Philaster sits "cross arm'd," sighs "away the day," makes the solitude reverberate with his mistress' name.[89] Amie, a shepherdess in Jonson's *The Sad Shepherd*, is infected by a young man's kiss. Soon she is ill and complains naïvely of this unfamiliar "disease" that torments her with alternate heats and chills.[90] There are many similar figures in the drama.

In later plays one occasionally finds a melancholy lover who does not suffer quite so pathetically and conventionally. Such a person is the hero of Jonson's *The New Inn*. Lovel, *"A compleat Gentleman, a Souldier, and a Scholer, is a melancholy Guest in the Inne."*[91] The shrewd host guesses, from his "drousie" demeanor and his "lethargie,"[92] that he is in love. The

---

[84] Lyly, *Campaspe*, in *Works*, II, 341–43, 352, 356. Concerning Alexander's love of Campaspe, see pp. 329–31. Other examples in Lyly's plays are Sapho in *Sapho and Phao* (*ibid.*, 392, 396 ff.) and three nymphs of Diana in *Gallathea* (*ibid.*, 446–49).

[85] *Works*, I, 35. The forsaken Oenone is also melancholy (pp. 37 ff.). In Peele's *David and Bathsabe*, Ammon becomes "amorously lean" (*Works*, II, 17).

[86] *Works*, I, 126, 129, 157.

[87] *Plays*, p. 119. In Chapman's *The Widow's Tears*, love renders Eudora melancholy (*Plays*, pp. 317–19).

[88] *Beaumont and Fletcher*, I, 4.

[89] *Ibid.*, p. 97. See also p. 115. There are several other lovesick persons in the Beaumont and Fletcher collection, among them Perigot and Amoret in *The Faithful Shepherdess* (II, 412–13, 418, 420–24), Frank in *The Captain* (V, 234, 238, 288), Hydaspes in *Cupid's Revenge* (IX, 245–46).

[90] *Jonson*, VII, 32.

[91] *Ibid.*, VI, 402.

[92] P. 414. The host refers to Lovel's "minde to be melancholy, and musty" (p. 408), his "daily dumps" (p. 409), his "sleepy humor / Of drousy, accidentall melancholy" (p. 459).

lady, also a guest in the inn, at first gives Lovel some encouragement, then wounds him with indifference. He describes the result in soliloquy:

> O my braine!
> How art thou turned! and my blood congeald!
> My sinewes slackned! and my marrow melted!
> . . . . Ile to bed, and sleepe,
> And dreame away the vapour of *Loue*.[93]

He finally wins the lady. Lovel is an intelligent and rather eloquent person who is able to regard his own state of mind with some detachment. Although his melancholy is due to love longing, it shows itself not in the conventional sighs, tears, and complaints, but in a certain somberness of deportment and asperity of thought and expression. In Ford's *The Lady's Trial* there appears a similar figure. Malfato, described in the *dramatis personae* as "a discontented lover," is in love with a lady who is happily married. His melancholy is "grounded and resolv'd / Receiv'd into a habit."[94] It makes him unsociable; he is in "hearty league / With solitary thoughts."[95] He can be vitriolically indignant.[96] He seems more like the honest and independent type of malcontent than like the melancholy lover.

Some of the cases in the drama are very definitely of medical interest. Among these is the lovesickness of Frank in *Monsieur Thomas*. Frank falls in love with Cellide, fiancée of his friend and benefactor Valentine, and, because he is honorable, suffers in silence. He becomes "much chang'd, extreamly alter'd, / His colour faded strangely too," and he "looks worse hourly." He "sweats too coldly," and his pulse is weak and slow. In the presence of Cellide, however, "He sweats extreamly: / Hot, very hot: his pulse beats like a drum now."[97] His friends discuss medical measures and put him to bed. Doctors are summoned, and they debate learnedly and futilely while the patient continues to decline.[98] A clever woman, however, observing the manner in which Frank grips Cellide's hand, guesses the truth.[99] A wise friend reveals the cause of the illness to Valentine. Valentine gives up the girl.

Antoninus, in Massinger's *The Virgin Martyr*, is rejected by the lady whom he loves and becomes very ill, so ill that he takes to his bed. Sapritius,

---

93 P. 476.
94 *Works*, III, 23.
95 P. 64. See also pp. 67, 87.
96 Pp. 25, 87–91.
97 *Beaumont and Fletcher*, IV, 107–8.
98 Pp. 116–17. We see the doctors vainly at work over the unwilling patient, pp. 120–21.
99 P. 109.

his father, is bewildered and alarmed. The physicians whom he summons report that the disease is "a deep melancholy," and they fear that "The grave must mock our labours."[100] A friend of Antoninus' reveals the cause of the malady to Sapritius:

> in his broken slumbers,
> Him shall you hear cry out on Dorothea
> . . . . let him hear
> The voice of Dorothea, nay, but the name,
> He starts up with high colour in his face:
> She, or none, cures him.[101]

Sapritius, being governor of the city, places the lady in his son's power, providing him thus with the means of cure; but Antoninus refuses to prostitute her. In the end he dies.

Ford's *The Lover's Melancholy* offers a study of love melancholy evidently indebted to Burton.[102] Palador, Prince of Cyprus, has for some time been pining for Eroclea, whose whereabouts he does not know. He is taciturn and sober,

> will smile, but seldom laugh;
> Will lend an ear to business, deal in none;
> Gaze upon revels, antic fopperies,
> But is not mov'd; will sparingly discourse,
> Hear music; but what most he takes delight in
> Are handsome pictures.[103]

He is in the condition of lethargic abstraction, then, that is a frequent result of melancholy. He dislikes company.[104] His physician, Corax, scolds him for neglecting the exercises which he has prescribed and for reading sonnets. Indignantly the doctor asks permission to leave the court: "it does infect me with the sloth / Of sleep and surfeit."[105] Clearly he knows what is the matter with the Prince. The Cyprian courtiers, however, do not know and are consequently puzzled and anxious. Corax' "Masque of Melancholy"

---

[100] *Plays*, I, 76. They mention music and sleep as curative measures (pp. 77–78).
[101] P. 77.
[102] See Chap. V, note 44. There is, however, little if anything in Ford's representation of love melancholy which he could not have found in literary sources. Ewing (*Burtonian Melancholy in the Plays of John Ford*, pp. 32–42, 60–64, 70–76, *et passim*) and Sensabaugh (*The Tragic Muse of John Ford*, pp. 62–93) have described the melancholy of Palador and of other lovesick characters of Ford's plays.
[103] Ford, *Works*, I, 12.
[104] See pp. 31, 84.
[105] P. 31.

(see above, pp. 125–27) is a device to reveal to them in a striking fashion the fact that the Prince is in love. At the close of the masque, Corax explains to the Prince that one kind of melancholy has been omitted, for " 'twas not in art" to represent "Love-Melancholy." The doctor then plunges into an eloquent description of love as a psychic disaster. The Prince, much moved, interrupts him, commands that "no man henceforth name the word again," and leaves abruptly. Corax has triumphantly demonstrated that "love pent ne'er so close, yet will be seen."[106] Palador is cured by reunion with Eroclea. Since this reunion has been arranged by another person, the physician can hardly be said to have contributed much toward the Prince's recovery.

In Brome's *The Queen's Exchange*, Osriick, King of Northumbia, sees a picture of Mildred, a maiden of Wessex, and falls in love with her. He forthwith complains that he is not well.[107] Because circumstances make his love dishonorable, he conceals it. He becomes very seriously distracted, and the doctors become "almost as mad as he, / Because they cannot find the cause."[108] The patient's moods and fancies are most changeable, eccentric, and unreasonable; his favorite occupation apparently is wandering alone in "solitary places . . . Groves and Thickets" where "he unheard by all may vent his passions"; he does not sleep for four consecutive nights.[109] Unable to stand it any longer, he finally sets out incognito for Wessex, woos Mildred, and wins her.

Secretiveness is a notably persistent trait among the melancholy lovers of Elizabethan literature. Sometimes the lover's stubborn silence is to be explained by the fact that he has reason to be ashamed of his passion, sometimes merely by the fact that the lover traditionally keeps his counsel. Elizabethan writers often use the lover's reticence to create bewilderment, anxiety, and complication. The solution of the problems which arise thus, as well as the cure of the lover's illness, depends upon discovery of his secret. The discovery is therefore a matter of considerable narrative interest. The manner in which the author brings it about frequently suggests the influence

106 Pp. 68–69. This scene was probably inspired by the stories told of Erasistratus and Galen and their dealings with lovesick patients (see Burton, *Anatomy*, III, 156). These two physicians, however, employ their ingenuity to good purpose in discovering the identity of the patient's beloved. Corax' masque accomplishes nothing beyond making the patient betray in public the fact that he is in love, a fact which Corax already knows. Indeed, since he is in league with the Prince's confident, Rhetias, he could hardly fail to know the identity of the lady.

107 *Works*, III, 476–77.

108 P. 497. They never discover it, yet they realize at least that the disease is melancholy. One of them thinks it advisable to humor what he supposes to be a melancholy caprice of the King's (p. 499); he brings the King a soporific (p. 509); he discourses on melancholic delusions (p. 526).

109 Pp. 498–99, 507. A fierce battle between love and right reason takes place in the mind of the king (pp. 500–1).

of the often repeated stories concerning the diagnostic methods of famous physicians.[110]

Stories of this category evidently were very popular. Shirley makes specific use of one of them in *The Witty Fair One*. To play upon a lady's sympathy, young Fowler feigns illness, while a friend masquerades as a physician in attendance. The lady visits the supposedly sick man. The doctor tells her that she is quite clearly responsible for Fowler's condition, for as soon as he saw her, "his labouring pulse, that, through his fever, did before stick hard, and frequent, now exceeds in both these differences; and this Galen himself found true upon a woman that had doted upon a fencer."[111]

VII

Some lovers in the early Stuart drama literally go insane. There is, for instance, the old general Memnon, central character of *The Mad Lover*. Memnon falls absurdly in love at first sight with the young Princess Calis. He stands in a trance and murmurs a declaration of love while the bystanders watch in astonishment.[112] Later he does not know what he has done or said. To parry his importunities, the girl says thoughtlessly that she will accept his proffered heart if she may have it in her hand. Memnon immediately becomes obsessed with the idea of cutting out his heart for her. They will enjoy their love, he believes, in Elysium. He goes so far as to summon a surgeon.[113] Memnon's officers and his brother Polydor attempt a cure, employing conventional devices. They raise rumors of new wars to divert the general's thoughts from his love. They humor his fancies and attempt to turn them to therapeutic use. Since he has been calling upon Orpheus to appear and discourse upon the joys of Elysium, an officer who can sing impersonates Orpheus and tries to soothe him with music and to dissuade him from his intended suicide.[114] A prostitute is engaged to impersonate

---

[110] See above, pp. 137–38. The influence of these tales seems apparent in the cases of Castania in Greene's *The Carde of Fancie* (*Works*, IV, 94–97), Apelles in Lyly's *Campaspe* (*Works*, II, 356), Palador of Ford's *The Lover's Melancholy* (*Works*, I, 68–69), Helena in *All's Well That Ends Well* (I, iii, 145–87), and others. The earliest example that I have found occurs in *Common Conditions* (registered 1576). A physician recognizes the symptoms of the love malady in his ailing daughter, persuades her to confide in him, and undertakes to get the man for her. See *Five Anonymous Plays, Fourth Series*, ed. J. S. Farmer (London, 1908), pp. 225–27.

[111] *Works*, I, 320. See Galen, *Opera*, XIV, 631–33.

[112] *Beaumont and Fletcher*, III, 5–7.

[113] P. 34.

[114] Pp. 47–50.

the Princess, and for a short time Memnon is deceived.[115] But nothing seems to do any good. Memnon finally comes to his senses when he learns that Polydor and Calis have fallen in love with each other. He retires in favor of his brother.

Shatillon, in *The Noble Gentleman*, has been distracted by the cruel treatment of his love. He has developed the delusion that his love is rightful heir to the French throne and has been imprisoned by the reigning usurper.[116] The usurping King, he believes, is pursuing him with plots and spies, fearing that he may marry the lady and claim the throne. His "Love," who is otherwise anonymous, is deeply repentant. She follows him about—without his recognizing her—anxiously humoring him and trying to restore his sanity. To aid her, a gentleman represents himself as an emissary with offers of reconcilement from the King. The King, he tells Shatillon, has released his love from prison and sends her to him. Thereupon the lady comes forward. Shatillon recognizes her and soon recovers his wits.[117]

The jailer's daughter, in *The Two Noble Kinsmen*, is tragically affected by her love of Palamon. She wanders in the forest deserted by her lover. "I am mop't," she says;

> Food took I non[e] these two daies.
> Sipt some water, I have not clos'd mine eyes
> Save when my lids scowrd off their [brine]; alas
> Dissolve my life, Let not my sence unsettle
> Least I should drown, or stab or hang my self.[118]

When she next appears she is mad. She sings songs and utters a great deal of pretty nonsense about flowers, about love, about Palamon.[119] When she is brought home, her father and his friends, all deeply distressed, are careful to humor her. A doctor is summoned. He diagnoses the case: " 'Tis not an engraffed madness but a most thick, and profound melancholly."[120] He instructs the maiden's wooer, who was prospering in his suit before she saw Palamon, to take upon himself the role of Palamon. The boorish young man plays the part very badly, but the maiden is easily convinced. The doc-

[115] Pp. 56–58.
[116] *Ibid.*, VIII, 181–83, 205–6, 210–12, 214–19.
[117] Pp. 236–39.
[118] *Ibid.*, IX, 328–29.
[119] Pp. 331, 333–34, 348–51, 356–57, 365–68. Her madness resembles that of Ophelia, who seems to have exerted a considerable influence on the lovesick maidens of the early Stuart drama. Yet Ophelia's madness apparently is due principally not to disappointment in love, but to grief for her father's death (*Hamlet*, IV, v, 4, 46, 76–77, 160–62, 184).
[120] P. 357.

tor then directs the wooer to "Lie with her if she ask you"; "it cures her *ipso facto,* / The melancholly humor that infects her."[121] In the final scene the jailer reports that she has recovered and is about to be married.

Penthea, of Ford's *The Broken Heart,* is prevented from marrying the man whom she loves and is compelled to marry Bassanes, an old man who torments her with his jealousy. She sinks charmingly and submissively into a melancholy. Sorrows, she suspects, have "dull'd my infected brain."[122] Her griefs drive her mad. She refuses food; for ten days she does not sleep.[123] At her last appearance she comes upon the stage *"with her hair loose"* and talks distractedly of sorrow and death, of the happy marriage that might have been, and of the children that she might have had.[124] There comes a lucid interval in which Penthea laments the fate which has forced her, "Widow'd by lawless marriage," to live what she considers a life of shame.[125] She dies of self-starvation.

Constance, heroine of Brome's *The Northern Lass,* has been mentally deranged by her love for Sir Philip Luckless. She is "full of melanchollie . . . sick in mind."[126] She sings prettily and talks pathetically of her love for Philip.[127] She will not be persuaded, as the jailer's daughter is, that another suitor is the man whom she loves. A witty servant who has assumed the disguise of a doctor discourses learnedly and accurately on her condition: "Her disease is melanchollie; the cause . . . love, which . . . hath overwhelm'd her spirits, and turn'd the faculties of all her senses into a rude confusion. . . . The partie that she loves, must be the Doctor, the Medicine, and the cure."[128] Constance finally marries her Philip.

Erotic distraction appears again in Brome's *The Antipodes.* Martha is married to Perigrine, but since he is mentally unbalanced (see above, p. 123), there has been no consummation of the marriage. Martha is consequently "sicke of her virginity" yet is so innocent that "she knowes not what it is."[129] Sometimes she weeps, sometimes laughs violently; now she is sullenly silent, again loudly talkative.[130] She is obsessed with a desire for children. She talks irrationally and pathetically of children and wonders how they are to be procured. Dr. Hughball undertakes the treatment of both Martha and her husband. The physician gives his attention especially to Perigrine,

---

[121] Pp. 364–65.
[122] *Works,* I, 263.
[123] Pp. 292–93.
[124] Pp. 289–90.
[125] P. 293.
[126] *Works,* III, 50.
[127] Pp. 51–53.
[128] Pp. 84.
[129] *Ibid.,* p. 257.
[130] P. 329.

for he believes that, if he can inveigle him into playing the part of the husband, both he and Martha will be cured. To be sure, after consummation of the marriage, "all their melancholly" is gone.[131]

VIII

There are many derisive portraits of the lover in Elizabethan satire, some drawn in a spirit of sharp disparagement, others in a mood of good-natured raillery. The lover of the satiric sketches is a conventional figure exhibiting the familiar melancholic traits. It might be hard to determine whether the writers took these traits from the amatory literature of their time or from lovers whom they actually saw. Just as there were many malcontents in Elizabethan England, there must have been many melancholy lovers whose behavior corresponded with the current ideas concerning the conduct proper to a man in love. Satiric treatment of the lover's manners, it should be noted, does not mean that the author doubts the reality of love melancholy.

A few illustrations will suffice. Marston challenges "Bedlam, Frenzy, Madness, Lunacy . . . to produce a more distracted man / Than is inamorato Lucian"[132] and describes his absurd behavior. Nicholas Breton repeats the tale of a sighing, moody lover who would "let fall a tear or two, with madame: and with that word, teare open his buttons, throw off his hat, fling away his pantoffles, breake all the strings of his lute, knocke the belly against the bedde poste and runne to his sworde."[133] John Davies of Hereford draws an unflattering portrait of "amorous Andrugio," who sits "in a corner with crost armes, / And with a sigh together brings his sides." Andrugio "Now seekes a rope, and then . . . a knife."[134] The Overbury characters include a caustic sketch of the amorous poser: "His armes are carelesly used, as if their best use were nothing but embracements. He is untrust and unbuttoned, ungartred, not out of carelesnes, but care. . . . He answers not, or not to the purpose . . . shortly hee is translated out of a man into folly."[135]

The lover's manners are ridiculed also in the drama. For example, Labesha, a gull in Chapman's *An Humorous Day's Mirth*, learns that his lady is false to him and declares:

---

131 P. 333.
132 *Satires*, in *Works*, ed. Bullen, III, 278.
133 From "A Farewell," published in 1599 with *The Wil of Wit* (*Works*, ed. Alexander B. Grosart [Edinburgh, 1879], vol. II), p. 63.
134 *The Scourge of Folly* (*Works*, vol. II), p. 17a.
135 *Overburian Characters*, pp. 21–22.

> I will in silence live a man forlorn,
> Mad, and melancholy as a cat,
> And never more wear hatband on my hat.

He grows "marvellous malcontent," takes upon himself "the humour of the young lord Dowsecer."[136] Hearing that his mistress has killed herself for love of him, he attempts to hang himself. At the opening of Marston's *What You Will*, Jacomo appears with his clothing in great disarray. He is "mad, starke mad, alasse for love."[137] In Field's *A Woman Is a Weathercock*, Sir Abraham Ninny, disdained by his lady, delivers a "doleful dump":

> Gush, eyes; thump, hand; swell, heart; buttons, fly open!
> Thanks, gentle doublet, else my heart had broken . . .[138]

Later he enters *"melancholy."*[139]

Like the less extreme forms of lovesickness, love madness is sometimes represented facetiously. Memnon, of *The Mad Lover*, and Shatillon, of *The Noble Gentleman*, are intended as ridiculous figures. An anonymous lover with a knack for verse draws a blithe picture of his own amorous distraction:

> Heard you not lately of a man
> That went beside his witt,
> And naked through the Citty rann
> Wrapt in a frantique fitt?
> Why honest neighbours it was I,
> Harke how the people showt mee;
> Heere comes the madd man when they cry
> With all the boyes about mee
>
> . . . .
>
> Tom Bedlam is a sage to mee,
> I speake in sober sadnesse,
> And more strang visions doe I see
> Then hee in all his madnesse.
> Nowe, when into my rage I happ
> About the markett walke I

---

136 *Plays*, p. 38–39. Dowsecer's melancholy humor has been described on p. 100.
137 *Plays*, II, 237.
138 *Old Plays*, ed. Dodsley and Hazlitt, XI, 30. See also pp. 54–56.
139 P. 34. Other gulls of the drama who become—or think that they become—melancholy for love are: Basilisco of *Soliman and Perseda* (Kyd, *Works*, p. 172), Gelasimus of the academic *Timon* (*A Supplement to Dodsley's Old Plays* [London, 1853], III, 48–49), Mallfort of *The Lover's Progress* (Beaumont and Fletcher, V, 75–77), Onos of *The Queen of Corinth* (*ibid.*, VI, 50–51), Geron of Brome's *The Love-Sick Court* (*Works*, II, 149–50).

With Capons feathers in my capp,
And to my selfe thus talke I.
Sawe I not Angells in her eyes? . . .[140]

IX

It seems best to deal separately with the love melancholy of Shakespeare's
plays, for Shakespeare's representation of the malady is not altogether typical. There is a good deal of lovesickness among the Shakespearean characters, to be sure, and it is evident that Shakespeare was well acquainted with
the current beliefs concerning it.[141]

In *Love's Labor's Lost*, love teaches King Ferdinand and his three companions in retirement "to rime, and to be melancholy" (IV, iii, 14).[142] Love
causes Proteus, of *The Two Gentlemen of Verona*, "to wreathe [his] arms,
like a malecontent," to walk alone, to sigh, to weep, to fast, to watch, "to
speak puling," to go "ungartered"; and Valentine, upon falling in love, be-
haves likewise (II, i, 20–27, 81).[143] In *A Midsummer Night's Dream* Helena
becomes

> All fancy-sick . . . and pale of cheer
> With sighs of love, that cost the fresh blood dear. (III, ii, 96–97)

In the same play Theseus classifies the lover with the madman and the poet
(V, i, 4–17). In these early comedies, however, Shakespeare seems to regard
lovesickness as something that calls for kindly mockery rather than serious
alarm. Romeo is melancholically in love with Rosaline (I, i, 122–244), but
this affair, which is lightly treated, is eclipsed by Romeo's love for Juliet,
which is not at all melancholic. Orlando, Silvius, and Phebe, of *As You Like
It*, are as woebegone as their prototypes in Lodge's *Rosalynde*,[144] but they
are so depicted that they provoke more amusement than sympathy. Orsino,
in *Twelfth Night*, languishes for love of Olivia (I, i), but one does not get
the impression that he is suffering greatly. Viola tells Orsino a tale about
her father's daughter, who, because of disappointment in love,

---

140 Commonplace book, Folger manuscript 1.21, fols. 44–45. The poem was probably
written in the early Stuart period.

141 See Draper, *The Humors & Shakespeare's Characters*, pp. 68–69.

142 Act IV, sc. iii, is very melancholic. In this play also there appears Armado, a
vainglorious gull who affects a ridiculous melancholy supposed to be due at least in
part to love. See I, ii; III, i, 1–140; IV, i, 60–96.

143 Cf. I, i, 29–69; II, iv, 129–36; III, ii, 62; IV, ii, 27–28; V, iv, 1–6.

144 See especially II, iv, 22–42; III, ii; III, v; IV, i; V, ii, 84–121. There are bantering
references to the love melancholy or lovesickness of various characters in *Much Ado
About Nothing*: II, i, 223; III, ii, 16, 54–55; III, iv, 41–42, 52–53, 71.

> pin'd in thought,
> And with a green and yellow melancholy,
> She sat like Patience on a monument,
> Smiling at grief. (II, iv, 114-17)

In reality, although Viola's father's daughter is in love, she is not in ill health. When Hamlet visits Ophelia in her closet, his disordered clothing and distracted behavior (II, i, 77-100) do indeed, as Polonius confidently observes, suggest "the very ecstasy of love" (II, i, 102). Polonius makes a very plausible diagnosis (II, ii, 146-51). But Polonius is wrong.

It is clear that Shakespeare does not take lovesickness very seriously.[145] Rosalind, in *As You Like It*, charmingly ridicules the common notions concerning the love malady in the well-known catalogue of the marks that distinguish a lover which she recites to Orlando: "A lean cheek . . . a blue eye and sunken . . . an unquestionable spirit . . . a beard neglected. . . . Then, your hose should be ungartered, your bonnet unbanded, your sleeve unbuttoned, your shoe untied, and everything about you demonstrating a careless desolation. But you are no such man" (III, ii, 397-406). It is Rosalind's belief, and probably Shakespeare's, that "men have died from time to time, and worms have eaten them, but not for love" (IV, i, 110-12). Shakespeare evidently approves the forthright love-making of King Henry V: "before God, Kate, I cannot look greenly nor gasp out my eloquence . . . if thou canst love me . . . take me; if not, to say to thee that I shall die, is true; but for thy love, by the Lord, no; yet I love thee too" (V, ii, 147-59).

Amid general belief in the lover's malady, then, one discovers a genial skeptic. I have found no definite evidence of such skepticism in the work of any other writer. Without question Shakespeare on the whole accepted the physiology, the medical science, and the psychology which other men of his time accepted. But when the teachings of the sciences were too obviously in conflict with the facts of experience, Shakespeare was a realist.

X

A gentleman in Field's *Amends for Ladies* complains that his sweetheart will not take his love seriously

---

[145] If anything in Shakespeare's plays indicates serious belief in love melancholy, it is Helena's languishing love of Bertram in *All's Well That Ends Well*. See especially I, iii, 112-225. The countess, holding Helena's wrist, accuses her of wishing to marry Bertram and uses the consequent irregular action of her pulse as evidence in extracting a confession of love from her (I, iii, 176-77). Love affects Pericles melancholically in a passage which is probably not Shakespearean (II, iii). Imogen's melancholy (*Cymbeline*, IV, ii, 1-60, 203-8) can hardly be classified as love melancholy. Concerning Ophelia's madness, see above, note 119.

'cause I do not weep,
Lay mine arms o'er my heart, and wear no garters,
Walk with mine eyes in my hat, sigh and make faces.[146]

Field's audience, like this lady, would expect a character in love to exhibit some of these symptoms. There is rather clear evidence that the actor in the role of lover appeared in disordered dress, stood with his arms folded and his hat pulled over his eyes, and indulged in unsociable musing. In dress and manner, there must have been little difference on the stage between the lover and the malcontent (see above, pp. 119–20). At the opening of Greene's *Friar Bacon and Friar Bungay*, Prince Edward enters *"malcontented"* and stands apart from his companions in "a melancholie dumpe," "all amort . . . malecontent."[147] One soon learns that his trouble is love. In Chapman's *An Humorous Day's Mirth*, Labesha, disappointed in love, grows "marvellous malcontent. . . . See where he comes."[148] In Marston's *What You Will*, Jacomo, in love, enters, "unbraced and careles drest."[149] When a stage direction indicates that a character in love enters "melancholy," it apparently means that the actor is to exhibit the familiar characteristics of dress, attitude, and behavior. I have found four instances.[150]

There is evidence also that a conventional manner of falling in love developed on the Elizabethan stage. The procedure apparently was to freeze into statuesque abstraction and to gaze in wide-eyed and speechless wonder at the newly beloved. As indicated in passages already quoted (p. 144), the King of Navarre *(Love's Labor's Lost)*, Orlando *(As You Like It)*, and Sir Francis Acton *(A Woman Killed with Kindness)* stand thus bedazed as they fall in love. When Memnon, of *The Mad Lover*, falls in love at first sight with Calis, he stands gazing fixedly at her ("how he looks"), then *"kneels amaz'd, and forgets to speak."*[151] Later Siphax, another warrior, sees the same lady for the first time. He exclaims, "Keep me ye blest Angels, / What killing power is this?" and immediately becomes stupidly tongue-tied. "Sure these Souldiers," says Calis, "Are all grown senseless . . . Are all dumb Saints."[152] In Marston's *The Insatiate Countess* there appears this stage direc-

146 *Old Plays*, ed. Dodsley and Hazlitt, XI, 96.

147 *Plays*, II, 17.

148 *Plays*, p. 39.

149 *Plays*, II, 237.

150 Dekker, *Old Fortunatus*, *Works*, I, 126; Heywood, *A Woman Killed with Kindness*, in *Works*, II, 108; Field, *A Woman Is a Weathercock*, in *Old Plays*, ed. Dodsley and Hazlitt, XI, 34; Webster, *Appius and Virginia*, in *Works*, III, 160.

151 *Beaumont and Fletcher*, III, 4–5.

152 Pp. 29–30.

tion: "*Isabella* fals in love. . . ."[153] The playwright seems confident that this will have a definite meaning to the actor.

XI

Learned writers sometimes classify jealousy loosely as a melancholic disorder (see above, pp. 140–42). Burton considers it a species of love melancholy. In Elizabethan literature, jealousy is often characterized as a mental disease[154] and is sometimes associated with melancholy. Greene refers to Pandosto's tragic jealousy as "a certaine melancholy passion."[155] In *Tell-Trothes New-yeares Gift*, an anonymous satire wholly devoted to the follies and evils engendered by jealousy, one reads that the jealous man's "mad fittes, once crossed with discourtesie, breed that vncurable melancholy which deadly grife and vntimely death do followe."[156] *The Man in the Moone*, a satire by "W. M.," contains a sketch of a jealous man: "One as melancholie as a Cat . . . who glared vpon me, as if he would haue looked through me."[157] Wye Saltonstall's characters include a jealous man, a person "possest with a mixt passion of love-melancholy. . . . His ielousy like vinegar dryes up his blood; hence his palenesse."[158]

The jealous men of the drama fall into two fairly distinct types. There are those who, like Othello and Leontes, are thrown into a sudden fury of jealousy which is presumably not normal to them. Then there are those who are chronically jealous—most of them, like Chaucer's January, old men with young wives. These are the melancholically jealous men. Such characters are almost necessarily comic figures. Zuccone, of Marston's *The Fawn*, is an example. He is "the onely desparatly rayling Lord at's Lady that ever was confidently melancholy," "a melancholy jealous asse."[159] Kitely, of Jonson's *Every Man in His Humour*, describes in some psychological detail the process by which jealousy, "like a pestilence," infects "The houses of

---

[153] *Plays*, III, 22.

[154] For instance, Gynecia, in Sidney's *Arcadia*, calls jealousy a "phrensie," a "flaming agonie of affection," a "fever" (*Works*, I, 309). Cf., Greene, *Pandosto*, in *Works*, IV, 233. In *The Merry Wives of Windsor*, Ford's jealousy is a "distemper" (III, iii, 230; III, v, 80; IV, ii, 28). His wife accuses him of "melancholy" (II, i, 155). Earl Lacy, in *Grim the Collier of Croydon*, becomes "*sick*" as a result of jealousy. St. Dunstan cures him of his "vain suspicious malady." (*Five Anonymous Plays, Fourth Series*, ed. J. S. Farmer [London, 1908], p. 160.)

[155] *Works*, IV, 237.

[156] London, 1593, sig. F2ᵛ.

[157] London, 1609, sig. F2ᵛ. A very similar passage occurs in *The Wandering-Jew* (London, 1640), p. 40.

[158] *Picturae Loquentes* (London, 1631), no. 17.

[159] *Plays*, II, 164, 170.

the braine," and he resolves manfully to master this passion which makes him so miserable.[160] He does not succeed in this, however, and his absurd suspicion is one of the chief sources of humor in the play.

In *The Broken Heart* Ford presents a somewhat elaborate study of psychopathic jealousy. Bassanes, an old man, has married a young woman, Penthea, who he knows does not love him. Her charms beget in him "a kind of monster-love, which love / Is nurse unto a fear."[161] He is subject to "megrims, firks, and melancholies"; in his jealous fits "he stares, / Struts, puffs, and sweats! most admirable lunacy!"[162] He has set an old duenna and a manservant to watch Penthea. He determines to have the windows next the street "damm'd-up" so that there may be no exchanges of amorous glances; he is afraid that some gallant is conveying "close packets"; he suggests removal to a "delightful island"; when a company comes to his house, he exclaims aside, "A tympany swells in my head already."[163] He suspects even his wife's brother when the two are closeted alone and bursts wildly in upon them with a poniard in his hand.[164] Bassanes, however, is not altogether a contemptible person. It is his misfortune to be old and in his age to love a young woman. Jealousy is one of the infirmities of melancholic senility. In Bassanes it is a disease. As he himself says,

> What can you look for
> From an old, foolish, peevish, doting man
> But craziness of age?[165]

His wretchedness is depicted too convincingly to be wholly ridiculous.

---

160 *Jonson*, III, 330. Other chronically jealous persons of the drama are: Labervele and Countess Moren of Chapman's *An Humorous Day's Mirth*, Cornelio of Chapman's *All Fools*, Bartolus of Fletcher's *The Spanish Curate*, Sir Martin Yellow of Glapthorne's *The Hollander*, Secco of Ford's *The Fancies Chaste and Noble*. Joyless, of Brome's *The Antipodes*, is represented as needing a doctor's ministration. Lysander, of Chapman's *The Widow's Tears*, is said to be predisposed to jealousy by melancholy: "That spark jealousy, falling into his dry, melancholy brain. . . ." (*Plays*, p. 317).

161 *Works*, I, 219.

162 Pp. 264–65. Cf. Burton, *Anatomy*, III, 322. Probably Elizabethan actors in jealous roles strutted, puffed, and glared, and probably this behavior crystallized into histrionic convention.

163 Ford, *Works*, I, 236, 240, 241.

164 Pp. 259, 263–65.

165 P. 317. Detailed discussions of Bassanes' jealousy occur in Ewing's *Burtonian Melancholy in the Plays of John Ford*, pp. 56–60, and in Sensabaugh's *The Tragic Muse of John Ford*, pp. 59–62, 82–84.

Chapter VIII. THE DIGNITY OF MELANCHOLY

I

IN THE PRECEDING CHAPTERS I have reviewed the scientific theories which constitute the background of the popular ideas concerning melancholy current in Elizabethan and early Stuart England. I have described the various forms in which melancholia appears in English literature: principally the malcontent types, the grief-distracted characters of the drama, and the melancholy lovers. I have incidentally pointed out some of the multifarious minor ways in which Renaissance physiology and psychology have insinuated themselves into the thought and expression of English writers. I have attempted to suggest also how greatly these scientific subjects interested educated Englishmen. I have tried to make it plain that, for the Elizabethan, *melancholy* had very definite physiological and psychological implications. These it has long since lost except perhaps in the language of the psychopathologist.

In its Elizabethan usage *melancholy* suggests so many and such diverse mental phenomena that generalization might seem impossible. Yet two rather definite and very different conceptions of melancholy emerge from the diversity. According to one, melancholy is a degrading mental abnormality associated with fear and sorrow. It may be a morose, brooding morbidity of mind, it may be a sottish lethargy, or it may be an insanity accompanied by sorrowful and fearful delusions, often ridiculous. This conception appears especially in the dramatists' representations of sorrow. Its source is the medical literature in the tradition of Galen. According to the second conception, melancholy is a condition which endows one with intellectual acumen and profundity, with artistic ability, sometimes with divine inspiration. This idea shows its influence especially in the malcontent types. Its source is the Aristotelian problem and its popularity is largely due to Marsilio Ficino.

Both of these conceptions appear continually in Elizabethan and early Stuart literature. Sometimes, as in the character of the malcontent, they seem satisfactorily merged. At other times they do not seem readily reconcilable. Because of the fundamental opposition between them, one finds among Elizabethan beliefs concerning melancholy certain obvious corollary antitheses.

Melancholy, for example, is both a very wretched state and a very happy state. There is, says Burton, "No torture of body like unto it! *Siculi non invenere tyranni Majus tormentum,* no strappadoes, hot irons, *Phalaris'* bulls. ... All fears, griefs, suspicions, discontents, imbonities, insuavities, are swallowed up & drowned in ... this Ocean of misery."[1] The dramatic characters overwhelmed by grief suffer unspeakable torment of mind. Yet melancholy is often praised and sought after as a great felicity. The melancholy man is a sober, even somber person, yet he enjoys subjective pleasures denied to ordinary men. This is the central thought of a popular Carolinian lyric entitled "Melancholly," probably by William Strode:

> Hence, hence, all you vaine delights,
> As short as are the nights
> Wherein you spend your folly:
> Ther's nought in this life sweete,
> If men were wise to see'te
> But only Melancholly:
>   O sweetest Melancholly!
>
> Welcome folded armes and fixed eyes,
> A sigh that piercing mortifies,
> A looke that's fastned to the ground,
> A tongue chayned upp without a sound.
> Fountains heads, and pathlesse groves,
> Places which pale Passion loves:
> [Moonlight walks], when all the Fowles
> Are warmly housde, save Batts and Owles:
> A midnight knell: a parting groane:
> These are the sounds wee feede upon.
> Then, stretch your bones in a still gloomy vally,
> Ther's nothing daynty, sweete, save Melancholly.[2]

According to one view, melancholy throws the human faculties into confusion, deprives man of the best use of his intellectual powers, degrades him mentally and morally. The melancholy person who appears among the Overbury characters "is a man onely in shew, but comes short of the better part; a whole reasonable soule, which is mans chiefe preheminence, and sole mark from creatures senceable."[3] According to another view, the melan-

---

[1] *Anatomy,* I, 498.

[2] Strode, *Works,* p. 14. This lyric is the familiar song on melancholy in *The Nice Valour (Beaumont and Fletcher,* X, 171–72). The poem has a companion piece, "Opposite to Melancholy" (*Works,* p. 15). These companion pieces might have suggested to Milton the writing of "L'Allegro" and "Il Penseroso" (see Dobell's preface to Strode's *Works,* pp. xxxviii–xxxix). The poems cannot be precisely dated. All that is definitely known is that the poem on melancholy existed in 1635 (Dobell, p. xxxvii).

[3] *Overburian Characters,* p. 22.

choly man, despite his unpleasing exterior, has intellectual qualities which deserve great respect. He has risen superior to the petty concerns of ordinary men and is continually occupied with thoughts of worth and dignity. His pleasures are intellectual and philosophical. Wye Saltonstall characterizes the melancholy man as

a full vessell which makes not so great a sound, as those that are more empty and answer to every knocke.... Hee can be merry without expressing it by an ignorant laughter.... If he walke and see you not, 'tis because his mind [is] busied in some serious contemplation.... [He] contemnes a gaudy outside as the badge of fooles. He goes therefore commonly in blacke, his Hat unbrusht, a hasty gate with a looke fixt on the ground, as though he were looking pins there, when yet his mind is then soaring in some high contemplation; and is then alwayes most busy, when hee seemes most idle.[4]

This man is absorbed in the "noble musing of the Melancholy" which Du Bosc[5] and others commend.

A similar antithesis appears among early Stuart opinions concerning the relation between melancholy and religion. As I have pointed out in Chapter III, many psychological and moralistic writers of the Renaissance insist that melancholic piety is simply the vagary of a diseased and debased mind, a mind likely to be under the influence of the Devil. Ben Jonson, evidently accepting this opinion as valid, tries to make it clear that his own pious contrition has no connection with melancholy:

> Good, and great God, can I not thinke of thee,
>   But it must, straight, my melancholy bee?
> Is it interpreted in me disease,
>   That, laden with my sinnes, I seeke for ease?[6]

Yet the idea that the deepest and most genuine piety dwells in melancholy minds occurs with some frequency in early seventeenth-century literature. John Donne offers his *Corona* of sonnets to the Deity:

> *Deigne at my hands this crown of prayer and praise,*
>   *Weav'd in my low devout melancholie.*[7]

---

[4] *Picturae Loquentes,* no. 8.
[5] *The Compleat Woman,* p. 41.
[6] *Jonson,* VIII, 122.
[7] *Poems,* ed. H. J. C. Grierson (Oxford, 1912), I, 318. Cf. "holy discontent," *ibid.,* p. 323; "holy *sadnesses of soule,*" *Devotions upon Emergent Occasions,* ed. John Sparrow (Cambridge, 1923), p. 48. Donne seems to believe, however, that melancholic piety or contrition is sometimes to be distrusted; see *Poems,* I, 222; *Sermons: Selected Passages,* ed. Logan Pearsall Smith (Oxford, 1920), p. 133.

An anonymous poet of the early Stuart period bids farewell to the "guilded follies" of the world and determines to live apart from mankind in "an holy melancholy."[8] James Day, in a poem called "The Melancholicke Soules comfort," writes that no music is more acceptable to the Lord than "*sobs and cries*."[9] A volume of religious verse by Humphrey Mill is entitled *Poems Occasioned by a Melancholy Vision, or A Melancholy Vision upon Divers Theames Enlarged.*[10] On the title page appears the motto "His gaudit musa tenebris." Mill is an exceedingly tame poet, yet the writer of a commendatory poem says,

> Had I but hope, that I so well could doe,
> I'd wish, that I were melancholy too.

Henry Vaughan addresses Christ:

> Fair and yong light! my guide to holy
> Grief and soul-curing melancholy.[11]

No two literary selections could better illustrate the dualism of the term *melancholy* as it was understood in the Carolinian period than Milton's "L'Allegro" and "Il Penseroso." In the first, melancholy is associated with hell and midnight, with "horrid shapes, and shrieks, and sights unholy"; is banished to an "uncouth cell" in a dark and forbidding desert; is rejected as utterly loathsome. Milton is exorcising the crucifying melancholy madness of the Galenic tradition. In "Il Penseroso," on the other hand, the poet personifies melancholy as a "pensive Nun" of sober and stately beauty, a "Goddess, sage and holy, . . . divinest Melancholy," and he invites her to be his companion and the ruling influence of his life. This is melancholy in the tradition of Aristotle and Ficino. The melancholy which Milton rejects in "L'Allegro" is not the same thing at all as that which he welcomes in "Il Penseroso."

"Il Penseroso" is a complete characterization of the scholarly, philosophic, and pious melancholy which was held in such high esteem during the early Stuart period. The goddess Melancholy is, appropriately, Saturn's daughter (24). She is dressed in "robe of darkest grain" (33); and since her "stately visage is too bright" for mortal eyes, it is "O'erlaid with black, staid Wisdom's hue" (14–16). She rewards her votaries with the sober pleasures of solitary meditation. She walks

---

[8] Grierson prints this as a spurious Donne lyric (*Poems*, I, 465–67). It appears in Izaak Walton's *Compleat Angler* (Part I, Chap. XXI).
[9] *A New Spring of Divine Poetrie* (London, 1637), p. 25.
[10] London, 1639. The vision is described in the first poem.
[11] *Works*, ed. L. C. Martin (Oxford, 1914), II, 513.

> With even step and musing gait,
> And looks commercing with the skies. (38–39)

The poet asks her to bring with her "calm Peace and Quiet" (45) and

>   retirëd Leisure,
>   That in trim gardens takes his pleasure
>
> . . . .
>
>   And the mute Silence hist along,
>   'Less Philomel will deign a song. (49–56)

Under the goddess' influence, the poet will take solitary nocturnal walks (65), or he will sit alone within doors before the glowing embers "Far from all resort of mirth" (81).

His life will be scholarly; he will walk "the studious cloister's pale" (156). He will apply himself to the study of recondite philosophy:

>   let my lamp at midnight hour
>   Be seen in some high lonely tower,
>   Where I may oft outwatch the Bear,
>   With thrice great Hermes, or unsphere
>   The spirit of Plato . . . (85–89)

He will be interested in the arts: in tragedy, in poetry, in sad or solemn music like the song of the nightingale or the clear anthems of "the pealing organ" and "the full-voiced choir" (161–62). "Spare Fast," the companion of Melancholy,

>   oft with gods doth diet,
>   And hears the Muses in a ring
>   Aye round about Jove's altar sing. (46–48)

Above all, Melancholy will encourage the contemplation of divine truth. She is a "Goddess, sage and holy" with

>   looks commercing with the skies,
>   Thy rapt soul sitting in thine eyes;
>   There held in holy passion still,
>   Forget thyself to marble . . . (39–42)

The poet asks her "first and chiefest" to bring with her

> Him that yon soars on golden wing,
> Guiding the fiery-wheelèd throne,
> The Cherub Contemplation. (51-54)

He looks forward to an old age spent as a religious recluse, to "The hairy gown and mossy cell" (169). He has his canny doubts about melancholic powers of prophecy, but he believes that, through "old experience," he will attain at least "To something like prophetic strain" (173-74). The melancholy of the Aristotelian tradition was never more beautifully celebrated.[12]

II

Englishmen were not troubled by the opposition between the two concepts of melancholy. They accepted both. Yet on the whole the more dignified connotations of melancholy determined England's attitude toward it. In general the attitude was definitely one of respect. This was true both in the late sixteenth century and in the early seventeenth century, but especially in the latter period.[13] Several of the passages already quoted in this chapter furnish evidence of England's high regard for the melancholy man. One finds further evidence in the fact that many English intellectuals, finding something attractive in the melancholic character, caught the malady.

Just how many of the more obscure and less articulate were afflicted, there is no way of knowing. There is evidence, however, that melancholy was common among the writers of the period. Sometimes their melancholy was apparently a passing fit, sometimes apparently a chronic condition. The malady seems to have touched even authors who were unmerciful in satirizing the malcontent.

---

12 *Melancholy* occurs four times in Milton's verse outside "L'Allegro" and "Il Penseroso." There is no suggestion of the pious and contemplative melancholy of "Il Penseroso," however, except in that poem. A pastoral musician's "pleasing fit of melancholy" is mentioned in *Comus* (546). In the same poem there is reference to "the lees / And settlings of a melancholy blood" and to the "drooping spirits" which result from them (809-12). In *Paradise Lost*, Milton associates melancholy with various sorts of brainsickness (XI, 485-86) and with the physical degeneration of old age (XI, 543-46). In *Samson Agonistes* a reference to the psychological effects of "anguish of the mind and humors black" (600) shows that Milton knew something of the psychology of grief. George W. Whiting plausibly suggests that Milton considered himself a melancholy man (*Milton's Literary Milieu* [Chapel Hill, 1939], pp. 129-76).

13 The idea that melancholy tormented and crazed its victims, however, persisted through many decades of the seventeenth century. See Samuel Butler's character of the melancholy man, *Characters and Passages from Note-books*, ed. A. R. Waller (Cambridge, 1908), pp. 59-60; Samuel Person's character of the melancholy man, *An Anatomical Lecture of Man* (London, 1664), pp. 78-80.

The roll of literary melancholics includes some rather impressive names.[14] Sir Philip Sidney reveals in his correspondence that he has his "melancholie times."[15] Robert Greene confesses to malcontentedness as a folly of youth.[16] Thomas Lodge writes of his "discontented thoughts," which have been "long inured to obscuritie" and divorced "from vaine glories inordinate follie."[17] Thomas Nashe, oppressed by poverty and by the neglect of his literary labors, rails "in a malecontent humor" at his fortune and his patrons, tears his papers, and rages "in all points like a mad man."[18] John Lyly[19] and Francis Bacon,[20] because of their failure to get on in the world, complain of melancholy. Edmund Spenser seems to have been melancholically disheartened by similar circumstances.[21] George Chapman, whose saturnine intellectuality suggests a melancholic spirit, declares that he is "drown'd in dark death-ushering melancholy."[22] Nicholas Breton, in *Melancholike Humours*, describes despondencies which are sometimes very painful. His "poore heart," he says,

> both day and night, in passions ouertoild;
> By ouerlabour of my braine doth finde my spirit spoiled.[23]

A sonnet of Ben Jonson's prefixed to the book assures the reader that Breton is no poser,

> Not wearing moodes, as gallants doe a fashion,
> In these pide times, only to shewe their braines.[24]

---

[14] G. B. Harrison believes that "most writers of any importance suffered from [melancholy] to some extent."—"An Essay on Elizabethan Melancholy," appended to Harrison's edition of Breton's *Melancholike Humours* (London, 1929), p. 70. He mentions Greene, Marlowe, Spenser, Chapman, Shakespeare, Marston, Ford. I find no definite evidence that Marlowe and Shakespeare considered themselves melancholic in the Elizabethan sense. It is worth noting that Chaucer complains of melancholy in *The Book of the Duchesse* (ll. 1–43).

[15] *Works*, III, 133. See also p. 84.

[16] *Works*, XII, 172. See above, p. 81.

[17] Dedicatory epistle, *Scillaes Metamorphosis* (*Works*, vol. I), p. 3.

[18] *Pierce Penilesse, Works*, I, 157. I am assuming that Pierce Penilesse is Nashe himself. See also *Lenten Stuffe*, in *Works*, III, 175.

[19] *Works*, I, 378.

[20] See James Spedding, *An Account of the Life and Times of Francis Bacon* (London, 1878), I, 125.

[21] *Prothalamion*, ll. 5–10; *Prosopopoia*, ll. 891-908.

[22] From the sonnet of dedication prefixed to *All Fools*, in *Plays*, p. 46. There is some doubt as to the authenticity of this sonnet, yet it is probably genuine. See Phyllis Bartlett's edition of Chapman's *Poems* (New York, 1941), p. 470.

[23] "An Extreame Passion," *Melancholike Humours* (*Works*, vol. I), p. 10.

[24] P. 5.

John Marston invokes Melancholy, as others have called upon Calliope, to assist him in the task of exposing and lashing the fools and sinners of England:

> Thou nursing mother of fair Widsom's lore,
> Ingenuous Melancholy, I implore
> Thy grave assistance: take thy gloomy seat,
> Enthrone thee in my blood; let me entreat,
> Stay his quick jocund skips, and force him run
> A sad-paced course, until my whips be done.[25]

In spite of his unmerciful treatment of Bruto, Marston is evidently a malcontent himself.[26] There could be not better illustration of the malcontent's bitter and strident invective than his *Satires* and his *Scourge of Villainy*. In *The Return from Parnassus (II)*, Marston is said to be "a Ruffian in his stile, / Withouten bands or garters ornament."[27] John Davies of Hereford addresses an epigram "To acute Mr. Iohn Marston" in which he refers to the "Male-contentednesse" of Marston and his muse.[28]

John Donne's "constant infirmity," one learns from Walton's biography, was "vapours from the spleen."[29] Donne himself was highly conscious of his affliction: "I languish, prest with Melancholy."[30] During his critical illness of 1623, Donne's physicians took measures to draw noxious vapors from his head. The patient meanwhile reflected gloomily upon his condition: "But what have I done, either to *breed,* or to *breath* these *vapors?* They tell me it is my *Melancholy;* Did I infuse, did I drinke in *Melancholly* into my selfe? It is my *thoughtfulnesse;* was I not made to *thinke?* It is my *study;* doth not my *Calling* call for that? I have don nothing, wilfully, perversely toward it, yet must suffer in it, die by it."[31]

---

[25] From the "Proemium in Librum Primum" of *The Scourge of Villainy*, in *Works*, III, 307. Cf. "sanguis . . . est sedatior, propter melancholiam non viciosam."—Melanchthon, *Opera*, XIII, 86. At the opening of Book XI (p. 371), Marston exorcises Melancholy in language much like that of "L'Allegro." Marston's invocation and exorcism of Melancholy (personified) may have suggested to Milton the writing of "L'Allegro" and "Il Penseroso." Thomas Warton first pointed out these parallels (see Henry John Todd, *The Poetical Works of John Milton* [London, 1801], V, 73-74, 107).

[26] This is the opinion of Morse S. Allen; see *The Satire of John Marston* (Columbus, Ohio, 1920), p. 10. O. J. Campbell, while he recognizes the malcontent character of Marston's early satires, writes that, in *What You Will*, Marston "seems to repudiate the 'malcontent' critic and all his ways."—*Comicall Satyre and Shakespeare's Troilus and Cressida* (San Marino, Cal., 1938), p. 175.

[27] Parnassus plays, the Macray edition, p. 86.

[28] *The Scourge of Folly* (*Works*, vol. II), p. 33ᵃ.

[29] Walton's *Lives*, ed. George Saintsbury (Oxford, 1927), p. 60.

[30] *Poems*, I, 206.

[31] *Devotions*, p. 69.

A thumbnail portrait of John Ford has been handed down to us in a couplet which has been very often quoted:

> Deep in a dump Jack Ford alone was got,
> With folded arms, and melancholy hat.[32]

The gently satiric writer evidently considered this a characteristic attitude. However little we know about Ford, then, we know at least that he was bitten by melancholy. Apparently Ford believed, with one of his admirers, that "Black choler" is "reason's overflowing spring."[33] In his ethical treatise *A Line of Life,* Ford gives the impression that he is a sober, contemplative, and scholarly person. The very conventional moral principles which he expounds in this essay seem to me to be present also in his plays.

Robert Burton "writ of melancholy, by being busy to avoid melancholy." When he undertook the composition of the *Anatomy,* he says, his purpose was "to ease my mind by writing, for I had *gravidum cor, foedum caput,* a kind of imposthume in my head, which I was very desirous to be unladen of, & could imagine no fitter evacuation than this. . . . I was not a little offended with this malady . . . & for that cause . . . I would expel *clavum clavo* . . . make an Antedote out of that which was the prime cause of my disease."[34] Saturn, he says, "was the Lord of my geniture."[35] According to Anthony à Wood, Burton "was by many accounted a severe student, a devourer of authors, a melancholy and humerous person." Burton wrote his own epitaph: *"Paucis notus, paucioribus ignotus, hic jacet Democritus junior, cui vitam dedit, & mortem melancholia. . . ."*[36] In assuming the pseudonym Democritus Junior, Burton implies a likeness between himself and a famous melancholic of antiquity, the philosopher who was continually moved to laughter by the spectacle of human frailty and folly.[37]

---

[32] From Hemming's elegy on Randolph's finger, *Journal of English and Germanic Philology,* XIX (1920), 273.

[33] Commendatory verses on *The Lover's Melancholy,* Ford's *Works,* I, lxxiii.

[34] *Anatomy,* I, 17–18.

[35] *Ibid.,* p. 14.

[36] *Athenae Oxonienses* (London, 1691), col. 535.

[37] According to Burton, Democritus was a sanguine melancholic (*Anatomy,* I, 461). Democritus owes his very prominent place among famous melancholics to a document, widely known during the Renaissance, which was supposed to be a letter written by Hippocrates concerning an interview with him. Hippocrates had been summoned by Democritus' anxious fellow citizens, who, because of his continual hilarity, feared that he was mad. Littré reprints this letter, which he considers spurious, in his *Oeuvres Complètes d'Hippocrate* (Paris, 1839–61), IX, 349–81. Burton gives the substance of it (*Anatomy,* I, 48–53). Renaissance writers often contrast Democritus, the laughing philosopher, with Heraclitus, the weeping philosopher, in whom human vice and folly continually excited tears. Heraclitus also is regarded as a melancholy man. See Diogenes Laertius, *Lives,* IX, 6; Lucian, *Philosophies for Sale,* 13–14.

There is no evidence that any of these men of letters rejoice in their melancholy. Indeed most of them characterize it as a very wretched condition. Yet they are not ashamed of it. Greene is the only one of them who apologizes for it. Clearly the Elizabethan intellectual found satisfaction in the idea that he was melancholy.

III

The strangely persistent vogue of melancholy among English intellectuals was a complex phenomenon with various contributing causes, several of which I have discussed or suggested. Among them was the general diffusion of psychological information (especially information about melancholy), which suggested introspection and supplied the terms for thinking of one's own mental states and processes. Another cause was the adversity which many educated men suffered because of England's inability to provide dignified employment for all its cultivated citizens.[38] Several of the men of letters mentioned above attributed their melancholy to frustrated ambition. Another cause was the general currency of the idea that intellectual labor bred melancholy. The Elizabethan Englishman believed that in exerting his brain he was sacrificing the heat and moisture of his body. If he engaged in mental toil, he would expect to become at least a little melancholy. The principal reason for the popularity of melancholy, however, was the general acceptance of the idea that it was an attribute of superior minds, of genius. The Aristotelian concept had invested the melancholy character with something of somber philosophic dignity, something of Byronic grandeur.

There was undoubtedly some connection, furthermore, between the vogue of intellectual melancholy and the temper of the age. The late English Renaissance was a period of progressively deepening despondency.[39] God, says Donne, "hath reserved us to such times, as being the later times, give us even the dregs and lees of misery to drink. . . . God hath accompanied, and complicated almost all our bodily diseases of these times, with

---

[38] L. C. Knights has discussed the social and economic causes of discontented melancholy among educated men of the Jacobean period in "Seventeenth Century Melancholy," *Drama and Society in the Age of Jonson* (London, 1937), pp. 323–32. See also Phoebe Sheavyn, *The Literary Profession in the Elizabethan Age* (Manchester, 1909), pp. 19–21.

[39] Renaissance pessimism has been the subject of some able studies: George Williamson, "Mutability, Decay, and Seventeenth-century Melancholy," *Journal of English Literary History*, II (1935), 121–50; Charles M. Coffin, *John Donne and the New Philosophy* (New York, 1937), pp. 132 ff., 264 ff.; Don Cameron Allen, "The Degeneration of Man and Renaissance Pessimism," *Studies in Philology*, XXXV (1938), 202–27; Spencer, *Shakespeare and the Nature of Man*, pp. 21–50; and others.

an extraordinary sadnesse, a predominant melancholy, a faintnesse of heart, a chearlesnesse, a joylesnesse of spirit."[40] Many explanations for this joylessness have been offered: social, political, and religious turmoil, reaction after the surging enthusiasm of the earlier Renaissance, intellectual satiety and confusion, loss of faith in man's freedom and pre-eminence, bewilderment and uncertainty due to the discoveries of the new science, belief in the senility of nature and the degeneration of man. All of these explanations are doubtless partly right, and taken together they represent something like the truth. It is not strange that melancholy should have appealed so strongly to intelligent men in such an era. It offered—or seemed to offer—an avenue of retreat from a disheartening world. The melancholy man might retire within himself and find compensation for the ills of the world in sober contemplative pleasures. It is evident, however, that many thoughtful Englishmen found no escape from despondency. In that case the concept of melancholy gave them a name for their state of mind, a satisfying explanation of what was going on within them, and a dignified pattern of conduct.

Elizabethan melancholy began as a fashionable affectation, as an imitation of an Italian attitude. Unlike most fads, however, it did not flourish briefly and die. It established itself so firmly in English thought and literature during the late Renaissance period that it persisted for generations. Under new names (hypochondria, hysteria, spleen, and vapors), the melancholic malady continued to trouble English men and women until late in the eighteenth century.[41] Even the Age of Wordsworth was addicted to melancholy. By this time, however, the medical and pathological implications had faded. To Keats, *melancholy* meant simply "sadness."

---

[40] *LXXX Sermons* (London, 1640), pp. 671–72 (no. 66).

[41] See Amy Louise Reed, *The Background of Gray's Elegy* (New York, 1924); Oswald Doughty, "The English Malady of the Eighteenth Century," *Review of English Studies*, II (1926), 257–69; Margaret Bailey's edition of Boswell's *The Hypochondriack* (Stanford, 1928), I, 75–99; John W. Draper, *The Funeral Elegy and the Rise of English Romanticism* (New York, 1929), pp. 64–69, 143 ff., 203, 230–31, 281, *et passim;* Eleanor M. Sickels, *The Gloomy Egoist: Moods and Themes of Melancholy from Gray to Keats* (New York, 1932); Lawrence Babb, "The Cave of Spleen," *Review of English Studies*, XII (1936), 165–76.

BIBLIOGRAPHY

BIBLIOGRAPHY

I

Principal Primary Sources

Aëtius of Amida. *De Melancholia ex Galeno, Rufo, Posidonio, et Marcello, Sicamii Aetii Libellus.* Included in *Galeni Opera,* ed. Kühn (herein cited), XIX, 699–720. Aëtius was a medical compiler of the late fifth and early sixth centuries.

Agrippa, Cornelius. *Henrici Cornelii Agrippae ab Nettesheym . . . de Occulta Philosophia Libri Tres.* Cologne, 1533. This work was first published in 1531.

Alexander of Tralles. *Alexandri Tralliani Medici Absolutissimi Libri Duodecim.* Venice, 1555. Alexander lived during the sixth century.

Anton, Robert. *The Philosophers Satyrs.* London, 1616. A series of seven verse satires, each devoted to the human failings associated with the influence of one of the seven planets. A second edition appeared in 1617.

Aretaeus. *The Extant Works of Aretaeus, the Cappadochian.* Translated and edited by Francis Adams. London, 1856. According to the editor, Aretaeus was probably a contemporary of Galen who practiced medicine in Rome.

Aristotle. *The Works of Aristotle.* Translated under the editorship of W. D. Ross. 11 vols. Oxford, 1908–31.

Avicenna. *Avicennae Medicorum Arabum Principis, Liber Canonis.* Tr. Gerard of Cremona. Basel, 1556. Avicenna's dates are 980–1036. The title above is an accurate indication of his reputation during the Renaissance.

Barckley, Sir Richard. *The Felicitie of Man, or, His Summum Bonum.* London, 1631. Earlier editions appeared in 1598 and 1603.

Barrough, Philip. *The Method of Phisick, Conteining the Causes, Signes, and Cures of Inward Diseases.* London, 1590. The first of the nine editions appeared in 1583. This is a work of popular character by a physician.

Bartholomaeus Anglicus. *Batman uppon Bartholome, His Booke De Proprietatibus Rerum.* London, 1582. This is a compendium of medieval lore by an English Franciscan of the thirteenth century. Stephen Batman's sixteenth-century English version (containing additions from other authorities) is apparently based upon the late fourteenth-century translation of John Trevisa, printed in 1495 and 1535.

Beaumont, Francis, and John Fletcher. *The Works of Francis Beaumont and John Fletcher.* Ed. Arnold Glover and A. R. Waller. 10 vols. Cambridge, 1905–12.

Bernard of Gordon. *B. Gordonii . . . Lilium Medicinae.* Paris, 1542. Bernard was a celebrated physician of the School of Montpellier in the late thirteenth and early fourteenth centuries. He enjoyed probably a greater reputation among Renaissance physicians than any other medieval European medical writer.

Bishop, John. *Beautifull Blossomes, Gathered . . . from the Best Trees of All Kyndes.* London, 1577.

Boaistuau, Pierre. *Theatrum Mundi. The Theatre or Rule of the World.* Tr. John Alday. London, 1581. A pious work devoted mainly to the sins and miseries of mankind. The Latin original appeared in Paris in 1558. The first of the three English editions appeared *c.* 1566.

Breton, Nicholas. *The Works in Verse and Prose of Nicholas Breton.* Ed. Alexander B. Grosart. 2 vols. Edinburgh, 1879.

Bright, Timothy. *A Treatise of Melancholie. Containing the Causes Thereof, & Reasons of the Strange Effects It Worketh in Our Minds and Bodies: with the Phisicke Cure, and Spirituall Consolation for Such as Haue Thereto Adioyned an Afflicted Conscience.* London, 1586. I have used the first of the two editions of 1586, printed by Thomas Vautrollier and reproduced by the Facsimile Text Society (New York, 1940). A third edition appeared in 1613.

Brome, Richard. *The Dramatic Works of Richard Brome.* 3 vols. London, 1873.

Bullen, A. H. (ed.). *A Collection of Old English Plays.* 4 vols. London, 1882–85.

Burton, Robert. *The Anatomy of Melancholy.* Ed. A. R. Shilleto. 3 vols. London, 1926–27.

Chapman, George. *The Works of George Chapman: Plays.* Ed. R. H. Shepherd. London, 1889.

Charron, Pierre. *Of Wisdome Three Bookes.* Tr. Samson Lennard. London, *c.* 1606. Later editions appeared in 1630 and 1640. The French original was published in 1601. Charron (1541–1603) was a distinguished preacher and a friend of Montaigne.

Coeffeteau, F. N. *A Table of Humane Passions. With Their Causes and Effects.* Tr. Edward Grimeston. London, 1621. The French original appeared in 1619. The author was a bishop (1574–1623).

Cogan, Thomas. *The Haven of Health: Chiefly Made for the Comfort of Students, and Consequently for All Those That Have a Care of Their Health.* London, 1589. The first of the six editions was published in 1584. Thomas Cogan (1545?–1607) was a physician of Manchester.

Constantine of Africa. *Constantini Africani . . . Opera.* Basel, 1536. Constantine (eleventh century) is known especially for his translations (or plagiarizations) of Greco-Arabic medical works. He was associated with the School of Salerno.

Dariot, Claude. *A Briefe and Most Easie Introduction to the Astrologicall Judgement of the Starres.* Tr. F. W. London, 1598. The Latin original was published in 1557. An earlier English translation appeared in 1583 (?). The author (1533–94) was a French physician.

Davies, Sir John. *The Poems of Sir John Davies.* Ed. Clare Howard. New York, 1941. Reproduced in facsimile.

Davies, John, of Hereford. *The Complete Works of John Davies of Hereford.* Ed. Alexander B. Grosart. Edinburgh, 1878.

Dekker, Thomas. *The Dramatic Works of Thomas Dekker.* 4 vols. London, 1873.

Dodsley, Robert (ed.). *A Select Collection of Old English Plays.* Revised by W. Carew Hazlitt. 15 vols. London, 1874–76.

Donne, John. *Devotions upon Emergent Occasions.* Ed. John Sparrow. Cambridge, 1923.

——. *The Poems of John Donne.* Ed. H. J. C. Grierson. 2 vols. Oxford, 1912.

Du Bosc, Jacques. *The Compleat Woman.* Tr. N. N. London, 1639. This volume is a translation of the first part of Du Bosc's *L'Honneste Femme.* The first part was originally published in French in 1632. It consists of eighteen edifying essays, purportedly for women, including one "Of the pleasant and Melancholy humour" (pp. 29–43).

Du Laurens, André (Laurentius). *A Discourse of the Preservation of the Sight: of Melancholike Diseases; of Rheumes, and of Old Age.* Tr. Richard Surphlet. London, 1599. (Shakespeare Association Facsimiles, no. 15, 1938.) This work appeared first in French in 1597. It is a popular work written purportedly for a noble patroness who was suffering from the various infirmities named in the title. Du Laurens was the principal physician of Henry IV and chancellor of the faculty of Montpellier. He died in 1609.

Earle, John. *Micro-Cosmographie.* Ed. Edward Arber. Westminster, 1895. First published in 1628.

Edwards, Edward. *The Analysis of Chyrurgery, Being the Theorique and Practique Part Thereof.* London, 1636.

Elyot, Sir Thomas. *The Castel of Helth.* London, 1541. (Scholars' Facsimiles and Reprints, New York, 1937). The book was probably first published in 1534. The *Short Title Catalogue* lists fifteen editions, 1539–1610.

Ferrand, Jacques. *Erotomania or a Treatise Discoursing of the Essence, Causes, Symptomes, Prognosticks, and Cure of Love, or Erotique Melancholy.* Tr. Edmund Chilmead. Oxford, 1640. The original French edition appeared in 1612. The author was a physician of Agen.

Ficino, Marsilio. *De Vita Libri Tres.* Basel, 1549. First published 1482–89.

Fletcher, John. See Beaumont.

Ford, John. *The Works of John Ford.* Ed. William Gifford, with additions by Alexander Dyce, reissued with further additions by A. H. Bullen. 3 vols. London, 1895.

Foreest, Peter van (Forestus). *Observationum et Curationum Medicinalium sive Medicinae Theoricae & Practicae, Libri XXVIII.* Frankfurt, 1602. Foreest (1522–97) was a Dutch physician of considerable reputation who practiced in Delft.

Fracastoro, Girolamo. *Turrius siue de Intellectione Dialogus.* Included in *Opera Omnia,* Venice, 1555. Fracastoro (1483–1553) was a leading medical writer of his day. He is known especially for his poem *Syphilidis, sive Morbi Gallici Libri Tres* (1530), from which the term *syphilis* is derived.

Galen, Claudius. *Claudii Galeni Opera Omnia*. Ed. Carolus Gottlob Kühn. 20 vols. Leipzig, 1821–33.

Garzoni, Tommaso. *The Hospitall of Incurable Fooles*. London, 1600. The Italian original appeared in 1586.

Glapthorne, Henry. *The Plays and Poems of Henry Glapthorne*. 2 vols. London, 1874.

Goulart, Simon. *Admirable and Memorable Histories Containing the Wonders of Our Time*. Tr. Edward Grimeston. London, 1607. The French version was originally published in 1600.

Greene, Robert. *The Life and Complete Works in Prose and Verse of Robert Greene*. Ed. Alexander B. Grosart. 15 vols. London and Aylesbury, 1881–86.

——. *The Plays and Poems of Robert Greene*. Ed. J. Churton Collins. 2 vols. Oxford, 1905.

Hemming, William. Elegy on Randolph's finger. Reprinted by John J. Parry in "A Seventeenth Century Gallery of Poets," *Journal of English and Germanic Philology*, XIX (1920), 270–77. See also G. C. Moore Smith, *William Hemminge's Elegy on Randolph's Finger*, Oxford, 1923.

Henderson, Robert. *The Arraignement of the Whole Creature, at the Barre of Religion, Reason, and Experience*. London, 1631.

Heywood, Thomas. *The Dramatic Works of Thomas Heywood*. 6 vols. London, 1874.

Hippocrates. *Hippocrates*. With an English translation by W. H. S. Jones. 4 vols. London, 1923–31. (Loeb Classical Library.)

Huarte, Juan. *Examen de Ingenios. The Examination of Mens Wits*. Translated by R. Carew from Camillo Camilli's Italian translation from the Spanish original. London, 1594. This was the first of four editions of Carew's translation. The Spanish original was published in 1580.

Jonson, Ben. *Ben Jonson*. Ed. C. H. Herford, Percy Simpson, and Evelyn Simpson. 10 vols. Oxford, 1925–50.

The Kalendar & Compost of Shepherds. Ed. G. C. Heseltine. London, 1930. This is a popular compilation of scientific lore first published in French in 1491. The *Short Title Catalogue* lists seventeen editions of various English translations, 1503–1625. The basis of Heseltine's text is the translation of R. Copland, first published *c*. 1518.

Kyd, Thomas. *The Works of Thomas Kyd*. Ed. Frederick S. Boas. Oxford, 1901.

La Primaudaye, Pierre de. *The French Academie. Fully Discoursed and Finished in Foure Bookes*. Tr. T. B. C. London, 1618. The French original was written by a nobleman, whose letter of dedication is dated 1577. The first book was published in English in 1586.

Lemnius, Levinus. *The Touchstone of Complexions*. Tr. Thomas Newton. London, 1576. The Latin original appeared first in 1561; Newton's translation in 1565. There were four English editions. Lemnius was an eminent physician of Zeeland who gave up medicine to enter the ministry (1505–68).

Lodge, Thomas. *The Complete Works of Thomas Lodge.* 4 vols. 1883. Printed for the Hunterian Club with a memoir by Edmund W. Gosse.

Lust's Dominion. Ed. J. Le Gay Brereton. Louvain, 1931. (*Materials for the Study of the Old English Drama,* new series, vol. V.) Originally printed in 1657.

Lyly, John. *The Complete Works of John Lyly.* Ed. R. Warwick Bond. 3 vols. Oxford, 1902.

Marlowe, Christopher. *The Works of Christopher Marlowe.* Ed. C. F. Tucker Brooke. Oxford, 1910.

Marston, John. *The Plays of John Marston.* Ed. H. Harvey Wood. 3 vols. Edinburgh, 1934–39.

——. *The Works of John Marston.* Ed. A. H. Bullen. 3 vols. London, 1887.

Massinger, Philip. *The Plays of Philip Massinger.* Ed. William Gifford. 4 vols. London, 1813.

Melanchthon, Philipp. *Liber de Anima.* In vol. XIII of *Philippi Melanthonis Opera Quae Supersunt Omnia,* ed. Carolus Gottlieb Bretschneider, Halle, 1834–60. *Liber de Anima* was originally published in 1540.

Mercado, Luis. *Opera.* 2 vols. Frankfurt, 1619–20. There is an earlier edition of 1608. The author was a Spanish physician (1513–1606).

Middleton, Thomas. *The Works of Thomas Middleton.* Ed. A. H. Bullen. 8 vols. London, 1885–86.

Milles, Thomas. *The Treasurie of Auncient and Moderne Times.* London, 1613.

Milton, John. *The Poems of John Milton.* Ed. James H. Hanford. New York, 1936.

Mornay, Philippe de. *The True Knowledge of a Mans Owne Selfe.* Tr. Anthony Munday. London, 1602.

Nabbes, Thomas. *The Works of Thomas Nabbes.* Ed. A. H. Bullen. 2 vols. London, 1887.

Nashe, Thomas. *The Works of Thomas Nashe.* Ed. Ronald B. McKerrow. 5 vols. London, 1910.

Overbury, Sir Thomas. *The Overburian Characters.* Ed. W. J. Paylor. Oxford, 1936.

Parnassus plays. See *Pilgrimage.*

Paul of Aegina. *The Seven Books of Paulus Aegineta.* Tr. Francis Adams. 3 vols. London, 1844–47. The author was a Greek medical writer of the seventh century.

Peele, George. *The Works of George Peele.* Ed. A. H. Bullen. 2 vols. London, 1888.

The Pilgrimage to Parnassus with the Two Parts of *The Return from Parnassus.* Ed. W. D. Macray. Oxford, 1886.

Plater, Felix. *Praxeos seu de Cognoscendis, Praedicendis, Praecauendis, Curandisque Affectibus Homini Incommodantibus Tractatus.* Basel, 1602. Plater (1536–1614) was a Swiss physician noted for his psychiatric studies.

——. *Observationum ... Libri Tres.* Basel, 1614.

Plato. *The Dialogues of Plato.* Tr. Benjamin Jowett. 2 vols. New York, 1937.

Regimen Sanitatis Salerni. Tr. Thomas Paynell. London, 1575. This volume presents a popular medieval Latin poem on medicine (known variously as *Regimen Sanitatis Salerni, Flos Medicinae, Regimen Virile, Schola Salernitana,* etc.) with commentary by Arnold of Villanova. Paynell has translated the commentary (which is of greater length than the poem) and has retained the original Latin of the poem itself. Nine editions of Paynell's translation are listed in the *Short Title Catalogue,* the first dated 1528. Sir John Harington's verse translation of the poem was published five times, 1607–24. Another translation appeared in 1613. For the history of this work, see Fielding H. Garrison, "A Note on the Prehistory of the Regimen Sanitatis," appended to Francis R. Packard's edition of *The School of Salernum . . .* , New York, 1920.

Reynolds, Edward. *A Treatise of the Passions and Faculties of the Soule of Man.* London, 1640. Reynolds became Bishop of Norwich.

Rhazes. *Continens Rasis.* Venice, 1529. This is the best-known work of an Arabian physician whose reputation during the Renaissance rivaled even those of Avicenna and Averrhoës. Rhazes (860–930) was head of a large hospital in Bagdad. His *Continens* consists mainly of quotations from earlier writers.

Rich, Barnabie. *Faultes Faults, and Nothing Else but Faultes.* London, 1606.

Rogers, Thomas. *A Philosophicall Discourse, Entituled, the Anatomie of the Minde.* London, 1576. Rogers was a divine who died in 1616.

Rowlands, Samuel. *The Complete Works of Samuel Rowlands.* 3 vols. Glasgow, 1880. Printed for the Hunterian Club with a memoir by Edmund W. Gosse.

Rufus. *Oeuvres de Rufus D'Éphèse.* Ed. Charles Daremberg and Charles Émile Ruelle. Paris, 1879. The editors have brought together the somewhat fragmentary remains of the work of a medical writer who enjoyed considerable fame in the ancient world. Rufus flourished toward the end of the first century A.D.

Salerno. See *Regimen.*

Saltonstall, Wye. *Picturae Loquentes. Or Pictures Drawne Forth in Characters.* London, 1631.

Scot, Reginald. *The Discoverie of Witchcraft.* Ed. Brinsley Nicholson. London, 1886. The original was published in 1584.

Shakespeare, William. *The Complete Works of William Shakespeare.* Ed. W. J. Craig. London, 1922.

The Shakespeare Apocrypha. Ed. C. F. Tucker Brooke. Oxford, 1908.

Shirley, James. *The Dramatic Works and Poems of James Shirley.* Ed. William Gifford with additions by Alexander Dyce. 6 vols. London, 1833.

Sidney, Sir Philip. *The Complete Works of Sir Philip Sidney.* Ed. Albert Feuillerat. 4 vols. Cambridge, 1922–26.

Silvaticus, Joannes Baptista. *Controversiae Medicae Numero Centum.* Frankfurt, 1601. The author was a Milanese physician (1550–1621).

Strode, William. *The Poetical Works of William Strode . . .* [with] *The Floating Island.* Ed. Bertram Dobell. London, 1907.

Tourneur, Cyril. *The Works of Cyril Tourneur*. Ed. Allardyce Nicoll. London, 1930.

Valleriole, François. *Enarrationum Medicinalium Libri Sex*. Lyons, 1604. The author, a physician, died in 1572.

Van der Velde, Jason (Pratensis). *D. Iasonis Pratensis Zyricei Medici Clarissimi de Cerebri Morbis ... Curandis Liber, non tam Medicis quam Studiosis Omnibus ... Apprime Utilis*. Basel, 1549. This Dutch medical writer (1486–1559) was physician to the Duke of Bevern.

Varchi, Benedetto. *The Blazon of Jealousie*. Translated with commentary by Robert Tofte. London, 1615. Tofte's narrative poem *The Fruits of Jealousie* is included in this volume. Varchi's book first appeared in Italian in 1561 (?).

Vaughan, William. *Approved Directions for Health, Both Naturall and Artificiall*. London, 1612. The first of the seven editions appeared in 1600. Vaughan (1577–1641) distinguished himself principally as the promoter of settlements in Newfoundland. He was not a physician.

Venner, Tobias. *Via Recta ad Vitam Longam*. London, 1628. This work (which is written in English) was first published in 1620. There were six editions. Venner (1577–1660) was a physician of Bath.

Walkington, Thomas. *The Optick Glasse of Humors or The Touchstone of a Golden Temperature, or the Philosophers Stone to Make a Golden Temper*. London, 1639. This is the third of four editions, the first published in 1607. Walkington was a minister (d. 1621).

Wanley, Nathaniel. *The Wonders of the Little World: Or, a General History of Man*. London, 1678.

Webster, John. *The Complete Works of John Webster*. Ed. F. L. Lucas. 4 vols. London, 1927.

Webster, John. *The Displaying of Supposed Witchcraft*. London, 1677. This John Webster (not the dramatist) was a Puritan minister, a physician, and an exponent of Baconian views. His dates are 1610–82.

Weyer, Johann. *Ioannis Wieri de Praestigiis Daemonum, et Incantationibus ac Veneficijs Libri Sex*. Basel, 1568. The first edition appeared in 1563. Weyer, a native of northern Brabant, was a physician who won considerable notoriety by his scientific and humane views concerning witchcraft. Seven editions of *De Praestigiis* appeared during the author's lifetime (*c.* 1515 to 1588).

Wirtzung, Christopher. *Praxis Medicinae Universalis; or a Generall Practice of Physicke*. Tr. Jacob Mosan. London, 1598. This is the second issue of the first edition (1597). There were three English editions. Wirtzung (or Wirsung) was a physician of Augsburg (1500–71).

Wright, Thomas. *The Passions of the Minde*. London, 1601. This was the first of five editions.

II

A Selected List of Modern Studies

Anderson, Ruth Leila. *Elizabethan Psychology and Shakespeare's Plays.* Iowa City, 1927.

Bieber, Gustav Arthur. *Der Melancholikertypus Shakespeares und Sein Ursprung.* Heidelberg, 1913.

Bradley, A. C. *Shakespearean Tragedy.* London, 1905.

Brett, George S. *A History of Psychology.* 3 vols. London, 1912–21.

Bundy, Murray Wright. "Shakespeare and Elizabethan Psychology," *Journal of English and Germanic Philology,* XXIII (1924), 516–49.

———. *The Theory of Imagination in Classical and Mediaeval Thought.* Urbana, Ill., 1927.

Campbell, Lily B. *Shakespeare's Tragic Heroes: Slaves of Passion.* Cambridge, 1930.

Campbell, Oscar James. *Shakespeare's Satire.* London and New York, 1943.

Craig, Hardin. "Ethics in the Jacobean Drama: The Case of Chapman," *The Parrott Presentation Volume* (Princeton, 1935), pp. 25–46.

———. *The Enchanted Glass: The Elizabethan Mind in Literature.* New York, 1936.

Cumston, Charles Greene. *An Introduction to the History of Medicine.* London and New York, 1926.

Dessoir, Max. *Outlines of the History of Psychology.* Tr. Donald Fisher. New York, 1912.

Draper, John W. *The Humors & Shakespeare's Characters.* Durham, N. C., 1945. This volume includes, in somewhat abbreviated form, material previously presented in several short articles.

Evans, Bergen. *The Psychiatry of Robert Burton.* New York, 1944.

Ewing, S. Blaine. *Burtonian Melancholy in the Plays of John Ford.* Princeton, 1940.

Fink, Zera S. "Jaques and the Malcontent Traveler," *Philological Quarterly,* XIV (1935), 237–52.

Forest, Louise C. Turner. "A Caveat for Critics Against Invoking Elizabethan Psychology," *Publications of the Modern Language Association,* LXI (1946), 651–72.

Garrison, F. H. *An Introduction to the History of Medicine.* Philadelphia and London, 1929.

Harrison, G. B. "An Essay on Elizabethan Melancholy," appended to Harrison's edition of Nicholas Breton's *Melancholike Humours* (London, 1929).

John, Lisle Cecil. *The Elizabethan Sonnet Sequences: Studies in Conventional Conceits.* New York, 1938.

Jordan-Smith, Paul. *Bibliographia Burtoniana: A Study of Robert Burton's* The Anatomy of Melancholy *with a Bibliography of Burton's Writings*. Stanford and London, 1931.

Knights, L. C. "Seventeenth Century Melancholy," in *Drama and Society in the Age of Jonson* (London, 1937), pp. 315–32.

Kreider, Paul V. *Elizabethan Comic Character Conventions as Revealed in the Comedies of George Chapman*. Ann Arbor, Mich., 1935.

Loening, Richard. "Ueber die Physiologischen Grundlagen Shakespeare'schen Psychologie," *Jahrbuch der Deutschen Shakespeare-Gesellschaft*, XXXI (1895), 1–37.

Lowes, John Livingston. "The Loveres Maladye of Hereos," *Modern Philology*, XI (1914), 491–546.

Panofsky, Erwin, and Fritz Saxl. *Dürers 'Melencolia I': eine Quellen- und Typen-Geschichtliche Untersuchung*. Leipzig and Berlin, 1923. In abbreviated form, much of the material in this monograph appears in Panofsky's *Albrecht Dürer* (Princeton, 1945), I, 156–71.

Robin, P. Ansell. *The Old Physiology in English Literature*. London, 1911.

Rogers, Carmen L. *Elizabethan Melancholy in the Writings of the University Wits*. Unpublished Cornell dissertation, 1933.

Russell, Harry Kitsun. *Certain Doctrines of Natural and Moral Philosophy as an Approach to the Study of Elizabethan Drama; with an Appendix Containing Illustrative Material from the Plays of Ben Jonson*. Unpublished North Carolina dissertation, 1931.

———. "Elizabethan Dramatic Poetry in the Light of Natural and Moral Philosophy," *Philological Quarterly*, XII (1933), 187–95.

———. "Tudor and Stuart Dramatizations of the Doctrines of Natural and Moral Philosophy," *Studies in Philology*, XXXI (1934), 1–27.

Sensabaugh, George F. *The Tragic Muse of John Ford*. Stanford, Cal., 1944. This volume includes materials and conclusions previously published in articles on Ford's ethics and relation to Burton.

Spencer, Theodore. *Shakespeare and the Nature of Man*. New York, 1942.

Stoll, Elmer Edgar. "Jaques, and the Antiquaries," *Modern Language Notes*, LIV (1939), 79–85.

———. *John Webster: The Periods of His Work as Determined by His Relations to the Drama of His Day*. Cambridge, Mass., 1905.

———. "Shakespere, Marston, and the Malcontent Type," *Modern Philology*, III (1906), 281–303.

Walker, Albert L. "Convention in Shakespeare's Description of Emotion," *Philological Quarterly*, XVII (1938), 26–66.

Williamson, George. "Mutability, Decay, and Seventeenth-century Melancholy," *Journal of English Literary History*, II (1935), 121–50.

Zilboorg, Gregory. *The Medical Man and the Witch During the Renaissance*. Baltimore, 1935.

Zilboorg, Gregory, and George W. Henry. *A History of Medical Psychology*. New York, 1941.

INDEX

INDEX

INDEX